How To Rule Your Own Country

HARRY HOBBS is a Senior Lecturer in the Faculty of Law at the University of Technology Sydney. As a constitutional and human rights lawyer his work explores questions of sovereignty and statehood. His books include *Indigenous Aspirations and Structural Reform in Australia* and, with George Williams, *Micronations and the Search for Sovereignty.*

GEORGE WILLIAMS AO is a Deputy Vice-Chancellor and Professor of Law at UNSW Sydney. He has written widely on constitutional law and public policy, including *Australian Constitutional Law and Theory, The Oxford Companion to the High Court of Australia* and *Human Rights under the Australian Constitution.* As a barrister he has appeared in the High Court in cases on freedom of speech, freedom from racial discrimination and the rule of law. He is a media commentator on legal issues and a columnist for *The Australian.*

How To Rule Your Own Country

THE WEIRD AND WONDERFUL WORLD OF MICRONATIONS

HARRY HOBBS & GEORGE WILLIAMS

NEWSOUTH

A NewSouth book

Published by
NewSouth Publishing
University of New South Wales Press Ltd
University of New South Wales
Sydney NSW 2052
AUSTRALIA
https://unsw.press/

First published 2022

10 9 8 7 6 5 4 3 2 1

NATIONAL LIBRARY OF AUSTRALIA
A catalogue record for this book is available from the National Library of Australia

ISBN 9781742237732 (paperback)
9781742238500 (ebook)
9781742239408 (ePDF)

Internal design Josephine Pajor-Markus
Cover design Peter Long
Printed and bound by CPI Group (UK) Ltd, Croydon, CR0 4YY

This book is printed on paper using fibre supplied from plantation or sustainably managed forests.

UNSW
SYDNEY

CONTENTS

1

THE WEIRD AND WONDERFUL WORLD OF MICRONATIONS

On 15 November 2004, Sydney artist Paul Delprat strode into Mosman Town Hall. For over a decade the former Mosman Citizen of the Year had waged a one-man battle against his local council in the affluent harbourside suburb. The saga stretched back to 1993, when Delprat lodged an application to build a 25-metre driveway through a bushland reserve to improve access to his home on Balmoral Bay. His application was approved, but Mosman Council changed the planning rules to protect the bushland and the approval was overridden. The land was rezoned and Delprat's driveway plans shelved.

Delprat was not about to take this lying down, lodging several protests with the council. However, by 2004 Mosman Council had rejected every single one of his objections. What more could he do? There seemed only one possibility, as Delprat explained: 'Having been cut off from Mosman we could only reciprocate'.

Sporting a gold-leaf crown and dressed in a flowing white robe, Delprat marched into Mayor Shirley Jenkins' office. Accompanied by local print media journalists and a national

TV crew, Delprat handed over a formal-looking document. It announced his house had seceded to create a new nation named Principality of Wy (after the neighbouring Wyargine Point).

In an instant, Paul Delprat became Prince Paul, and his struggle for a driveway a diplomatic stoush between two nations. Prince Paul hoped the situation could be resolved amicably. Unfortunately, local government authorities were dismissive. In 2010, Anne Connon, the new mayor, remarked, 'I look at it with a degree of wry amusement. But it's not of any great importance'.

Prince Paul has not (yet) convinced the council to allow construction of his driveway. Nonetheless, the war has been expensive for all sides. Reports suggest that the council has spent more than $130 000 defending its actions in the NSW Land and Environment Court. While the council was successful in that foray, it finds itself arrayed against a creative enemy. Prince Paul has sketched preliminary plans for a medieval-style drawbridge to finally improve access to his home without damaging the protected bushland.

Perhaps the greatest challenge to the principality comes from within. Prince Paul admits that his adult children are 'somewhat embarrassed' by the royal titles he has conferred upon them. Prince Paul is unmoved. As he explains, the Principality of Wy continues to thrive today, standing 'as a beacon of hope to all those oppressed by bureaucracy'.

Delprat's actions may be bizarre and even extreme. However, they are far from unique. Eccentric and enterprising individuals around the world have created their own micronations for these and many other reasons.

Prince Paul delivers secession documents to Shirley Jenkins, Mayor of Mosman
Newspix

* * *

In 1969, a letter was delivered to Canadian prime minister Pierre Trudeau. The letter's contents were alarming: 'Unless immediate action is taken on your part, we shall have no alternative but to regard your occupation as the commencement of hostilities and we shall therefore order total mobilization of our citizenry'.

Despite the ominous warning, Trudeau did not respond personally. He left that for his correspondence secretary, Olga Maxwell. Maxwell sought to placate the author of the letter, acknowledging that Canada 'would have trouble beating you in a war, for I know that your strength is that of a million men, as your hearts are pure'. Nonetheless, Maxwell was clear. The Canadian government was unable to comply. The author of the

Republic of Rathnelly street sign
Claire Millgate

letter needed to contact the city of Toronto if it wanted funding to build a playground.

The letter was written by the Republic of Rathnelly, a 'nation' whose territory neatly mapped onto the neighbourhood of Rathnelly in Toronto, Canada. In the 1960s, concern over an expressway being built through their homes led residents to band together. During celebration of Canada's centennial on 1 July 1967, they declared the formation of their nation. Although a republic, the community elected a queen. They issued passports, organised a parade and even conscripted children between the ages of 5 and 14 into a broom-wielding militia. They also composed a national anthem, titled 'Rathnally the Brave'. Curiously, in the song Rathnelly is spelled with an 'a':

Rathnally we will faithful be
Strong determined to be free
We will fight with all our might
So onward friends for liberty ...
So onward friends to victory

Two years after the republic was formed, its citizens wrote to Trudeau asking for foreign aid to build a playground in exchange for letting the city use the republic's parkland. Foreign aid may not have arrived, but the Republic of Rathnelly survived and prospered. The proposed expressway was abandoned, and Rathnelly Day continues to be celebrated every second June.

* * *

In an April 1973 press conference in New York, John Lennon and Yoko Ono introduced the world to Nutopia:

We announce the birth of a conceptual country,
    NUTOPIA.
Citizenship of the country can be obtained by declaration
    of your awareness of NUTOPIA.
NUTOPIA has no land, no boundries [*sic*], no passports,
    only people.
NUTOPIA has no laws other than cosmic.
All people of NUTOPIA are ambassadors of the country.
As two ambassadors of NUTOPIA, we ask for diplomatic
    immunity and recognition in the United Nations of
    our country and its people.

Diplomatic immunity was important. The previous month, Lennon had been denied permanent residence in the United States on account of a British conviction for drug possession. If he was an ambassador of a country, it would be much harder for American authorities to deport him. The assembled journalists were not sure whether Lennon and Ono were serious. At the press conference, Lennon waved a white tissue, exclaiming 'This is the flag of Nutopia – we surrender, to peace and to love'. A reporter for the *New York Times* noted that Lennon then used the tissue to blow his nose.

* * *

More than 40 years later, reports emerged of a new nation in North Africa struggling to find its feet. A poetic Declaration of Sovereignty read:

> For countless millennia our planet has witnessed the rise and fall of peaceful societies and those of cruel heartlessness; with a thousand shades in between ...
>
> In this moment, in this newly formed nation we seek to be the exemplar for a new form of government. A government that is centered on science not subjugation. A nation driven by charity not consumption. A people driven by social and environmental stewardship.
>
> Our nation is established on the last *terra nullius* land remaining on Earth. Forgotten by both time and humanity, the ancient land of Bir Tawil, placed between Egypt and Sudan, is ungoverned by any nation.

Jeremiah Heaton stakes his claim to the Kingdom of North Sudan in June 2014.
Credit unknown

> The dawn of our nation begins as a blank slate in an arid, desolate desert. Through the charity of the world community and the disciples of modern science, we will construct the most fertile, ecologically sensitive nation on Earth.
>
> In the spirit of peace and progress, with the date of 16th of June, 2014 and in accordance with international law, I, Jeremiah Heaton lay claim as Sovereign Monarch for the Kingdom of North Sudan.

In keeping with this declaration, Jeremiah Heaton, a 38-year-old American farmer, planted a flag in the Bir Tawil desert and proclaimed the creation of the Kingdom of North Sudan.

Bir Tawil is a 2060-square-kilometre area of uninhabited land along the Egyptian and Sudanese borders. The land is claimed by neither Egypt nor Sudan because of an inconsistency between the political and administrative borders that separate the two countries. Egypt follows the 1899 political boundary that places Bir Tawil in Sudan (and the much larger Halayib Triangle within Egypt). Sudan follows the administrative boundary, based on the actual use of land by tribes in the region. Its boundary places Bir Tawil within Egypt (and the Halayib Triangle within Sudan).

Heaton discovered this anomaly and decided that he would take advantage of it by creating his own country. Why? Several answers have been given. In one account, Heaton was fulfilling a promise he made to his daughter Emily to make her a princess (film rights to the story have been bought by Disney). Other accounts suggest different motivations. In conversations with a journalist from *The Guardian*, Heaton explained that his Kingdom 'could offer the world's great innovators a place to develop their products unencumbered by taxes and regulation, a place where private enterprise faces no socially prescribed borders of its own'.

You can find out more on the kingdom's website. There you can buy citizenship, a knighthood, cryptocurrency and even the right to name fictional streets. The kingdom has applied for observer status at the United Nations and appointed ambassadors across Europe. It is also seeking an audience with both Egypt and Sudan. So far, neither state has responded, let alone recognised the kingdom.

Heaton had other challenges on his hands. In 2019, a rival Kingdom of the Yellow Mountain also laid claim to Bir Tawil.

A Russian-based Kingdom of Middle Earth and an Indian 'Kingdom of Dixit' also assert sovereignty over the same desert. Egypt and Sudan may not be keen on Bir Tawil, but many others are.

* * *

People all over the world want their own country. Since 2010, independence referendums of various legality have been held in South Sudan (Sudan), Puerto Rico (the United States), Veneto (Italy), Scotland (the United Kingdom), Catalonia (Spain), Sint Eustatius (Netherlands), South Brazil (Brazil), Kurdistan (Iraq), New Caledonia (France) and Bougainville (Papua New Guinea). More independence votes are planned in these and other parts of the globe.

And yet, there is a great difference between Catalonia and Wy, Scotland and Rathnelly, Puerto Rico and Nutopia, and South Sudan and the Kingdom of North Sudan. The first of each pair has some legitimate basis for statehood, whether based in history, culture, ethnicity or something else. The second of each pair does not. The United States may not have been able to deport John Lennon, but this is not because he was an ambassador for Nutopia. Nutopia was not a real country. It was a micronation.

In contrast to true independence or secessionist movements, micronations are generally considered trivial. They might simply be ignored by the state, like the Principality of Wy is ignored by the Mosman Municipal Council or the Kingdom of North Sudan is ignored by Egypt and Sudan. In other cases, real countries may play along and humour the founders, like

Olga Maxwell's letter to the Republic of Rathnelly. Sometimes the state may be unsure how to respond, perhaps because it is not clear if the micronation's statehood is the real goal. Inventing a country might instead be part of an attempt to attract media attention and political support.

Even if it is just for play, micronations dress in the language of statehood and perform acts of sovereignty. They draft constitutions, issue passports, mint coins, print stamps, compose national anthems, design flags, and write letters to countries and the United Nations seeking recognition of their status as a state. Sometimes they even declare war on real countries.

This book shines a light on the global phenomenon of micronations. We examine the stories behind the eccentric and committed people who decide 'enough is enough' and form a new country.

What is a micronation?

The best way to define what it means to be a micronation is to consider what it is *not*. Micronations look a bit like nation-states – such as Australia or Japan – but they are not states under international law. Their defining feature is that they lack the same qualities as proper nations, even though they mimic them.

So what does it mean to be a 'nation-state'? There is no universally accepted legal definition. In the 1940s, the International Law Commission – a body of experts elected by the United Nations General Assembly charged with the responsibility for developing international law – looked at this question. British international lawyer James Brierly argued that a definition of 'state' 'would be difficult to establish and highly controversial'. According to Brierly, the word 'was commonly used in documents and speech, and its meaning had been understood without definition'. At best, he said, 'I know it when I see it.'

French international lawyer Georges Scelle agreed. He believed 'that it would be almost impossible' to reach a satisfactory definition. As Scelle explained, 'He himself had been active in international law for more than fifty years, and still did not know what a state was; and he felt sure that he would not find out before he died. He was convinced that the Commission could not tell him'.

The Commission resolved its work by avoiding the problem. It concluded that its failure to reach a definition was a good thing as 'no useful purpose would be served by an effort to define the term "state"'.

The challenge in developing a clear definition of a state has not prevented people from trying. The most common definition comes from a 1934 treaty between countries in North, South and Central America. The Convention on Rights and Duties of States (known as the Montevideo Convention, as it was agreed to in the Uruguayan capital), outlines four criteria of a state: (1) a defined territory; (2) a permanent population; (3) a government; and (4) a capacity to enter into relations with other states. On the face of it, the list seems clear, but there are complications.

First, the criteria are flexible. There is no rule prescribing a minimum area of territory, size of population or effectiveness of government. As such, a wide 'variety of entities with differing circumstances' fall within the definition. For example, entities with a very small territorial footprint, like Vatican City (0.49 square kilometres), Monaco (2.1 square kilometres) and Nauru (21 square kilometres) are all regarded as states.

The same is true for some entities that possess no territory. Poland and Czechoslovakia were both recognised by France in World War I despite not possessing any land because their territory had been taken over during the war. As this example shows, governments exiled from their territory because of wartime occupation, civil war, revolution or military coup remain states. Countries with minuscule resident populations are also recognised. Only around 800 people live within the borders of Vatican City. Tuvalu and Nauru are both recognised as countries, despite possessing fewer than 11 000 people.

The requirement that a country have a government is also elastic. There is a strong presumption that a state will continue to exist even if it loses control of its territory or its government can no longer function. Hence, a state that no longer possesses an effective government is unlikely to immediately lose its status. Between 1991 and 2006, there was no central government in Somalia, but this did not mean Somalia was no longer a state. After elections in Belgium in 2010, it took more than 500 days for a new administration to be sworn in, during which time there was no government. Even so, there was no danger that Belgium would lose its status.

Second, there is an inherently political aspect to statehood. Some entities that easily satisfy the Montevideo Convention requirements are not considered to be states. Take Taiwan as an example. Taiwan has a defined territory, a permanent population and a government, and it freely enters into agreements with a host of countries. However, very few countries consider it a state. The reason is because the People's Republic of China asserts that it is the sole legitimate government of all China – including Taiwan. In 1971, the United Nations General Assembly agreed, voting to eject representatives of Taiwan from the United Nations and admitting the People's Republic of China as 'the only legitimate representative of China to the United Nations'.

Under its 'One China' policy, the People's Republic of China refuses to maintain diplomatic relations with any nation that recognises Taiwan. Owing to mainland China's political, economic and military strength, many states have broken off formal diplomatic relations with Taiwan. Australia formally switched its recognition from Taiwan to the People's Republic of China in 1972. In late 2021 Nicaragua also switched its recognition to the People's Republic of China. Today, only 14 nation-states, including Vatican City, recognise Taiwan. Nonetheless, many countries that formally recognise the People's Republic of China maintain unofficial consular links with Taiwan.

Finally, there are also other requirements of statehood that are not included in the Montevideo Convention. Most significantly, a state cannot have been established in breach of international law. For this reason, the Turkish Republic of Northern Cyprus is not a state, even though it meets the Montevideo Convention definition, because it was formed as a result of the illegal use of force. The same is true of Rhodesia. In 1965 the white minority government unilaterally declared independence with the aim of creating an apartheid state. Denounced by the United Nations Security Council as an 'illegal racist minority regime', Rhodesia was not formally recognised by any country. In the words of Christian Hillgruber, the claim to statehood of these political communities was defeated by an 'error at birth'.

The International Law Commission was right. There is no straightforward definition of what a state is, and it is unlikely that one can be established. However, this only gets us part of the way to an understanding of micronations. The Montevideo Convention definition allows room for a variety of entities to qualify as states. So is there enough room for micronations?

In his ground-breaking examination of the creation of states in international law, James Crawford explained that the key to statehood is 'governing power with respect to territory'. That is, 'to be a state, an entity must possess a government or system of government in general control of its territory, to the exclusion of other entities not claiming through or under it'. This position reflects the distinction between ownership of land and the authority to exercise sovereignty over that land. While you may own your apartment or house, you are not able to create laws for that territory – only the state is allowed to do that.

The important point is that a state is independent or sovereign when it is not 'under the legal authority of another state'. It is here that micronations fail the test of statehood.

Micronations may declare their independence, but they are unable to do so to the exclusion of other entities. The lack of a legitimate foundation for their claim means that their assertion of authority over territory is contested by real states and not recognised in law, even if they physically occupy territory. Micronations are self-declared nations that perform and mimic acts of sovereignty and adopt many of the protocols of nations. However, micronations do not have a foundation in domestic and international law for their existence, and are not recognised as nations in domestic or international forums.

Could our understanding of what a state is evolve to encompass micronations? It is worth recalling that 'states are not innate or physical truths'; a 'state is not a fact in the sense that a chair is a fact'. There is no reason that our definition of 'state' must always exclude micronations. Nevertheless, their inclusion in the definition seems highly unlikely, at least in the short term. No state is likely to accept micronations into their club by pushing for a change in what it means to be a state.

If understandings of statehood are unlikely to adapt to include micronations, is it possible that a micronation could evolve to become a state? Again, this is unlikely, though a possibility remains. As we explore in this book, many micronations – particularly those inspired by libertarian political philosophies – prioritise the creation of an effective (albeit limited) government. In some cases, micronations do so on land or sea they claim no state exercises lawful authority over, either because the area is unoccupied, or because the micronation has reclaimed land in international waters. Assuming that their legal basis for possession is correct and that they build a functioning government capable of exercising legitimate authority over defined territory, the micronation may come to constitute a state.

Statehood is a question of fact. Whether another state recognises an entity as a state or not is immaterial to its status. If a micronation is able to satisfy the criteria of statehood, the fact that other states do not recognise it as a state would not prevent it from actually being a state. It would become a real nation. Once again, however, its ability to *function* as a state would be limited if other countries refuse to accept it.

Why do people set up micronations?

Micronations are established for many reasons. Wy, for example, was established in an attempt to build a driveway. Rathnelly was founded to protest against the construction of an expressway that would break up a community. While Wy has so far not had its intended effect, Rathnelly continues today as a celebration of the success and vitality of the neighbourhood. Neither of these micronations appear to genuinely want statehood or the powers and privileges that come with it, such as a seat at the United Nations.

Nutopia also did not seek statehood, but was established in an attempt to avoid John Lennon's deportation from the US. It did not claim any physical territory and it continues to exist in name only: a gold plaque engraved with the words 'Nutopian Embassy' was installed at the kitchen entrance to the apartment where Lennon and Ono lived. The Kingdom of North Sudan, by contrast, seems to desire the creation of an actual country. However, it exists solely online. Understandably, Egypt and Sudan are not excited about the prospect of an American setting up shop on their borders.

Micronations try to act like nations, but lack any domestic or international legal basis for statehood. Beyond these common features, they are incredibly diverse. Some micronations are established as conceptual art projects designed to critique understandings of statehood and sovereignty. For example, the Kingdom of Elgaland-Vargaland, created by two Swedish artists, claims sovereignty over the areas between the borders of countries. It also asserts authority over other intervals, such as the transition from sleep to wakefulness.

The Empire of Atlantium is also a vehicle to explore the idea of sovereignty and statehood. Initially set up by three Australian teenagers in 1981, the micronation was revived by George Cruickshank when he purchased an apartment in Potts Point, Sydney, in the 1990s. Although the empire has interest in three plots of land, it does not maintain any formal territorial claims, instead conceiving itself as a 'non-territorial' state. As His Imperial Majesty George II of Atlantium explains, 'In an age where people increasingly are unified by common interests and purposes across – rather than within – traditional national boundaries Atlantium offers an alternative to the discriminatory historic practice of assigning nationality to individuals on the basis of accidents of birth or circumstance.' Many people agree. Today, Atlantium claims more than 3000 citizens spread across 100 countries.

Lots of micronations are founded in a combination of frustration with regulation and a burning sense of a political injustice. Many are formed in a battle against local councils. Australian Peter Gillies created the Principality of United Oceania, located in Port Stephens in New South Wales, after several rejected planning applications on his property. The Independent State of Rainbow Creek in Victoria emerged as part of a decades-long compensation dispute between Victorian farmers and the state government's State Rivers and Water Supply Commission. The Hajduk Republic of Mijat Tomić in Bosnia and Herzegovina owes its existence to bureaucratic inertia. Vinko Vukoja-Lastvić's motel was located on the border of three councils. No council could agree who was responsible for connecting his property to the electrical grid, so none acted.

NATO-led peacekeeping forces were initially alarmed at the sudden emergence of this new republic, but quickly realised it had no secessionist ambitions.

Other micronations owe their formation to their creators' sense of personal expression and desire for attention. British filmmaker Danny Wallace created the Kingdom of Lovely (situated entirely within his flat) for a BBC documentary series. The Republic of Molossia, in the US state of Nevada, is expressly styled as a backward and politically unstable 'banana republic'. President Kevin Baugh explains: 'It's an expression of personal sovereignty, creativity, imagination, and political satire ... It's a nice way to look around the world. You can see what countries are doing and say, "I can do that."'

Some micronations are founded for a laugh, others because of boredom. The Great Bitter Lake Association was a micronation created by the crews of 15 ships stranded in the Suez Canal because of the 1967 Six-Day War. The war lasted less than a week but conflict between Egypt and Israel continued, and Egypt blocked the canal to all shipping. It took eight years before the canal was cleared and the flotilla could continue their journey.

Where a town or small community supports the idea, micronationalism can also promote tourism and deliver an economic boost to a region. The Republic of Whangamōmona on the North Island of New Zealand emerged when regional council boundaries were changed. Upset about the potential of having to play rugby for their neighbours, the residents decided to secede. Initially a symbolic act aimed at drawing political and media attention to their concerns through humour, the

Tourists have a celebratory drink at the only pub in the Republic of Whangamōmona
Darcy Pietersma

motivation has shifted over time. Republic Day is now celebrated every second January, attracting thousands of tourists.

There can also be a dark side. Micronations may be created to scam unsuspecting people. The 'most audacious fraud in history' centred around the fictional nation of Poyais. More stock-standard scams exist too. The now defunct New Age International University claimed to be a leading university of Seborga, licensed by the Principality's Department of Education. However, Seborga is not a real country. Admissions, licensing and certification for the university were controlled by an institute in Kolkata, India, and the university was not accredited. The 'university' was a diploma mill established to sell illegitimate academic degrees.

How many micronations are there?

Micronations are a global phenomenon, and the ease with which they can be established (and abandoned) makes it difficult to work out the total number around the world. The growth of the internet makes an accurate assessment even more challenging. A brief survey reveals that thousands of micronations exist entirely on social media platforms like Facebook, Reddit and MicroWiki. Cyber, simulationist or conceptual micronations are extraordinarily rich and diverse, but they do not give rise to the same sorts of questions as micronations that claim real territory.

Several lists of territorial micronations exist. The academic journal *Shima*, which serves as a forum for research into island cultures, insular communities and imaginations of autonomy, has published 20 academic articles on 15 micronations. *Atlas Obscura*, an online magazine and travel company that specialises in providing guides to strange and odd places around the world, has written 44 articles on around 30 micronations. *Micronations: The Lonely Planet Guide to home-made nations*, published in 2006, features detailed discussion on 50 micronations.

User-edited lists have also been developed. An online Micronations World Map, which allows people to tag micronations on parts of the globe, catalogues 67 different micronations. At the time of writing, a list on Wikipedia stretches to 89 entries. Another user-edited online map created by Matthew Hubbard (formerly the ruler of the now defunct online Republic of Matthewopia) identifies more than 100 micronations.

Compiling an accurate number remains challenging. Each of these lists includes several micronations that others do not. Adding these up to produce an estimated total number suggests a figure of at least 135, though many of these entities are no longer active and it is unlikely that even this tally is comprehensive. Indeed, while writing this book, the authors were contacted by emperors, kings, dukes, presidents and other heads of state letting us know of their existence. The archduke and prime minister of the Parliamentary Monarchy of Duckionary (established in 2018) explained how his country preaches tolerance across Central and Eastern Europe; the president of the Free Republic of Verdis (founded in 2019) noted his desire to develop a modern, environmentally conscious and humanitarian state.

Protecting the environment is a popular motivation. Daniel Racovolis is the leader of Urabba Parks, an incorporated micronation that works with Landcare and is located in Rankins Springs, central New South Wales.

Two points are clear. First, micronations can be found all over the world. Micronations claim territory from Antarctica to the Arctic, and from Tonga to Jamaica. Some even claim territory in space. Nevertheless, they appear to be predominantly located in wealthy western countries, like Western Europe, the United States and Australia – perhaps a reflection of the time that one needs to invest in creating a state. Second, despite their breadth, a disproportionately high number of micronations are in Australia. Some estimates suggest that one-third of all micronations are located there.

Why is Australia micronation central?

Australia's relaxed approach to micronations is part of why it hosts so many of these wannabe countries. As we will see throughout this book, while many countries might try to put down would-be rebels either through force of arms or force of law, Australia largely tolerates the strange, earnest and eccentric people who claim to create their own country – so long as they continue to pay tax and follow the road rules. The Australian approach reflects three main themes.

First, the act of seceding from the state and declaring one's own country is consistent with an Australian culture that celebrates the underdog, larrikinism and mocking authority. The 'Aussie larrikin' emerged in the second half of the 19th century as respectable society was increasingly preoccupied with attempting to shed the 'stigma of convict origins'. Initially an object of alarm and derision, the larrikin figure was the subject of an attitude shift around the turn of the 20th century. Today, the larrikin stands for 'the rejection of received opinion and defiance towards insensible authority'. A larrikin is 'almost archly self-conscious, too smart for his or her own good, witty rather than humorous, exceeding limits, bending rules and sailing close to the wind, avoiding rather than evading responsibility, playing up to an audience, mocking pomposity and smugness'.

The generally supportive public reaction to government restrictions imposed in response to the Covid-19 pandemic demonstrates how Australians are ordinarily content to follow the rules. However, even if Australians are 'very obedient' towards authority, we remain 'suspicious of persons in authority'. As social scientists have found, we are highly sceptical of hierarchy.

This attitude can be seen in those we choose as our national heroes. One iconic figure in Australian history is the bushranger Ned Kelly. Born to poor Irish parents, the Victorian outlaw eluded police for two years, thanks largely to a network of supporters and sympathisers. In his Jerilderie Letter, Kelly justified his actions and outlined a political manifesto. Describing instances of police corruption, Kelly called for justice to the Irish families of north-west Victoria and demanded that squatters share their property and wealth with the poor. His famous last stand at Glenrowan – complete with a suit of bulletproof armour – is immortalised in the work of celebrated Australian artist Sidney Nolan. Convicted of murder and sentenced to hang, Kelly's reputed last words, 'Such is life', cemented his status as a cultural icon. Today, Kelly denotes 'a romantic and rebellious aspect of national identity in contemporary Australia', and he remains the 'historical embodiment of Australian larrikinism'.

What better way to exemplify larrikinism than by 'thumbing your nose' at the nation and founding your own country? After all, as Prince Paul of Wy notes, 'Deep in the psyche of Australians is a little bit of Ned Kelly. We all look at Ned in his armour and his defiance of authority and let's face it, there's a little bit of him in all of us.' His Imperial Majesty George II of Atlantium agrees, arguing that micronationalism in Australia stems 'from our convict heritage and disrespect for authority. American groups like the Davidian Branch tend to be more violently whacko, whereas Australians are just quaintly eccentric'. Some micronations like the Empire of Atlantium, His Imperial Majesty continues, are more like a 'sustained performance art project'. These differ 'from what most people

Emperor George II of Atlantium
Richard Price

understand micronations to be. Which is some crazy guy, in the middle of nowhere, declaring himself independent of Australia and shooting up the feds'.

Australian voters do not seem to worry. In the early 1980s, John Rudge established the Grand Duchy of Avram, a micronation based around his home in the small seaside town of Strahan in Tasmania. Rudge also legally changed his name to recognise his new status, becoming John His Grace the Most Noble the Duke of Avram. In 1989, the Duke was elected to the Tasmanian Parliament.

A second reason for the remarkable number of micronations in Australia draws on notions of security and stability. Australia occupies an entire continent, and its sovereignty is unthreatened. For this reason, it sees micronations as irrelevant or, at worst, a nuisance rather than a genuine threat. This perspective is very different from the attitude that countries with troubled histories of secessionism and rebellion may adopt. The approach in Australia is a product of legal factors and the nation's history and culture.

There is no federal law concerning secession, but it is clear that it is prohibited by the Australian Constitution. There is simply no right to secede. The preamble to the Australian Constitution speaks of an 'indissoluble Federal Commonwealth', so micronations that claim to secede are therefore not granted any legal status. They remain subject to Australian law and are required to follow that law.

Secession may be illegal, but threats of secession have a long history in Australia, contributing to a broader political and cultural climate that views secessionism as not serious. This was not always the case. In the 1930s, the prospect of Western Australia seceding was treated with alarm in Canberra. In 1933, amid an economic crisis caused by the Great Depression and a belief that the Commonwealth was dominated by eastern Australian interests, the state held a referendum on the issue. More than 66 per cent of Western Australians voted to withdraw from the Commonwealth. To complicate matters, the

Western Australian state election was held the same day as the referendum, and it was won by the anti-secessionist Labor Party. Nonetheless, the Labor Party promised to act in accordance with the referendum result.

The Australian Constitution is an Act of the British Parliament. For Western Australia to secede, the United Kingdom would have had to change that law. In 1934, Western Australia sent a delegation to London to petition the UK Parliament to amend the Constitution to allow the state to become a self-governing Dominion within the British Empire. Its 439-page report, *The Case for Secession*, comprehensively detailed the state's position that secession was the only option.

The UK Parliament was desperate to avoid getting caught between Western Australia and the Commonwealth. Rather than rule on the petition, the parliament set up a committee to determine whether it could even receive and consider the request. In 1935, after hearing arguments from both Western Australia and the Commonwealth, the committee concluded that it could not entertain the petition. As economic conditions improved and the Commonwealth began making special financial assistance grants to Western Australia, support for secession dissipated.

The movement never completely died out and secessionist threats continue. In the 1980s, Tasmanian premiers from both the Labor Party and the Liberal Party suggested secession as a response to clashes with the federal government over environmental regulation. Queensland and Western Australian premiers often invoked the notion too. More recently, in 2017, the Western Australian Liberal Party passed a resolution at its state conference calling on the establishment of a committee to 'examine the option of Western Australia becoming a financially independent state'. In the midst of the coronavirus pandemic, interest in secession again rose; according to one 2020 survey, 28 per cent of Western Australians want to secede. A new political party, WAxit, was even formed in the hope of cashing in on this support.

Nonetheless, perhaps because secession has never occurred, or because of the 'ritual' nature of its invocation, the idea of secession in Australia is today largely regarded as 'an essentially ceremonial challenge, rarely meant seriously by the State from which it issues, and never received seriously by those whom it is intended to impress'. The call for secession is not meant to be taken literally. Rather, it is meant to indicate displeasure with policies or actions undertaken and adopted by the federal government – as well as a healthy disrespect for their claim to authority.

Micronations in Australia can take advantage of this attitude. The Principality of Snake Hill, a micronation centred around a house in Mudgee, New South Wales, declared independence on 2 September 2003. Princess Paula explained what happened next:

> We did fully expect the response that most people do get around the world when they try to secede: they usually get a letter or some visits from government employees who try to mediate the situation, Paula says. Mum even said that they'll send tanks. I said: 'Relax, this is Australia, no one reads anything.' And it's true. They just sent a letter saying, 'Thank you very much for the letter', and that was it.

This approach is also manifested in response to Indigenous assertions of sovereignty. Consider the Murrawarri Republic's declaration of independence. The Murrawarri people are an Indigenous nation whose traditional lands stretch across northern New South Wales and south-western Queensland. On 30 March 2013, the newly formed People's Council of the Murrawarri Republic issued letters to Queen Elizabeth II, prime minister Julia Gillard, and state premiers Barry O'Farrell and Campbell Newman asking them to provide documents by 8 May 2013 demonstrating that the Murrawarri Nation had ceded their sovereignty and land to the British Crown. No response was received. For the Council, the failure to produce these documents meant that the Crown 'affirmed the Murrawarri Republic to be a continued Free and Independent State, in line with International law and covenants'.

The Murrawarri Republic's declaration received attention internationally. But it is hard to find much discussion in Australian media. The first official response was made in response to an inquiry from an American journalist. A spokesperson for the Attorney-General's Department noted that the government had not replied to the Council's assertion of sovereignty 'because "there are no constitutional means available for the establishment of separate political communities in Australia", adding that the Australian Commonwealth's sovereignty over the continent is recognised in international law'.

A final reason for the prevalence of micronations in Australia is spatial. Australia is a large country with a relatively small population. With 25 million people occupying more than 7.6 million square kilometres, Australia has a population density of three people per square kilometre. This ranks Australia

192 out of 194 countries in the world for population density, ahead only of Namibia and Mongolia.

Population density figures are complicated by the location of Australia's population centres. Australia is one of the most urbanised countries in the world, with 86 per cent of the population living in urban centres (data from 2018), and 85 per cent living within 50 kilometres of the coast (data from 2001). In practice, this means that vast areas of the continent are sparsely populated. For instance, approximately 79 per cent of the Western Australian population lives within the Greater Perth area, leaving around 550 000 people spread over the remainder of the state's 2.6 million square kilometres. There is a lot of space for people who want to create their own country. Let's hear from one of them now.

2

'WHILE I BREATHE, I HOPE': THE PRINCIPALITY OF HUTT RIVER

A little after 5 pm on the afternoon of Friday 2 December 1977, a telegram was delivered to Government House, the official residence of Australia's governor-general, in the leafy Canberra suburb of Yarralumla. The contents of the telegram were ominous:

> Confirming my letter of 28th November re your governments lack of respect of the laws not only on my people but also on people of your own country ... it is my official responsibility to declare that a state of war now exists between our respective countries and diplomatic relations are at this time now severed.

There is no evidence that Governor-General Sir John Kerr responded to the telegram. It is also not clear whether it was passed on to prime minister Malcolm Fraser, defence minister Sir James Killen or the chief of defence force staff Sir Arthur MacDonald. With Australia's political and military leaders apparently unaware that the nation was the target of a declaration of war, the sender of the telegram could strike.

Just two days later, however, the war concluded. At half past three on Sunday 4 December 1977, a second telegram was cabled to Sir John Kerr, announcing that 'the state of war between our countries has now ceased'. What was going on? Had Australia dodged a bullet?

The author of the telegram was Prince Leonard Casley of the Hutt River Province. With his province having a permanent population of fewer than 20 residents, no standing army, and its 75-square-kilometre territory entirely enclosed by the state of Western Australia, Prince Leonard had a change of heart. The Australian government does not appear to have replied to either message. Prince Leonard suggests that the government was 'pondering its predicament'.

There have been many short wars. On 14 July 1969, El Salvador launched an attack on neighbouring Honduras that persisted until a ceasefire was negotiated four days later. In 1896, the United Kingdom launched an assault on Zanzibar to force the accession of a puppet government. Faced with the overwhelming power of the Royal Navy, the Sultan of Zanzibar fled, and the conflict lasted somewhere between 38 and 45 minutes. The war between the Hutt River Province and Australia stretched for almost two days, but unlike the colonial Anglo-Zanzibar War or the 100 Hour War in Central America, no shots were fired.

What then was the purpose of Prince Leonard's declaration of war? He certainly had no intention of engaging in hostilities. Instead, war was a means to secure recognition for his fledgling principality. According to his reading of the Geneva Conventions of 1949, a state should show full respect to a nation undefeated in war. As the Hutt River Province was undefeated, Prince Leonard argued that Australia must recognise its sovereignty. This provided a foundation for his assertion of the independence of his principality over the following decades. That Casley sought this was a reflection of his own background and – strangely enough – arose out of his concerns with mismanagement of the Australian wheat market.

The Principality of Hutt River is one of the world's most famous micronations. Under the dogged determination of Prince Leonard, Hutt River became well known across the continent and the globe. In thousands of letters to politicians and government officials – both in Australia and overseas – Prince Leonard and his growing family explained the reasons for their declaration of independence and attempted to gain international recognition as a real country. Although Prince Leonard was unsuccessful – no country ever officially recognised Hutt River as a state – the sheer volume of correspondence reveals his persistence and the way that micronations can rely on the ignorance and goodwill of others to bolster their claims. The subject of thousands of newspaper articles, magazine profiles and television reports, Hutt River helped to popularise the idea that anyone can rule their own country. How did he do it?

The birth of the principality

Prince Leonard was born Leonard Casley in the small gold mining town of Kalgoorlie, Western Australia, in 1925. Dropping out of school at age 14, he moved almost 600 kilometres west to Perth and picked up work for a shipping company. When he turned 18, he joined the Royal Australian Air Force and served in Borneo during World War II.

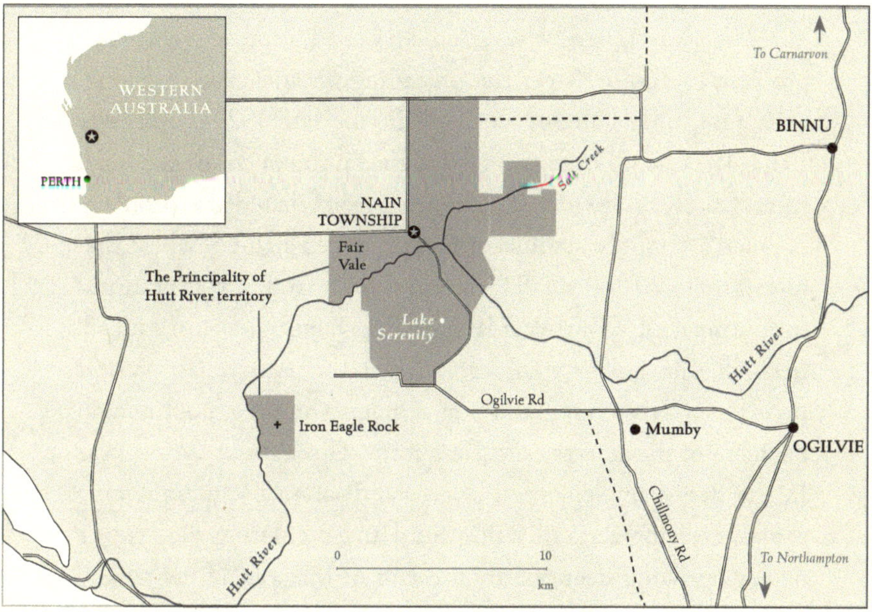

Location of the Principality of Hutt River

Perhaps it was there that he refined his independent streak. In an interview with the *New York Times* in 2011, his wife Shirley noted that Leonard did not enjoy having to follow orders. At least he spent his spare time productively; Casley taught himself accounting and claimed to have mastered 'the regulations surrounding agricultural exports'. This study proved valuable. In the 1960s, Casley bought a property in outback Western Australia, situated at Hutt River in the district of Yallabatharra, about 500 kilometres north of Perth. Casley wanted to build a wheat farm. Unfortunately, his timing was far from ideal.

The Australian wheat industry had lurched from one problem to another over the preceding decades, causing long-term resentment among farmers. In the late 1920s and early 1930s, the Great Depression led to the failure of countless small farms. Sadly, government responses exacerbated the problem. A failed attempt to stabilise prices produced a glut of wheat that forced up to 20 000 small farmers off their land. It was not until the outbreak of World War II that some stability was introduced. In 1939, the government established the Australian Wheat Board to oversee the marketing, storage, shipping, pooling and payment of the country's wheat output. Throughout World War II, the Board implemented price stabilisation by guaranteeing prices, creating a stabilisation fund and regulating the issuing of new growing licences. By the end of the war, industry and government accepted the need to maintain price stabilisation during peacetime.

When Casley bought his property in 1965, the Australian Wheat Board still regulated and managed the industry. National and state boards sought to shelter growers from volatility by stabilising prices and incomes. The Board compulsorily acquired and pooled all wheat produced in Australia, established a home consumption price, and had the sole authority to market wheat domestically and internationally. Following a bumper harvest in 1968, industry sought the introduction of production quotas to reduce stock build-up and maintain pricing levels. The Western Australian government agreed, shepherding the *Wheat Delivery Quotas Act 1969* through the parliament. The Act established a three-member Wheat Quotas Committee and empowered the body to impose quotas for the summer harvest.

The quotas had a detrimental effect on many farmers, including Casley. In the spring of 1969, while preparing to harvest around 6000 acres of wheat, Casley received a letter notifying him that he would be permitted to sell only 100 acres' worth. The quota had been reached based on the average production of the property over the previous seven years. There was no appeal mechanism or compensation available under the Act. As Casley explained in a letter to the Wheat Quotas Committee:

> This Quota will not pay the interest on machinery being purchased by H.P. [hire purchase] at present.
>
> The bulk of the land when purchased were in new land condition or undeveloped.
>
> Developing the properties has been costing $50,000.00 Per Annum, apart from the purchase costs ...
>
> You must realise that when one is developing a property they expect to be out of pocket initially, they do however expect to see a reasonable income in the future. To take away future prospects of reasonable income is of course to be strongly rebuked, and action against same must be taken.

On the same day, Casley wrote to the state governor, Sir Douglas Kendrew, and the premier of Western Australia, Sir David Brand, reiterating his concerns:

> Our families in receiving a quota of 1647 bushels of Wheat which wont even pay the interest on machinery

> purchased on H.P. and who will have spent by March 1970 around $400,000.00 in purchasing and developing our properties are very gravely concerned as to our future.
>
> We consider that the Government is depriving us of our rights to duly farm and market our produce.

Casley continued to press for a change in the quota. In these and other letters he argued that the quota 'protects primarily those who have created the wheat surplus in Australia' and would lead to 'more farmers put off the land'. Declaring that 'I will not have my family reduced to a state of begging', Casley suggested a compromise whereby quotas could be assessed 'on a percentage of acreage basis', which would assure all farmers 'of a basic minimum income depending on season and marketing factors'.

Casley was concerned that the quota would wreck his business and force him off his property. In addition to filing complaints, he hatched an alternative plan. Considering that 'a claim of compensation is justified', he offered a solution in a letter to the premier – the governor could gift him land. He outlined this plan in an accompanying letter to the governor:

> The land we would propose is a reserve and station country in large which would inco-operate our existing holdings. Have sea frontage and a reasonable balanced source of income from its various sources and potentials ...
>
> I respectfully trust that you recommend same to Her Majesty the Queen and that she in turn will give her approval.

Casley used the wheat quota ratio to calculate what he considered appropriate. To crop the 6000 acres of wheat to which he felt entitled, the government would have to give him 1.8 million acres at a cost of around $52 million.

Unsurprisingly, Casley's call fell on deaf ears. He was not only unsuccessful at forcing a change in the wheat quota, but the governor and premier would not entertain his 'compromise'. In fact, there is no evidence that they even replied.

Events would soon become more concerning. Casley and his family became worried that the state government would act to compulsorily acquire their farm. Citing the introduction of a bill permitting the state to acquire land without consent, Casley determined to act. As Leonard's son Graeme Casley explains, 'that was the real catalyst'. Leonard Casley concurs: 'We seceded to protect our lands. To stop our lands from being taken from us.' On 21 April 1970, Leonard Casley served a formal notice of secession to the federal and Western Australian governments.

Independence

On 23 April 1970, Leonard Casley mailed four letters. Addressed to the governor-general Sir Paul Hasluck, prime minister John Gorton, Western Australia premier Sir David Brand and the state's governor Sir Douglas Kendrew, Casley's letters set out his legal basis for secession. The statement read:

> Fate Accompli
>
> In accordance to the rights of the Magna Carta and the rights of the Atlantic Treaty and the International rights to,

> newly form, "Self Preservation Governments." Resulting from actions deterent from the Principles of Unjust Enrichment and the Western Australian Governments further enforcement of a Retrospective Penal Act contrary to the Commonwealths Government Promise to the people of Australia thru the United Nations.
>
> It is herewith declared that as no objections has been directly lodged with myself during the last five months against ceding from the State of Western Australia accordingly to reasons given and the area of Independence to be negotiated accordingly to the compensation claim.

Casley invited the prime minister and governor-general to 'give formal recognition to our independence in formal accord to the Queens Prerogative under Section 61 of the West Australian Constitution'. He warned the premier:

> I would rather that a position of mutual co-operation were to prevail than to have to fight your Government purely for the purpose of gaining Justis which I am determined to achieve.
>
> I believe that you have a lot to gain by resolving the matter into one of progressing co-operation. If the matter goes into its next stage it will not be possible to achieve that which can be achieved from this point ...
>
> In the circumstances I feel that I can not be any more generous than I have to date to avoid embarrassment and at the same time resolve this matter.

Casley purported to establish his nation based upon the Magna Carta, the Atlantic Treaty, other unspecified international rights, and section 61 of the Constitution of Western Australia. None support his assertion of independence, meaning that there was no sound legal basis for his action.

The Magna Carta is a peace settlement signed between King John of England and a group of rebel barons in 1215. There is nothing in the document supporting the right of a person to pack up and leave the Australian nation. There is also no 'Atlantic Treaty', but Casley may have meant to refer to the North Atlantic Treaty, an international military alliance between ten founding Western European countries plus the United States and Canada. Signed in 1949, the treaty forms the legal basis for the North Atlantic Treaty Organisation (NATO). The treaty does not recognise a right to form anything akin to a 'self-preservation government', nor any other rights that would assist Casley. Finally, section 61 of the Constitution of Western Australia provides that the British monarch may divide the 'Colony of Western Australia' into separate colonies as Her Majesty 'thinks fit'. However, no monarch has taken such steps, and the secession of any part of the state would be inconsistent with the creation of an 'indissoluble Federal Commonwealth' by the Australian Constitution.

Even though there was no legal basis for Leonard Casley's secession, his flurry of letters sparked confusion. It was clear the Hutt River was not a sovereign state, but government officials were concerned that Casley would rely on the goodwill and ignorance of others to press his claims. On 6 August 1970, the acting secretary of the Prime Minister's Department, R.N. Townsend, wrote to the director-general of the Postmaster-

General's Department explaining the general rule that had been set down:

> Mr. Casley has written to the Prime Minister on a number of occasions since 23 April 1970. Mr. Casley's claim has not been taken seriously and consequently, in drafting replies for the signature of the Prime Minister's Private Secretary, we have been careful not to include any reference to Mr Casley's self-imposed title. The replies from the Prime Minister's office take the form of a simple acknowledgment of Mr. Casley's correspondence.

It seemed that not everyone got the memo. Many government officials were unsure how to respond. On 19 June 1970 the acting official secretary to the governor-general, D.R.M. Thompson, wrote to the 'Administrator' of the 'Hutt River Province', informing Casley that the official secretary to the governor-general, Sir Murray Tyrrell, had read his communication 'with interest'.

In October 1970, the Leader of the Opposition in Western Australia, John Tonkin, addressed Casley as 'Administrator, Hutt River Province'. That same month, Ian Thompson, the state member for Darling Range, also addressed Casley as the Administrator of Hutt River Province. Thompson noted further, 'Your comments on the constitutional aspects of the Hutt River Province are of interest. I look forward to a harmonious relationship.'

Casley seized upon loose or diplomatic language from government officials. He sent countless photocopies of letters addressing him as the Administrator of the Hutt River

Province to other state agents in an attempt to bluff them as to the legitimacy of his claim. However, the Commonwealth remained resolute. On 10 December 1971, prime minister William McMahon wrote to John Tonkin, now premier of Western Australia: 'I would like to make it quite clear that the Commonwealth Government does not recognise either legally or in any other way the existence of a self-styled Province of this nature nor can I envisage any circumstance in which it would do so.'

The premier reiterated this forceful dismissal a week later. In a press release, Tonkin explained: 'The Commonwealth Government has removed any shred of credibility from the claims of the so called "Hutt River Province" proclaimed by the Casley family of Western Australia.'

This has since remained the formal position of the Western Australian and federal governments. In July 1973, Tonkin again rejected any suggestion that the Hutt River Province was independent, declaring that 'Mr. Casley's land is just as much a part of the State of Western Australia, and of the Commonwealth of Australia, as is my block in Preston Point Road, East Fremantle'. 'The so-called province,' he added, 'can never hope to have any legal or political existence.'

The following year, the new Liberal premier Sir Charles Court echoed his predecessor. In answering questions on the citizenship status of Leonard Casley in the Western Australian Parliament, Court noted: 'The State's jurisdiction is beyond question, and Mr Casley's pretension to the contrary is manifest nonsense.' In March 1975, prime minister Gough Whitlam patiently reiterated this in a letter addressed to Casley:

> I should like to make perfectly clear to you that the Australian Government does not recognise legally or otherwise, the existence of the "Hutt River Province".
>
> The area concerned is part of the Australian nation and the Constitution and laws of Australia apply in the self-styled "province" just as they apply to other parts of the Australian nation.

Nonetheless, Casley continued to act as though his claim was lawful. Consistent with the British diplomatic laws of recognition, following independence a flag was chosen and correspondence delivered to the governor-general of the neighbouring Australia. In March 1971, a Hutt River Bill of Rights was adopted, promising all persons the full protection of the law. Hutt River coins were minted, banknotes issued, postage stamps and passports designed and printed, and vehicle registration plates established. A national anthem was recorded:

> There is a giant lying in the sun
> Where people welcome everyone
> It's a land where dreams can all come true
> And people strive until they do
> Where wealth in rivers wide can flow
> And there is room enough to grow
> This land of hope, this land of dreams
> This land I call my own.

Casley sent numerous letters to other countries and the United Nations seeking diplomatic recognition, and claimed to have set up consulates in Vienna and Sydney. He attempted to set

10 MAR 1975

Dear Mr Casley,

I have received your letter of 7 February 1975.

I should like to make perfectly clear to you that the Australian Government does not recognise, legally or otherwise, the existence of the "Hutt River Province".

The area concerned is part of the Australian nation and the Constitution and laws of Australia apply in the self-styled "province" just as they apply to other parts of the Australian nation.

I should also add that Australian diplomatic missions overseas have been advised of the position and, as necessary, have conveyed this advice to the governments of countries to which they are accredited. You should understand, therefore, that in the event of your seeking to present the "province" overseas, the Australian diplomatic representative in the country concerned would make it clear that the "province" has no legal standing.

Yours sincerely,

E. G. WHITLAM

E. G. WHITLAM

Mr L. G. Casley,
10 Lockhart Street,
COMO W.A. 6152

Prime Minister Gough Whitlam dismisses Prince Leonard's assertion of sovereignty
Courtesy of the National Archives of Australia. NAA: A1838, 1490/3/1656/ PART 1

up a register for international shipping under the Hutt River Province flag. In 1977, he even laid a sovereign claim to part of Antarctica.

Casley also continued to harvest wheat in open defiance of the quota. Fearing prosecution and the resumption of his farm, he and his family searched for a legal defence. They believed they found one in an obscure law passed in England during King Henry VII's reign. The *Treason Act 1495* was passed to heal resentment following the War of the Roses. Aiming to encourage former advocates of Richard III to support Henry VII, it provided that anyone serving or fighting for the new king would not be guilty of any offence. Drawing on this provision, Casley invested himself as His Royal Highness Prince Casley and transformed the Hutt River Province into the Principality of Hutt River. As he (wrongly) understood it, because he was a prince, the law would preclude Australia prosecuting him or his family for any offences they committed while he attained his throne, and would prevent the Australian government from interfering with him 'in the discharge of his Princely duties'.

Prince Leonard's actions made no legal difference, and it is not clear whether the Australian or Western Australian authorities appreciated the reasons for the change in nomenclature. Nonetheless, believing his title more secure, Casley persisted in engineering attempts for inadvertent and implicit acts of recognition. In letters to members of the federal government and opposition, he used the title 'Prince Leonard' and designed his letterheads to invite replies addressed to him using that title. He was often successful. In March 1975, the federal Treasurer, Jim Cairns, wrote to 'Dear Prince Leonard'.

Prince Leonard Casley in front of the flag of the Hutt River Province
Courtesy of the National Archives of Australia.
NAA: A1838, 1490/3/1656 PART 1

In September 1975, opposition leader Malcolm Fraser also wrote a reply to 'Dear Prince Leonard', addressing the letter to 'Prince Leonard, Administrator, Hutt River Provinces, via Western Australia'. Letters like this have no legal effect, but Casley acted as if they did.

While these letters addressed Casley as a prince, they did not definitively 'recognise' his farm as a principality. However, Casley soon had more luck. In a letter dated 23 December

1975, Peter Nixon, the incoming minister for transport in the new federal government led by Fraser, wrote to 'My dear Prince Leonard', and addressed his correspondence to 'Prince Leonard, Sovereign, Hutt River Province'. Nixon and the Fraser government had not decided to shift from Whitlam's approach, and Nixon's letter addressed to 'Hutt River Province' did not recognise a new sovereign country. However, Casley used this to bolster his claims with other governments by sending photocopies around the world.

The situation had become so troubling that it forced an internal response. In January 1976, John Menadue, the secretary of the Department of the Prime Minister and Cabinet, warned all departmental heads that Casley was writing letters to members of the new government to elicit replies that inadvertently recognised his sovereignty. Menadue asked each department to ensure that any reply from their minister would be addressed to Leonard Casley's two-bedroom home in the riverside Perth suburb of Como.

Other challenges soon emerged. The Australian Postmaster-General refused to accept Hutt River stamps, characterising them as 'stickers'. The post office also refused to deliver mail addressed to the province (as opposed to Casley's Como home), instead returning it to sender. Casley sent hundreds of letters to government officials and parliamentarians demanding that they end the 'economic embargo' and used the media to drum up support against his 'belligerent' neighbour.

An attempt to route Hutt River mail through Canada failed, but not without embarrassment to the Australian government. Australia Post officials were forced to explain to their North American counterparts that the principality had no legal status.

Bemused Canadian officials issued a nationwide staff bulletin that led to the interception of articles bearing Hutt River stamps. Internal correspondence records that Australian postal officers considered Casley a 'crank' and 'eccentric'. Eventually the post office relented, determining to deliver mail to Casley so as not to depart from the tradition of doing its utmost to deliver inadequately or inaccurately addressed mail. Australian officials might not recognise Hutt River, but they lost the will to continue the fight with the relentless and persistent Casley.

A media sensation

The Principality of Hutt River had no legal existence separate from the Commonwealth of Australia, but its story soon attracted a storm of interest. Prince Leonard proved an adept media performer, making comparisons to David and Goliath and Leonard Wibberley's satirical novel *The Mouse that Roared* to draw attention to Hutt River. Playing on community fascination, Leonard Casley invested his entire family with royal titles and appointed them to key positions in his government. His wife Shirley became Her Royal Highness Princess Shirley of Hutt, Dame of the Rose of Sharon. His eldest son, Ian, became Prince Ian, Grand Duke of Hutt, Earl of Fairvale, Grand Bailiff of the Royal Order, and Knight Commander of the Most Worthy Order of The Crusaders Cross of Jerusalem. Prince Ian was also the Postmaster General of the fledgling province.

Prince Leonard and his principality became a media sensation, attracting tourists and money, and frustrating Commonwealth officials in Canberra and diplomatic posts overseas. Even schoolchildren across Australia got in on the act. In August 1971, Western Australia premier John Tonkin wrote to prime minister William McMahon informing him that schoolchildren around the country wanted to treat the subject as a school project. The premier sought advice as to how this could be shut down lest children gain the mistaken belief that Hutt River had a valid existence.

The excitement and attention lavished on Hutt River is reflective of Australians' tendency to celebrate the underdog. Leonard Casley was adept at styling himself as the honest farmer toiling away, refusing to be crushed by an unthinking government. This image attracted sympathy and support, as did the fact that some could see a faint outline of the Eureka Stockade legend in a farmer choosing to take on the government. Others just loved the story of a man telling the authorities to get stuffed.

Perth folk band The Ranting Lads recorded a song celebrating the principality and Prince Leonard's determination:

Broken Serenity: The Ballad of Hutt River

Well I'll tell you a tale of a farmer's long fight,
A man who could not rest until he's won his right:
To work on his land to live a good life,
With his four strapping sons, his three daughters
and the wife.

Chorus:
Tis of the rebel Casley a story will be told,
A man who valued freedom more than any sum of gold.
He settled in Hutt River, it was his chosen land.
Twas there the rebel farmers will fight and make a stand.

Well the government decreed with one wave of its hand:
'We don't want your wheat, but we will take your land.'
'Never!' cried the farmer. 'This action is unjust.
You have betrayed the honest fold; you've broken your
trust.'

Chorus

'Well listen, my family, to what I have to say:
Under this tyranny our land it will decay.
Our own separate land for us will be the need –
We'll wait thirty days, and then we'll secede.'

Chorus

Well the politicians muttered. He did what he meant.
'We'll raise your wheat quota twelve hundred percent!'
'Too late,' said the farmer. 'Too long you did lag;
It's Hutt River Province. We've raised up our flag.'

Chorus

Well the tale of his battle it was spread far and wide.
He would not be beaten nor run off and hide.
Let others take examples of this courageous man:
'They said we can't make it. We showed them we can.'

Chorus

'The Royal Family', *Sunday Times*, 14 November 1971
WA Newspapers/The West

Whether or not journalists truly believed Casley's claims, they often repeated them without qualification. In television and radio broadcasts and articles in newspapers and magazines from all over the globe, the principality was playfully described as a 'breakaway province' and Leonard Casley a 'remarkable Australian'. In 1971 the Western Australian *Sunday Times* featured a portrait of 'The Royal Family'.

In 1973, the ABC show *Weekend Magazine* described the province as a 'royalist's utopia': 'Here there are no peasants, serfs or even a middle class. The royal family makes up the total population.' For those who doubted the legality of secession, Prince Leonard always had a quick reply; in an interview with a journalist for *The Australian* newspaper, Leonard quipped: 'Andorra has been having legal arguments for 800 years. We expect a few bumps.'

International journalists soon picked up the story. In 1975, *Time* magazine interviewed the man 'the government was trying to make ... a pauper' and who became 'a prince' instead. Discussing his plans and skirmishes with the authorities, the story concluded by noting that 'as the legend of Prince Leonard grows, the Canberra government and the Western Australia state government are finding his quixotic tilts at their bureaucracy increasingly nettlesome'.

The following year, major Swiss newspaper *Neue Zürcher Zeitung* featured a story on the 'farming Don Quixote', reporting that thousands of tourists were 'rushing to the self-styled aristocrat in this egalitarian immigrant country'. The Swiss paper spoke to Perth publican Pat O'Dwyer – ennobled by Prince Leonard as Sir Brendan, Earl of Auburn – who discussed Casley's motivations: 'It began as a protest and a great laugh ... At first I thought the Prince was a big nut. But people like his protest against a stupid bureaucracy and that is why he is becoming more popular.' Unlike many breathless pieces in the Australian media, the article recognised that the Principality of Hutt River relied on media attention for its success:

> The 'Sovereign' of Hutt cannot want the intervention of 'bureaucratic fungus'. For Prince Casley earns much more and more effortlessly than farmer Casley. He would, however, be quite pleased if the authorities were to become somewhat tougher with his mini-state. As O'Dwyer admits: 'We must remain in the public eye.' But the Government of Western Australia has so far only let itself be provoked to the dry statement that 'Mr Casley is no different to any other citizen.'

These and other stories increased Casley's national profile and Prince Leonard was soon invited to speak to events all over the country. In 1976, the Launceston Liberal Forum introduced the prince to their luncheon: 'Who among us in Tasmania has not said, "If only we could secede?". Here then is a man who has not only said so, but he has done so. It is only in Australia that such an unusual thing could take place.'

The Hobart *Mercury* was perhaps a little too naïve in believing Leonard's story:

> Though small in stature, Prince Leonard came up big with a sincere talk of how he led the people of the 30-square mile Hutt River Valley from a situation which threatened

> ruin to a lucrative enterprise whose economy is constantly growing stronger ...
>
> He did his homework very well, and was able to meet every challenge to the sovereignty of his tiny principality. Now, people are travelling the world on Hutt River passports 'with no problem at all, and in many respects we are receiving full recognition from Australian governments'.

Other journalists proved just as receptive to Leonard Casley's claims. In 1974, the *South China Sunday Post-Herald* breathlessly reported on Casley's plans to transform the 'tiny independent state' from a 'backwater'. The journalist explained that 'a well-known Hongkong firm with massive banking and travel interests' was eager to facilitate the transformation by supporting the construction of 'a casino, a yachting and water-skiing lake, Australia's first artificial ski slope and a fully equipped riding school'. According to the story, 'Pan American Airways have said they would "more or less" be their official airline, and plans are in hand to create an airport big enough to take 737s and other jets'. As if the tale was not sufficiently fantastic, the journalist also discussed the legality of the province: 'The "secession" came after a dispute with the Western Australian government over a wheat quota – and astonished Government officials found it was legal because it did not contravene anything in the constitution.'

Even if Casley's plans for a casino and ski fields never came to fruition, he constructed several government buildings, a secession monument, and the 'Pyramid of Hutt' that contained healing crystals. Casley also erected a giant stone bust of himself.

A steady stream of tourists, and national and international media attention, ensured he remained an icon, with people from all over the world marvelling at his tenacity as the leader of his new nation.

Businesses soon tried to cash in. In 1979, the owners of a tourism resort on Magnetic Island in Queensland issued Prince Leonard and Princess Shirley two first-class return tickets from Perth to Townsville in an effort to drum up publicity. While in Queensland, Prince Leonard met Premier Joh Bjelke-Petersen on what Leonard described as 'a State visit'. The meeting was recorded in official photographs.

Of course, not everyone appreciated Prince Leonard or considered the principality an eccentric but harmless joke. The Thirtyniners' Association, a group of World War II veterans, wrote several letters to successive prime ministers in the 1970s calling on the federal government to end Casley's pretensions, 'before others with similar ideas to theirs break this country up into hundreds of small provinces, giving free access to those considered by the majority of our citizens today as undesirable immigrants'. Thos Parker, the federal secretary of the Association, concluded with a warning, 'Should it be your decision to ignore our position, we have the right as citizens to remedy the matter our own way.' In 1979, Michael Hodgman, the Liberal member for Denison in Tasmania, called upon prime minister Malcolm Fraser to act: 'The continuance of the so-called "Hutt River Province" is, in my judgment – and I have no doubt that you would share this view – a source of embarrassment to the Commonwealth Government. I believe it should now be brought to a halt.'

Fraser's secretary replied curtly: 'There has never been a

"Hutt River Province" and it follows that its existence cannot be terminated.'

International recognition

In his attempts to garner international attention, Prince Leonard appointed hundreds of 'honorary consuls' and 'ambassadors' all over the world. The sudden presence of individuals seeking to enter states or conduct businesses on Hutt River passports caused confusion and requests for clarification from Australian embassies. A flurry of diplomatic cables sent back to Canberra record serious alarm within the Department of Foreign Affairs. Canberra was warned that 'the issue of these "passports" must eventually cause some embarrassment to the Commonwealth Government':

> You will notice that the 'passport' is well produced, has a look of authenticity and is in effect a copy of an Australian passport except that the word Australia in no way appears in the document. The phrase 'independent sovereign state' appears under the crest on the cover and on the first page and 'diplomatic passport' only on the cover.

Canberra demurred. Embassies were advised to explain that the Hutt River was not a sovereign state and to leave it at that.

This tactic did not work in all cases. The cables reveal that Australia's approach to the Hutt River was treated with candid bemusement by foreign states. The Bolivian government was 'puzzled' that Leonard Casley 'has been able to obtain letters signed by the Prime Minister while Leader of the Opposition, and the Minister for Transport, addressing him as "Prince Leonard"'. The Swiss government was 'genuinely puzzled' by the 'degree of toleration the province seems to enjoy'. They considered that, under Swiss law, Leonard Casley's actions would amount to offences worthy of prosecution and wondered whether Casley had ever been prosecuted and if not, why not. Perhaps it suggested some acquiescence on Australia's part? In May 1976, the Department of Foreign Affairs issued a memo to all diplomatic posts reiterating three points:

> nothing has altered with respect to the "Province's" legal status;
>
> that the not taking of any legal proceedings against the "Province" by the Commonwealth has not stemmed from any acquiescence on its part to the "Province's" attempts to acquire legal personality;
>
> and
>
> the various Government instrumentalities in Australia are taking appropriate action at every opportunity to thwart such attempts.

That diplomatic memo also sought to explain the Australian government's approach to the principality. Although Casley had not been prosecuted for his apparent secession, this did not mean that the government accepted his independence. Rather, because the Hutt River was still part of the Commonwealth, no law had been broken. The Australian government would prevent Leonard Casley from acting like a state and attempting to attain international recognition. It would also ensure that Casley complied with all Australian laws, whether they be on taxation or the road rules. While many countries questioned the wisdom of this approach, the Australian government stuck to it.

The Western Australian government was also alarmed at the prospect that Leonard Casley was confusing people overseas. In April 1976, premier Sir Charles Court explained in parliament:

> I think some people are misled. Whilst the average citizen of this State would be fully aware of the stupidity of Mr Casley's claims, people in, and from other places have less cause to realise that they are being duped. As certain elements of the media seem intent on sustaining this hoax, it may become necessary to consider what special action can be taken, if only to save visitors to this State, and people in other places, from being misled and commercially exploited.

Ultimately, the Australian government refrained from taking any further steps, perhaps because he was not technically breaking any laws or because the Australian public may have seen a crackdown as mean-spirited and unnecessary. As Patrick O'Neill explained on ABC show *This Day Tonight* in 1976, 'the Government may look stupid, while he exists, but it will look even more stupid when it tries to dismantle him'.

People connected to Hutt River took advantage of the confusion. A Canadian newspaper dedicated an entire page to 'Hutt's Alberta Consul', a 16-year-old high school student named Jack Geiger. The story concluded, 'there are indications the Australian government is accepting the principality. Prime minister Malcolm Fraser address[ed] the ruler as Prince Leonard, not Mr Casley, while the Commonwealth has helped Hutt River with its tourist promotions'. Some who had taken out Hutt River citizenship and been awarded royal titles proclaimed it on their business cards.

Journalists loved these stories. The apparent diplomats explained that the 'response was incredible'; on international flights 'they are often upgraded to first class', while in hotels 'they are moved from standard rooms to suites'. Others claimed to use Hutt River passports to travel internationally. In an article from 1982, retired Australian detective and supposed Hutt River ambassador, Sir Tom Ericksen, explained what happened when he tried to enter Orly Airport in Paris on a diplomatic passport:

> 'Hutt River Province?' [the Immigration Officer] asked in heavily-accented English, his eyebrows rising to meet his cap. 'Where is Hutt River Province?'
>
> Ericksen recalls the conversation because he is fond of recalling it. 'It's 18 times bigger than Monaco,' he replied. 'Second-biggest country in Australia.'
>
> 'One moment,' said the passport officer, not at all happy with the green and gold embossed document in his hand, nor apparently with the knighthood it proclaimed for its 20-stone owner.
>
> Ericksen stood politely in the queue while the officer conferred with his superior. Presently the two men

> returned to the counter. 'Yes, excuse me, Your Excellency,' said the more senior man, ushering Ericksen through the desk and slapping his underling at the same time. 'Right this way, Your Excellency,' he said as he led Victoria's ambassador to Hutt River Province into France, pausing only to stamp his passport on the way through.

Whether or not this story is true, it is difficult to imagine it occurring now, given the increase in border security around the world since the September 11 attacks in 2001.

Hutt River may have fooled individuals from time to time, but Prince Leonard did not obtain official recognition of the sovereignty and independence of his province from another state. He did, however, continue to receive letters that addressed him as 'Prince Leonard'. In 1974, he claimed to have received a card from the Shah of Iran wishing him all the best for the next 12 months and continued success. In 2016, he received a letter from Queen Elizabeth II. The Palace replied to a letter Casley had written wishing the Queen a happy ninetieth birthday, conveying 'Her Majesty's good wishes to you and all concerned for a most enjoyable and successful celebration on 23rd and 24th April to mark the forty-sixth anniversary of the Principality of Hutt River'.

Although these letters were of no legal import (and sometimes of questionable veracity), Prince Leonard used them to add a veneer of legitimacy to his claims. Indeed, in 2016, several journalists reported that the principality had 'finally received an official nod from [the Queen as] Australia's head of state'.

In at least one instance, Prince Leonard did manage to successfully fool a state – if only for a week. In 1981, Hong Kong

Prince Leonard Casley shaking the hands of Japanese tourists at the Western Australia–Hutt River border
Hemis / Alamy Stock Photo

became the first government in the world to extend diplomatic recognition to Hutt River. A public notice published in the Hong Kong Government Gazette announced the appointment of 'a Mr Raymond Sacklyn as Ambassador for Hutt River Province', declaring that Mr Sacklyn 'enjoyed the special trust and confidence of the Prince as his personal representative in Hong Kong'. Following inquiries by journalists, 'embarrassed officials' in Hong Kong admitted that they had made 'a frightful mistake'. A special gazette was issued ending the recognition of the principality and Mr Sacklyn's tenure as ambassador.

At another time, Prince Leonard himself was fooled. In 1974, Leonard received notice that the Sultanate of Occussi-

Ambeno would officially recognise the Hutt River. The sultanate was located on the west coast of Timor and had itself declared independence from Portugal in 1968. The Sultan, Sir Waals Abdullah I, invited Prince Leonard's government to negotiate on the establishment of mutual diplomatic relations and on the development of mutual cooperation and assistance programs. In an article in the *Sunday Times*, Prince Leonard announced, 'this is a complete surprise – we had never approached the sultan's government'. Perhaps this was because the sultanate itself was a hoax, a creation of New Zealand anarchist and stamp collector Bruce Grenville. It is not clear if Hutt River ever joined Grenville's International Council of Independent States – a United Nations for micronations.

The end of Hutt River

Over the years, Leonard Casley and his family appeared in Australian courts numerous times charged with avoiding various tax and other laws. In 1972, his son Wayne Casley was fined $40 for failing to register for national service, while Leonard and another son, Ian Casley, were fined $2 for failing to vote in a federal election. The next year, Leonard defied an order from the Northampton Shire Council to stop building an art gallery, motel, chapel and administration block without a permit and was fined $125. In 1974, he was convicted of selling wine on his farm, fined $40 and ordered to pay another $60 in costs. The conviction was recorded despite Casley informing the Magistrates Court that Hutt River 'did not recognise or submit to its jurisdiction', leaving him to issue a strongly worded 'diplomatic protest'.

A few years later Casley had a successful court battle. In 1977 he was convicted of failing to provide documents to the Australian Taxation Office, was fined $4 and ordered to pay $50 in costs. Casley refused to pay, and a warrant was issued for his arrest. After attending a police station at Northampton to discuss the matter, he was transferred 50 kilometres south to Geraldton to spend the night in jail. His son Ian 'acted without delay and almost immediately set off for Geraldton' to pay the fine but arrived at 4:05 in the afternoon – five minutes after the police station had closed. The station officer explained that he therefore could not accept the fine.

Leonard was discharged at 8:45 am the following day, 'after having been kept in prison for 16 or 17 hours'. He was apoplectic, declaring to journalists that 'your country has seriously erred' and 'someone in Australia has made a terrible mistake'. The Supreme Court of Western Australia agreed. Casley was successful in an action of false imprisonment against the state of Western Australia and the superintendent of Geraldton Regional Prison on the basis that he should have been released when his son attempted to tender the fine the previous day. Leonard Casley was awarded $200.

Graciously, Leonard Casley wrote to prime minister Malcolm Fraser, offering his expertise to assist Fraser in fixing a host of Commonwealth laws which, according to Leonard, were both unconstitutional and 'in a mess'. His biographer remarks, 'Only a Prince amongst Princes would make such a kind offer of help to an apparent foe.' It does not appear that Fraser responded.

More recently, Casley had less success in the courts. Despite purporting to secede on the basis of a restrictive wheat quota, the Hutt River farm stopped growing wheat and instead focused on tourism. The move was fruitful; by 2010, supposedly around 40 000 tourists were visiting each year. However, that again drew the attention of the Australian Taxation Office, which became interested in the income generated from tourism within the principality – Casley had apparently stopped paying tax on income generated within Hutt River in 1970.

In 2007, the High Court of Australia dismissed an application by Casley to appeal against a judgment against him for failing to file tax returns. Justice Dyson Heydon found that arguments that the principality is 'not part of Australia and not subject to Australian taxation laws' are 'completely unarguable', 'fatuous, frivolous and vexatious'. In 2017, Justice Rene Le Miere of the Western Australian Supreme Court added that they were 'gobbledygook'. His Honour explained: 'Anyone can declare themselves a sovereign in their own home but they cannot ignore the laws of Australia or not pay tax.'

The WA Supreme Court decision proved particularly consequential. Leonard Casley was ordered to pay income tax of more than $2.7 million, covering several years, while his son, Graeme Casley, was ordered to pay more than $242 600. Although Leonard Casley sought to negotiate, the Australian Taxation Office and federal government would not budge. With pressure mounting on the aging prince, Leonard Casley abdicated in 2017, and his youngest son Prince Graeme acceded to the throne. In 2019, Prince Leonard passed away at the age of 93. One year later, with tourism drying up as a result of the Covid-19 pandemic, Graeme announced that the farm would be sold to pay their tax bill. He sold it in 2021, bringing an end to the half-century existence of 'the second biggest country in Australia'.

Death and taxes

The demise of the Principality of Hutt River demonstrates that no one can outlast the two certainties in life: death and taxes. On this account at least, the future of the principality was written the very day that Leonard Casley purported to secede. As ABC journalist Patrick O'Neill noted in 1976, 'One day someone will do something about him and he can huff and puff and rattle his toy sabre as much as he likes, but Australia has the ultimate authority.'

O'Neill was proven correct, but there was much more to this story than a final, overwhelming assertion of authority by Australia. Reflecting on Prince Leonard's actions decades later, Pastoralists and Graziers Association of Western Australia president Tony Seabrook explained that Casley 'stuck his nose up, even his finger, at the Federal Government, and most people were not only amused by what happened but a little bit on his side'. Seabrook continued:

> he challenged the bureaucracy of the day and he gave a lot of people a lot of food for thought ... One day he was a wheat farmer, doing what the rest of us do, getting covered in dust and chaff, and the next day he was a prince. You don't find a lot of people today in our society now that are prepared to differentiate themselves with the daring and the dash that he did. I don't know that he changed the world but he certainly added a lot of colour to it.

In at least one way, Casley did change the world. The Principality of Hutt River became an inspiration for thousands of people in Australia and across the world. His actions inspired many others frustrated with bureaucracy to cast off the shackles of the state and rule their own micronation. As the Principality of Hutt River's motto recorded, 'While I Breathe, I Hope'.

3

'FROM THE SEA, FREEDOM': THE PRINCIPALITY OF SEALAND

On a rainy and gloomy Saturday afternoon in September 1967, a small but dignified ceremony was held to mark the independence of the world's newest country. Although no national anthem had yet been composed, a few solemn words were uttered, and the nation's red, white and black tricolour flag was raised. Under the stewardship of Prince Roy Bates, a World War II veteran and former major in the British Army, and his wife Princess Joan, the Principality of Sealand greeted the world.

All newly independent countries face immediate challenges. Leaders need to consider how to provide for their citizens, build infrastructure to promote development and secure the safety of their nation. However, the challenges facing Sealand were particularly daunting. To begin with, the entirety of the principality's territorial claim consisted of a 4100-tonne decommissioned naval installation located 13 kilometres off the coast of Essex in the River Thames estuary.

Initially built in 1942 to guard the United Kingdom port of Harwich from invasion, the naval fort possessed no arable land. In fact, it possessed very little habitable land at all. The

Principality of Sealand resembled an abandoned oil rig. It comprised a pontoon about the size of two tennis courts, supported by two 18-metre hollow reinforced concrete towers of around 7.3 metres in diameter. During the height of World War II, some 200 men called the fort home.

The fort – officially known as Fort Roughs, and colloquially as Roughs Tower – was not the only one sitting abandoned off the coast. Seven Maunsell forts (named for their designer Guy Maunsell) were deposited in the Thames estuary in 1942 and decommissioned in the late 1950s. Alarmed by Bates's move, the UK government decided to act. A couple of months after Bates took control of Roughs Tower, the Ministry of Defence blew up a second fort located nearby. Operation Sunk Head involved almost 1500 kilograms of explosives and was carried out to make the fort unsuitable 'to interests other than the Ministry'. The demolition crew sailed past Roughs Tower and yelled 'You're next!'

The demolition crew's warning did not come to fruition, and the UK did not wrest the abandoned fort from Roy Bates and his family. The Principality of Sealand continues to operate today, more than half a century later. But why did Bates seek to create his own country? Why did he choose such an unpromising location? And how on earth is his family still occupying the site?

Meet Roy Bates

If anyone could it make work, Roy Bates could. Born in 1921, he grew up in the coastal town of Southend on the north bank of the Thames estuary. The only surviving child of six siblings,

Bates was always eager to broaden his horizons – and engage in a scrap. As a 15-year-old he dropped out of boarding school to fight for the International Brigades in the Spanish Civil War – though not for ideological reasons. As Bates explained much later, 'I fought for both sides. I didn't care, I just wanted to fight.'

Eventually Bates was deported back to England. Once home, he picked up work as a rancher with the Vestey family, who owned a gigantic meat-packing business that operated across three continents. Bates was about to be sent to Argentina with the Vesteys when war broke out in Europe in 1939. Informed that as an essential worker he would not be allowed to enlist, he simply stopped turning up to work. Initially joining the Coastal Battalion, Bates agitated for a transfer so he could see action. He was accepted into the Royal Fusiliers and served in North Africa, the Middle East and Italy.

From there it gets a little difficult to separate fact from fiction. Several newspaper articles record that he saw action at the Battle of Monte Cassino in 1944. While advancing, a stick grenade exploded in his face, smashing his jaw and showering him in shrapnel. The timeline is unclear, but Bates apparently later crash-landed on the German-occupied island of Rhodes and was taken prisoner by Greek fascists. Bates claims to have escaped but was recaptured and set to be shot when a German officer arrived and stopped the firing squad. It is not clear when or how he was released from German custody. He was officially discharged from the army in 1946 at age 25, his thirst for adventure unsated.

Returning home to Southend, Bates bounced around for a while. He found a job at a company that imported poultry meat from the Republic of Ireland, but the work and commute did not satisfy him, so he went looking to buy a fishing boat. In late 1948, Bates met 21-year-old Joan Collins at a dancehall in Southend; he proposed three days later, and the couple were married in February 1949. Over the next three years, Roy and Joan had two children, Penelope and Michael, but Roy was not yet ready to settle down. After leaving the fishing industry, frustrated at the low pay, Bates tried his hand at all manner of things. Some of his ventures included running a butcher shop and a real estate business, and importing latex from Malaysia. It was only Joan's objections that blocked his plan to buy a farm and move the family to Kenya in the middle of the Mau Mau rebellion in the 1950s. Looking back, perhaps that life would have been simpler.

Roy may have given up on the fishing business, but he would often take Michael out on the water. It was on one of these trips in early 1965 that the pair first set foot on the Maunsell forts. Scrambling up a rusty 20-metre ladder, Roy and Michael stood atop the decrepit fort, among a litter of cormorants, and looked out across the North Sea. Then and there, Bates decided to try his hand at radio broadcasting.

Pirate radio

Many micronations are created when people grow frustrated with bureaucracy and government regulation. The Principality of Sealand is no different. What is unique about Sealand, however, is that the bureaucracy that Roy Bates fought against concerned radio broadcasting. The Principality of Sealand was born out of a struggle to broadcast pop songs in the UK.

The British Broadcasting Corporation (the BBC) was set up in 1922 and granted a monopoly as the only organisation legally allowed to broadcast over the radio in the United Kingdom (this would not change until 1973). The BBC took this public trust seriously. For its first director-general, John Reith, the BBC had a civilising mission; its purpose was 'cultural improvement'. BBC broadcasts upheld the rhythm of the church calendar, and aimed to inform and educate the public by offering a carefully curated selection of programming. That programming was financed by a broadcast licence levied on listeners.

Imaginative and resourceful people sought to evade the licensing fees and the BBC's legal monopoly. Several commercial radio stations were set up across the English Channel on continental Europe in places like Normandy and Luxembourg. Others adopted even more ingenious evasions. In 1928, for instance, the owners of the London *Daily Mail* newspaper chartered a yacht called the *Ceto*. They installed a radio transmitter on the boat and set sail, intending to broadcast music and advertisements into the country from outside territorial waters. The transmitter did not work particularly well at sea, so the plan was adapted. The radio transmitter was replaced by four gigantic loudspeakers and the *Ceto* toured the UK, anchoring off holiday resorts and coastal towns, and blasting gramophone records from the deck. Despite being a 'technical failure', the experiment proved to be a publicity coup. *Daily Mail* correspondents reported that 'thousands of people' flocked to hear the 'musical yacht'.

Other ships began transmitting radio broadcasts into Northern Europe in the late 1950s. By 1964, the first ship broadcasting into the UK, Radio Caroline, was established. A week later, it was joined by Radio Atlanta. The pirate radio stations distinguished themselves from the BBC by offering pop music in addition to more traditional fare. They had another advantage. The UK's Copyright Act prevented the BBC from broadcasting more than 28 hours of records across all its stations each week, whereas Radio Caroline and Radio Atlanta broadcast more than 12 hours of records each day.

The success of Radio Caroline and Radio Atlanta brought competition. Ten more pirate radio stations emerged over the next two years, attracted by the considerable advertising revenue; 'some stations were said to individually bring in upwards of £20,000 each month' (around £370,000 in 2022). While most operated from ships specially fitted to broadcast radio, several set up shop on decommissioned naval forts in the Thames estuary. Dylan Taylor-Lehman notes that 'the enterprise also became so popular that the pirate radio was said to influence the outcomes of local elections, and the Beatles even recorded Christmas greetings for Radio London and Radio Caroline'. Their popularity placed government in a bind; Cabinet papers suggest that prime minister Harold Wilson was a fan of the pirate radio stations. As one government official remarked, 'They are beyond territorial waters. To stop them we will have to send a torpedo, but that's a bit drastic, isn't it?'.

Not everyone supported the pirate radio operators. In one letter to the editor, the chairman of the British Copyright Council lambasted the 'mumbling Ministers' for permitting 'the fort squatters' to remain. According to the Council, 'the forts are a scandal at law-abiding Britain's own front-door. Every liner passes close to them: the stranger can almost hear the lawless laughing at the Crown'.

As the letter writer intimates, during this period 'a kind of mild anarchy ruled the airwaves'. It is not surprising that by

1965 Roy Bates would enter this electric atmosphere. Unlike most of his competitors who operated from ships, Bates decided to try a different tactic. He would transmit Radio Essex from an abandoned World War II–era anti-aircraft gun platform called Knock John, located at the mouth of the Thames estuary. The plan was simple, but there was a catch. A rival pirate radio station, Radio City, was already operating out of Knock John. After a brief struggle, the Radio City crew were dispatched; as one displaced member noted, 'a disc jockey has to be many things – but a prize-fighter isn't one of them'.

Radio Essex did not survive for long. The UK government tolerated the existence of pirate radio operators largely because public opinion supported their exciting programming. However, the government felt compelled to act in the aftermath of the highly publicised shooting of June 1966, when a dispute over the ownership of a radio transmitter between Reg Calvert, the manager of Radio City, and retired Major Oliver Smedley turned violent. During a scuffle at Smedley's home, Smedley shot and killed Calvert. Smedley was cleared on the grounds of self-defence, but the killing spurred the government to act.

The government began enforcing the *Wireless Telegraphy Act 1949*, which prohibited unlicensed broadcasts within the UK's 3-nautical-mile territorial zone. Unfortunately for Bates, Knock John was located only one and a half nautical miles from the coast. Served with a summons, Bates was found in violation of the Act in November 1966 and fined £100. His appeal was dismissed the following year.

Bates may have been new to pirate radio, but he loved a scrap. On Christmas Day 1966, he dismantled the equipment on Knock John and moved to another decommissioned offshore

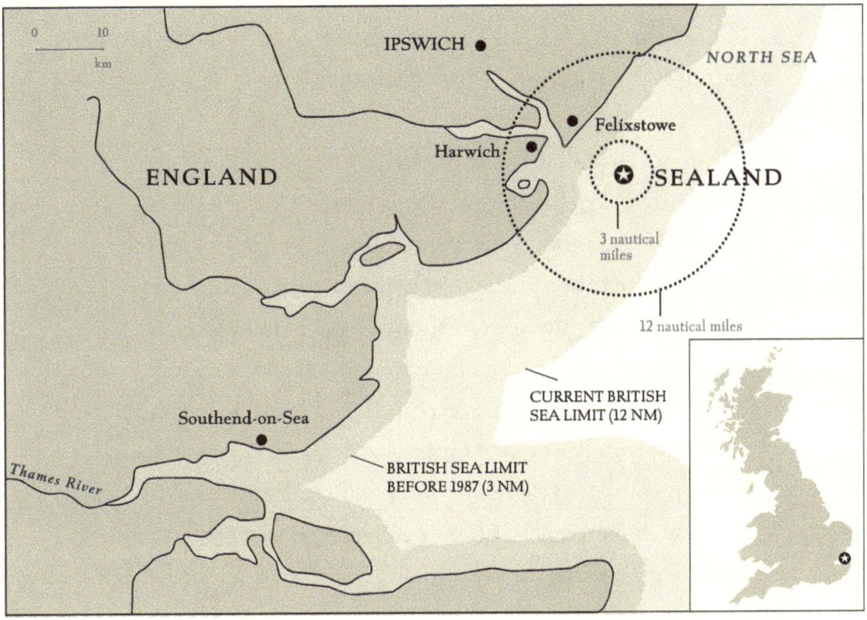

Location of the Principality of Sealand

naval fort, Roughs Tower. Located 11 kilometres off the coast of Suffolk, and 13 kilometres from Essex, Roughs Tower was therefore outside the UK's 3-nautical-mile territorial zone and so beyond British jurisdiction.

Roughs Tower may have been decommissioned but it was not abandoned. Anticipating that government intended to step up enforcement actions against pirate radio operators, Radio Caroline had already relocated to the remote fort. Over the first half of 1967, Bates struggled with the staff of Radio Caroline to wrest control. He eventually triumphed, evicting the crew from the tower and repulsing their attempts to return with an air-rifle, Molotov cocktails and perhaps even a flamethrower. The London *Times* reported one such incident:

> Mr. Bates said that Tuesday night's raid, in which a party of boarders was fought off, was 'a mere tickle' compared with the usual goings on. He said there had been several raids on the tower in the past three months. In one raid, Mr. Bates said, 'there were about 30 of them in foreign-looking boats, rather like Dutchmen, armed with knives and guns trying to take over. But they were repelled. After all, there is only one way up the ladder, and if you are at the top you are in a pretty good position. Some tried to swim with snorkels but they were spotted and given short shrift with a flame thrower.'

After another incident, 'one man was left hanging over the North Sea on a rope ladder for several hours' before being rescued by a lifeboat. Michael Bates notes that by this stage his father was 'getting himself a bit of reputation as an unstoppable nutter, which under the circumstances, was quite a useful reputation'. Unsurprisingly, the government faced questioning in parliament over what it intended to do 'to end gang warfare on pirate radio stations'.

In July, the government made its move. The *Marine & Broadcasting (Offences) Act 1967* closed the legal loophole that allowed pirate radio stations to operate. The Act prohibited British citizens from operating, participating in or assisting in broadcasts from the high seas, and banned advertising on these broadcasts. Advertisers abandoned the pirates and the industry crumbled. But the pirates had a victory of sorts. The government committed to reforming copyright law and the BBC was split into several radio stations – BBC Radio One, Two, Three and Four. While the latter three stations would continue to play the usual fare, BBC Radio One would broadcast pop. Many of the pirate radio DJs would soon be working at the BBC.

Rather than continue Radio Essex, Bates had a better idea. A few weeks earlier, while having a drink at a pub on the mainland to celebrate Joan's upcoming birthday, Roy remarked to his wife, 'Now you have your very own island.' Joan replied, 'It's just a shame it doesn't have a few palm trees, a bit of sunshine, and its own flag.' Everyone laughed, but Bates remembered the conversation. On 2 September 1967, Joan's birthday, he declared himself the ruler of the Principality of Sealand. It was a move he had foreshadowed earlier that year. Indeed, as he had told *The Times* in June:

> 'My solicitors are studying the legal aspects of the entire affair,' Mr. Bates said. 'This will entail international law and until they have completed their work I do not intend saying what my plans are. They have nothing to do with commercial radio, although I have all my equipment on board.'

Bates, his family and a small band of supporters claimed to have established the world's newest country.

Securing the claim

Life was hard on Sealand. Many years later, Joan Bates remarked that the first few months were 'like hell on Earth. There were no windows, no doors, the wind howled through, and everything was covered with a thick layer of crumbling rust'. Even getting supplies – whether food, heating oil or building materials – to the principality was difficult. It required bundling everything up in their Southend apartment, catching a bus to the sleepy port town of Paglesham, walking a mile along an unpaved road to a dinghy, ferrying themselves to their boat, and sailing 72 kilometres out to the fort. All up, a one-way trip would take four and a half hours, or a lot longer in bad weather. As Penelope Bates recalled, 'It was hours and hours from Paglesham on the boat ... I used to sit there in a blanket and think, "For God's sake will someone kill me please?"' Michael, on the other hand, was glad that he did not have to go to school.

Making it to the fort was hard enough, but then you had to get the supplies up to the principality. In the early days, before a mechanised winch was installed, the only way to set foot on Sealand was via a rope ladder or a wooden crate connected to a hand-cranked winch. In both cases this involved dangling 20 metres above the raging North Sea. It is not surprising that rationing was the order of the day. When the tins of baked beans, corned beef and dried milk ran out, the family lived on hard tack biscuits made of flour and water. During the particularly cold month of November 1967, the resupply boat never arrived. With no heating oil, the family survived by wrapping themselves in blankets.

The UK government was not sure how it should respond to this strange turn of events. Some officials demanded the fort's immediate destruction, but the Navy was reluctant to intervene, wary of the improvised arsenal Bates had apparently stocked. Other officials found the whole thing ridiculous. The

Winch access to the Principality of Sealand
roberthardíng / Alamy Stock Photo

Ministry of Defence considered his actions bizarre rather than threatening, remarking that his behaviour was 'ludicrous. Mr. Bates is trespassing and it now looks as if he is being very foolish'. Complicating matters further were difficult questions of jurisdiction. As the fort was located outside the UK's 3-nautical-mile territorial waters and the government had abandoned the site some years previously, it was uncertain whether Bates was breaking any law.

Nonetheless, it was clear from newspaper reports that Bates was causing considerable trouble. In light of the Molotov cocktail incident, Cabinet decided it would be best to 'dislodge' Bates and his supporters, in order 'to prevent it falling into the hands of foreign interests'. The Ministry of Defence began planning for Operation Callow.

The plan was simple. Bates had to return to England from time to time to stock up on groceries and supplies. On one of these visits, government officials would meet Bates at his home, remind him that the fort belonged to the Ministry of Defence and ask that he leave. If Bates declined their request, the government would offer him £5000 and promise to pay for removal of his property. Once the Bates family had been safely escorted off the site, the fort would be demolished to prevent them or anyone else from attempting reoccupation. Unfortunately, things did not go to plan.

Bates refused to cooperate. Rejecting the government's offer, he demanded £90,000. When the government rebuffed this, Bates refused to entertain any suggestions that he give up possession. Learning that a detachment of Royal Marine commandos was preparing to seize the fort, Bates went to the press and accused the government of threatening the lives of his children – who were still located on Sealand. Anxious to avoid negative publicity, the government backed down.

Other strategies were considered. David Belasco, a disillusioned Bates supporter, approached the government proposing to betray his former leader and allow the military safe entry. While the Ministry of Defence considered the plan 'implausible', it did let Belasco know that it was 'prepared to take the Fort over' if he was able to obtain possession without force. Ultimately this too did not eventuate. The Ministry backed out when it became clear that Belasco wanted the navy to blow the fort up to provide a stunning finale to a book he was writing.

Perhaps frustrated that his book would not have its ending, Belasco blew the whistle on the whole project. He swore an affidavit claiming that the Ministry had asked him to capture the tower by force. Bates jumped on the news, leaking the story to the *Daily Telegraph*. Much to the government's embarrassment, the matter was raised in parliament.

Still other approaches were considered. To maintain provisions, Bates regularly sailed between the fort and his home on the UK mainland. To delay and frustrate Bates, H.M. Customs and Excise sometimes refused to clear his boat for departure, arguing that it lacked a load line certificate certifying the safety limit of the boat's load. With a flair for gaining media attention, Bates again approached the papers, alleging that the government had 'marooned' his children on the fort by dredging up 'some obscure bit of marine law'. Although Customs and Excise maintained that Bates had merely to 'hire another boat if his own does not conform to the regulations', they eventually relented. Another plan to prosecute Bates for failing to ensure that his 14-year-old son Michael attended school was also dismissed. So too was the suggestion that the UK government pass legislation to expand Britain's territorial waters to encompass the fort. As one official noted, such a 'huge undertaking for a relatively small purpose would be "a ponderous move, inviting ridicule"'.

This did not mean that the government had given up, and its legal advisers considered the situation over several months. They concluded that if Bates committed a criminal offence on the fort he could be brought to trial and the fort reoccupied by the Navy. In November 1967, Michael Bates fired several shots from the fort towards HMS *Egeria*, a Royal Navy survey minesweeper. However, no damage was recorded, and the evidence was uncertain, so the incident was ignored.

The Director of Public Prosecutions did not have to wait long for a clearer case. In May 1968, Michael Bates fired a pistol in the direction of lighthouse staff working on a buoy near the tower. When Roy and Michael were next ashore, they were both indicted for violations of the *Firearms Act 1937*. And yet, at the moment of its triumph, the government hesitated: 'It was decided not to take advantage of Mr Bates' attendance in Court to try and occupy the Fort, as this smacked of sharp practice.'

The government had missed its opportunity. The court disagreed with the government's legal advisers and dismissed the case, finding that it had no jurisdiction. Justice Chapman of the Essex Assizes held that the parliament possessed 'the power to make it an offense for a British subject to have a firearm with intent to endanger life in Istanbul or Buenos Aires, or where have you'. However, it had not done so in this case. The Firearms Act was held to 'operate only within the ordinary territorial limits', and did not apply on Roughs Tower as it was located outside the UK's 3-nautical-mile territorial waters. The Sealand website records Justice Chapman concluding: 'This is a swash buckling incident perhaps more akin to the time of Sir Francis Drake, but it is my judgment that the UK courts have no jurisdiction.'

This last line does not appear in the actual judgment of the court, and it is important to note that the court did not hold that Sealand was independent. In fact, Justice Chapman concluded that the parliament *could* extend its jurisdiction to encompass the offshore platform if it wanted to. However, Bates saw the decision as providing recognition of his principality.

Some journalists and lower-level officials were also uncertain of this distinction. In a feature on 'the beautiful Princess Joan of Sealand' published in the aftermath of the decision, the *Sunday Mirror* reported: 'Last week a British judge ruled that the tower was outside British legal jurisdiction, which means that Mr and Mrs Bates have sovereignty over their island fort.' Customs officials in Essex also apparently began 'treating Sealand ... as a foreign country', informing journalists that they were 'awaiting directives about the necessity of passports'. Amid the confusion, the Foreign Office remained firm: 'Of course we don't recognise it as a foreign state. It's a fort in the North Sea, that's all. It's not a state ... it's a building.'

Following Justice Chapman's October 1968 ruling, the issue was returned to Cabinet, which eventually reached a practical resolution. Bates's continued occupation may have been undesirable, but as he was 'doing no actual harm ... and the Ministry of Defence had not need of the Fort themselves ... there were no pressing reasons for evicting Mr Bates, certainly none that would justify the use of force or the passage of special legislation'. It was also agreed that, in any case, 'there was some advantage in refraining from prosecutions which would enhance Mr Bates's local reputation as a colourful adventurer persecuted by authority.'

The decision set in place the UK's approach to the Principality of Sealand over the following decades. The UK generally ignores Sealand on the basis that it is a non-state actor with no legitimate claim to jurisdictional authority – so long as it does not cause too much trouble. This approach has much to commend it, but it has allowed Sealand space to attempt to develop into a fully-fledged nation.

Hostages and high-stakes diplomacy

The United Kingdom reached an uneasy but pragmatic position with respect to the Principality of Sealand. So long as Roy Bates, his family and his supporters did not bother or harm anyone, the government would allow them to stay on Roughs Tower. The UK remained committed to this approach, though Bates's actions often provoked alarm.

Over the course of the late 1960s and early 1970s, Bates and his family began to repair and restore the principality. Installing generators, they brought power to the small rusty fort and set about creating a home. Windows were refitted and electrical wiring redone. A small kitchen was fitted out with tables, chairs, a kettle and even some house plants. The bedrooms were painted, electric lights added and gym equipment set up. Not every member of the family was so enamoured. In 1968, Penelope Bates decided that she did not want to live in the North Sea and returned permanently to Southend. Michael had no such qualms. While Roy and Joan travelled around the world, invited by curious journalists and wealthy investors, Michael often spent days and weeks alone on the fort. His longest stint was six months.

During this period, Roy Bates sought to use his growing notoriety to gain international recognition for his principality. In 1969, he and a group of French and Belgian entrepreneurs approached the Belgian government hoping to establish diplomatic and commercial ties. Unfortunately for the group, British officials assured their Belgian counterparts that Sealand was not a sovereign nation. As if to emphasise this point, the same British officials ignored the inquiries from Sealand's representatives.

Following this disappointment, Bates began to focus his attention on a group of Germans who had approached Sealand after seeing an advertisement in a newspaper. Among the group was a former diamond dealer and soon-to-be Sealand minister of foreign affairs named Alexander Achenbach, and a World War II secret agent called Walter Scheffel who collected big cats and claimed to have received a landed title from Queen Elizabeth II. The group quickly set about conducting a 'diplomatic offensive' by sending letters to 150 countries on Bates's behalf seeking recognition of Sealand's statehood. In 1973 and 1974 they contacted the British embassy in Bonn, and made direct entreaties to Scotland, Morocco and the Federal Republic of Germany. The Second Secretary in Bonn sent a memo to the German government: 'No one knows why various European businessmen should take such an interest in it ... It is possible that they wish to encourage the creation of a tax haven or even to be able to claim oil discoveries in the area.'

In 1976 they stepped up their efforts. They 'asked the Australian Embassy for visas in their Sealand passports, went to the Sri Lankan Embassy with a briefcase containing 100,000 Deutsche Marks to request a visa to set up a five-million dollar gem exhibition, and approached the Indonesian, Senegalese, Irish, and Nigerian embassies with similar requests'. Around the same time, Bates also contacted several international agencies. Armed with a legal opinion claiming that Sealand was a state under international law (authored by one of his supporters), Bates contacted the International Frequency Registration Board to reserve radio frequencies.

None of these efforts succeeded. States and international agencies that received attention from Bates and the Germans contacted the UK for advice on how they should proceed. The Foreign and Commonwealth Office was adamant that the principality was not a state. The United Nations was also not interested; as one spokesperson apparently explained, 'the United Nations is an organisation of governments, not gun platforms. The secretary-general has a nut file for such applications'.

It soon became clear that Bates and his German supporters had different ideas about the future of Sealand. The Germans had earlier established a business in Luxembourg called 'Sealand Information Gathering and Messaging Agency', through which they sought to sell Sealand stamps and coins. In 1976, Achenbach and several others were arrested in Luxembourg and charged with 'engaging in fraudulent business based in an imaginary country'.

Achenbach tried to raise Sealand's sovereignty as a defence by attempting to file a motion in the International Court of Justice at the Hague, hopeful that it would hold that the charges were an act of aggression. Not worried by this ploy, but nonetheless concerned that 'Luxembourg's financial name should not be sullied in any way', officials consulted the British government before reducing the charges. A court found the men guilty of selling stamps and coins without a licence and fined each around £400. Achenbach then adopted a different strategy. On 2 August 1976 he petitioned the Cologne Administrative Court to revoke his German citizenship on the grounds that he was a citizen of the Principality of Sealand. The court rejected his petition, finding that Sealand was not a state as it satisfied neither the territory nor population requirements of the Montevideo Convention.

The decision did not diminish Achenbach's interest in Sealand. The former diamond dealer had grand plans, commissioning an architect to expand the Roughs Tower site. The plans involved the creation of another platform adjacent to Sealand on which a casino, a duty-free shop, a bank, a post office, a hotel, restaurants, apartments and a tree-lined square would be built. Achenbach had one additional request: 'light weapons should be installed to fend off enemies, should that prove to be necessary. Better safe than sorry'.

Construction never began, but Achenbach had fixed upon the idea of using the principality as a tax haven. As he explained to a reporter from German radio station Südwestfunk, 'The main thing is to take advantage of the privileges that come with being a state.' Achenbach's plan relied on Sealand's ambiguous legal position. Germany considered Sealand to be part of the United Kingdom for the purposes of the tax treaty between the two states, but the UK did not levy taxes for activities that took place on Roughs Tower. As such, German citizens might be able to avoid paying taxes on income generated in Sealand. Unfortunately, Achenbach's ingenious plan was scuppered by a German court. Because Roughs Tower sat outside the UK's territorial waters, German taxes would apply.

One week after the judgment of the court, in August 1978, Achenbach invited Roy and Joan Bates to Austria to discuss his proposal to buy the fort. The bid was a scam. While Roy and Joan travelled to the continent, they left their son Michael alone on the platform. A group of Germans led by Achenbach's lawyer, Gernot Pütz, arrived at Sealand by helicopter, brandishing a forged document purportedly declaring that Roy had sold the principality. Michael was sceptical but let them enter. When

Michael turned his back to pour them a dram of whisky, the Germans slipped outside the room and locked him inside. After imprisoning Michael for a few days, they eventually put him in a boat and sent him to the Netherlands, from where he made his way home.

Becoming suspicious when the meeting was postponed, Roy and Joan returned to England and reconnected with Michael. Once there they launched their own assault from a helicopter flown by John Crewdson, a pilot who had worked on stunts for the 1969 James Bond film *On Her Majesty's Secret Service*. In a pre-dawn raid, Roy, Michael and two other men armed with sawn-off shotguns and semi-automatic weapons hurtled across the North Sea. Hovering above the platform, the men slid down ropes hanging from inside the helicopter and dropped onto the steel deck. Twenty-six-year-old Michael landed with a crash and dropped his shotgun. The gun went off, splattering grapeshot into a fuel tank. Bewildered, the Germans immediately surrendered, allowing Roy and his crew to take them as hostages. The commotion attracted several journalists, who sailed out to the fort to interview Roy.

Unsurprisingly, the action also drew the attention of the Netherlands and Germany. Dutch officials asked the UK to help secure the release of their citizen – Dutchman Hans Lavoo had sailed to the fort to help negotiate the release of the German prisoners but had himself been taken hostage by Bates. Dutch officials wondered whether the fort could be destroyed. In an internal letter, a British Foreign Office official asked, 'Is there any chance of a British patrol vessel "passing by" the Fort and somehow knocking it into the sea?' The German government

Armed Sealanders guard Gernot Pütz
Credit unknown

was perplexed. Officials wrote (quite accurately) to their British counterparts:

> The German national Gernot Ernst Pütz is being held prisoner by members of a so-called 'Principality of Sealand' on the former anti-aircraft fort 'Roughs Tower', off Harwich. Therefore, the imprisonment of Pütz is in a way an act of piracy, committed on the high sea but still in front of British territory by British citizens.

The British did nothing, replying flatly that any false imprisonment was taking place 'outside British jurisdiction'.

The British did not respond to further German correspondence. Within a few days all but one of the hostages were released.

Only Pütz remained. As a Sealand citizen, Roy Bates considered that Pütz had committed treason. Joan noted to a journalist that while the UK executed people for treason, Sealand did not. Roy explained later, 'I've killed a lot of Germans in my time. Another one wouldn't have made much difference, but I didn't want to kill anything else, really.' Pütz was fined 75 000 deutschmarks and ordered to remain on the fort until he could discharge the penalty.

In an interview with *The Times*, Hannelore Pütz, Gernot's wife, expressed considerable alarm. Hannelore 'could not understand why the British authorities appeared unable or unwilling to intervene'. Hannelore explained that she could not raise 75 000 deutschmarks and was afraid to visit her husband on the fort for fear of her own safety. The *Times* story concluded by noting (erroneously) that 'a court ruling 10 years ago declared the fort to be outside British jurisdiction'.

Growing frustrated with the UK's failure to resolve the issue, Germany dispatched a diplomatic official to Sealand to negotiate the release of their citizen. Dr Christoph Neimöller was unable to secure Pütz's release, but was baffled by the situation and wondered whether the entire event was an elaborate publicity stunt. If so, it appears to have worked. Sealand had hosted an official from an independent, recognised state, who negotiated with them as it would a peer. With that achieved, Bates released Pütz a few weeks later. The pair shook hands, smiled and posed for cameras. Bates even appointed Pütz Sealand's new foreign minister (having stripped Achenbach of the ministry), charging him with strengthening 'the island's links on the Continent'.

The situation may have resolved itself, but it provoked further questions for the UK government. In December 1978, Lord Kennet asked the Minister of State, Foreign and Commonwealth Office, 'is it not the case that what this time may be a harmless and colourful escapade could next time, in law, be a moderately dangerous act by an unfriendly foreign Power?'. Lord Kennet continued:

> My Lords, is it not the case that the British national on this tower has been reported in the press as having taken actions which, if they had been committed in a place where there was jurisdiction, would have been crimes, but that as there is no jurisdiction on this tower no action has been taken to restrain him from capturing or kidnapping people and holding them to ransom?

Others questioned whether the fort might be a navigational hazard and should be destroyed, or towed within the UK's territorial waters. The government acknowledged Lord Kennet's concerns but did not commit to taking any action. It was not until 1987 that the UK extended its territorial sea in line with the international standard of 12 nautical miles, thereby encompassing Roughs Tower and putting away doubt over its authority over the fort. Sealand maintains that as it was already a sovereign nation, the UK's actions do not affect the principality.

Lessons learnt

Bates learnt his lesson. Recognising that the survival of the principality relied on maintaining cordial relations with its much larger neighbour, for the next two decades Sealand kept its head down. Bates claims to have rebuffed several attempts by foreign governments to purchase the principality to embarrass the UK. In the late 1970s, representatives of the Spanish government apparently sought to purchase the principality to use as a bargaining chip in a bid to regain sovereignty over Gibraltar. Similarly, during the Falklands War a group of Argentinians supposedly asked to buy the fort and set up 'their own "Malvinas" right on Britain's doorstep'. At another point Muammar Gaddafi 'offered Roy a "pot of gold" to use the tower'. Roy dismissed each offer, explaining, 'I sent them away. I'd never do anything that would pose a threat to the UK.' Of course, doing otherwise would also have posed a threat to Sealand.

Roy Bates may have managed to wrest physical control of Sealand back from Achenbach and Pütz but more challenges awaited. The two Germans maintained a government in exile from Belgium, called the Sealand Rebel Government. From there they sold thousands of counterfeit Sealand passports that were used by criminal gangs to finance drug trafficking and money laundering. The extent of this criminal enterprise only became clear in the late 1990s.

In 1997, Andrew Cunanan murdered fashion designer Gianni Versace in Miami, Florida. Several days later, Cunanan broke into a houseboat and committed suicide. During the FBI investigation, the owner of the boat presented a forged Sealand passport and claimed to be a Sealand diplomat. Investigators traced the passport back to Spain. Later that year, Spain's paramilitary police arrested club owner Francisco Trujillo Ruiz for selling diluted petrol at a petrol station he owned in Madrid.

Trujillo Ruiz claimed diplomatic immunity, arguing that he was Sealand's consul to Spain. That set off a wave of further investigations. *The Guardian* reported:

> In a raid on the ring's offices, a bingo hall in Madrid, and a lawyer's chambers presented as a Sealand embassy, Spanish police seized hundreds of blank passports and a document issued by a German neo-Nazi organisation recognising Sealand's existence.
>
> Other documents related to money laundering operations involving Russians and Iraqis. Investigators believe that more than 4,000 fake Sealand passports were sold to Hong Kong citizens for $1,000 each before the former colony was handed over to China in 1997.

The Spanish police accused around 80 people of committing fraud, falsifying documents and pretending to be foreign dignitaries. Several countries appeared to have been taken in by Sealand 'ambassadors': 'the embassies of Gabon, Paraguay, Nepal, Syria, Haiti, Liberia, Honduras, Jamaica, Pakistan, Cyprus, Ethiopia, Jordan and Turkey all responded to requests for information from Sealand representatives who claim to be preparing lucrative investments in those countries'.

The group included Moroccan drug smugglers and Russian arms dealers. The Panama Papers later revealed that the Sealand Trade Development Authority Limited, a front company established by Achenbach and Pütz, led negotiations with the arms dealers to broker 'a $50 million deal to send 50 tanks, 10 MiG-23 fighter jets, and other combat aircraft, artillery, and armored vehicles from Russia to Sudan'. Roy and

Michael Bates maintained that the real Principality of Sealand had nothing to do with these enterprises. Roy explained, 'We're very vulnerable – we are the smallest state in the world. We are wide open for criticism, but we are very careful; we don't want to do anything wrong.' In 1997, the principality attempted to distance itself by cancelling all Sealand passports, including those they had issued themselves.

The difficulty of financing regular upkeep on a decaying World War II–era sea fort compelled the Bates family to consider another money-making scheme. In 2000, the principality reached agreement with HavenCo, a US data-hosting company, to host a web server outside the jurisdiction of any government. For an initial payment of US$250 000 and a share of the company, the Bateses would allow HavenCo to operate from Roughs Tower. HavenCo was interested in operating a 'data haven'. Similar to a tax haven, data havens offer 'no-questions-asked data storage web hosting and encrypted communication'. HavenCo's anarcho-libertarian directors promised their customers 'a combination of first-world infrastructure and third-world regulation'. As they explained, 'HavenCo will allow for gambling, pyramid schemes, adult porn, subpoena-proof email, and untraceable bank accounts. But not everything will fly. In addition to the spam and child-porn ban, corporate cybersaboteurs are forbidden.'

The directors fixed upon Sealand because of its uncertain status. Even if the law was and is clear – Sealand is part of the United Kingdom – the directors reasoned that in practice, the United Kingdom had tolerated and would continue to tolerate some level of criminality. Perhaps they were correct. As a US State Department official monitoring the situation explained, 'right now, we aren't even concerned with something like Sealand because they are not representing any kind of a threat ... It would not be an issue for us unless, for example, they are hooking up with Osama bin Laden'. Ultimately, the arrangement collapsed after only a few years. Concerned that HavenCo 'was bad for Sealand's image and quest for sovereignty', the Bateses ejected the original US directors and adopted an acceptable internet use policy consistent with international and European Union laws. To do otherwise might have invited a state response that could threaten the viability of Sealand.

Nonetheless, Sealand's strange position of being inside yet outside the UK remains attractive for certain people. In 2012, unconfirmed reports suggested that Julian Assange was planning on moving WikiLeaks servers to the principality. Michael Bates refused to be drawn on the reports, but some in the hacker community were excited: 'Then they can keep running WikiLeaks and nobody can touch them ... If you get a certain distance away from any land, then you're dealing with maritime law ... They can't prosecute him under maritime law. He's safe. He's not an idiot, he's actually very smart.'

Assange may be very smart, but the source misunderstood the law. The location of the servers would not prevent prosecution. WikiLeaks servers were not moved.

Becoming a nation

In the years following their declaration of independence, Roy Bates and his family set about creating the symbols of a state. Sealand already had its own tricolour flag – as Michael Bates explained, the red represents Roy, the black represents pirate radio and the diagonal white stripe marks the 'path of purity [they] would endeavour to walk'. Soon they added a motto – *E Mare, Libertas* (From the Sea, Freedom) – and a coat of arms. The principality also has its own national anthem. In 2005, the Slovak Radio Symphony Orchestra recorded the anthem as part of its anthology of the national anthems of the world.

In 1975, Bates introduced a Constitution for his principality. Consisting of 23 articles and purportedly based on the common law, its preamble reads:

> In consciousness of his responsibility before God and before man, and inspired by the will to serve the cause of Peace for his People and for all peoples in the world, the sovereign ruler of the PRINCIPALITY OF SEALAND, His Majesty Prince Roy of SEALAND, for himself and for his successors to the throne, by virtue of his constitutional authority resolves, swears and proclaims ...

Bates has adopted further state symbols. The principality mints its own currency – the Sealand dollar – issues its own passport, and sells noble titles. Anyone can become a Duke or Duchess for £499.99. Perhaps if money is a bit tight, you might like to become a Count or Countess (£199.99); a Lord, Lady, Baron or Baroness (£29.99); or just an ordinary citizen (£24.99). Micronational citizenship can be attractive: the principality notes that it received more than 200 inquiries about political asylum after the Brexit referendum and the election of Donald Trump.

Sealand has also issued thousands of postage stamps featuring famous maritime explorers, including Vasco da Gama,

Stamps from the Principality of Sealand
Onecanadasquarebishopsgate

Christopher Columbus, Ferdinand Magellan and Captain James Cook. An official post office was set up in the sixth subfloor of one of the concrete towers, 'replete with a teller window and a banner reading "Post Office"'. It also has a Facebook page, a Twitter account and a YouTube channel.

The Principality of Sealand has adopted other prominent symbols of nationhood. In 1989, musician Frank Zappa argued that 'you can't be a real country unless you have a beer and an airline – it helps if you have some kind of a football team, or some nuclear weapons, but at the very least you need a beer'. Sealand does not have a beer, an airline or nuclear weapons, but it does have a football team. In 2003, it created its own soccer team and soccer competition: the Sealand National Football Association.

The Sealand national team has played several matches. In 2004, it played a friendly against Åland Islands, a Swedish-speaking autonomous region of Finland (the teams drew 2–2). Unsurprisingly, Sealand is not a member of FIFA or UEFA. However, it was a member of the Nouvelle Fédération-Board – a federation of football associations that represented nations, dependencies, unrecognised states, minorities, stateless peoples, regions and micronations not affiliated to FIFA. In this capacity it has competed against teams from the Chagos Islands, Alderney (the third largest of the Channel Islands off the coast of Normandy), Raetia (a province of the Roman Empire located in present-day Germany), Tamil Eelam (the proposed independent state in north and east Sri Lanka) and Occitania (a region of southern France, western Italy and northern Spain), as well as micronations such as Somaliland and the Principality of Seborga.

And yet, the future of the Sealand football team is unclear. The Nouvelle Fédération-Board became defunct in 2013, replaced by the Confederation of Independent Football Associations (CONIFA). CONIFA has rejected Sealand's application to join the successor organisation as 'frivolous'. This meant Sealand did not participate in the most recent 2018 CONIFA World Cup (Kárpátalja, a team representing the Hungarian minority in Carpathian Ruthenia, defeated Northern Cyprus 3–2 on penalties).

The Sealand national team has not played a game since 2014. However, it claims many athletes compete for the nation across a range of sports, including curling, minigolf, table football and athletics. Several mountaineers have also carried the Sealand flag on their expeditions. In 2004, Slader Oviatt raised the Sealandic flag on the summit of Muztagh Ata, the second highest mountain on the Tibetan plateau. Nine years later, Englishman Kenton Cool unfurled the flag on the summit of Mount Everest.

The future of Sealand

Micronations are usually short-lived, often surviving as long as their charismatic or eccentric founder. Those rare entities that persist beyond their creator largely do so because they become a symbol for something much larger. The Principality of Sealand was set up to bypass restrictions on radio broadcasting but it quickly became something more. As Prince Michael explained to the BBC in 2020, 'Our story still fires people up. We don't live in a society where people like being told what to do, and everybody loves the idea of liberty and freedom from government. The world needs inspiring territories like us – and there aren't many places like this that exist.'

Nonetheless, the future of the principality is uncertain. In its heyday in the early 1970s around 50 people – family, friends and guards – lived on Sealand at times. Conditions were

Sealand on the wedding day of Prince Michael Bates, May 1979
Goddard Archive / Alamy Stock Photo

cramped but nice enough. Each of the two concrete towers are stacked with circular rooms about 6.7 metres in diameter. Most of the rooms are below the waterline, which fills them 'with a faint gurgling sound' and leaves a persistent clammy smell. The towers house guest rooms, a kitchen, a gym, a recreation room with a pool table, and a meeting room. It even hosts an ecumenical chapel. Today, only two people live on the fort: caretakers Mike Barrington and Joe Hamill alternate two-week shifts, doing just enough to make sure the principality keeps going and the rust is kept at bay. After a diesel generator caught fire and caused extensive damage in 2012, power is now supplied by solar panels and wind turbines.

Roy Bates passed away in 2012 at the age of 91, having ruled Sealand for 45 years. He was succeeded as the Prince of Sealand by his son Michael. Desiring an education for his own children, Michael and his family had left the decommissioned fort many years earlier, preferring to settle in an Essex seaside town where Michael built a shellfish business to support his family – and to pay for upkeep of the installation. Michael has now retired from the business, and although there are several heirs to the throne of Sealand, it is possible that his children and grandchildren will lose interest in the 4100-tonne abandoned naval fort sitting off the UK coast.

4

LIBERTARIAN PARADISE: THE REPUBLIC OF MINERVA

In August 1971, two members of the US-based Ocean Life Research Foundation sailed into the tranquil waters of the Minerva Reefs in the Pacific Ocean. Located around 500 kilometres south-west of Tonga and about 700 kilometres south-east of Fiji, the two submerged atolls are a long way from any country. The Ocean Life Research Foundation hoped to change that.

After mooring their 54-foot pleasure yacht within the lagoon that separates the north and south reefs, the men – 38-year-old oilman Tad Weed and 48-year-old timber dealer Bob Marks – set about their plans. They first dredged up several mounds of sand, soil and coral to above the high-water mark. Encasing their rudimentary land reclamation project with reinforced concrete, they then erected an 8-metre-high marker with beacons and radar reflectors. On the top of the marker, they raised a flag: a gold torch inside a gold circle on a blue background. The Republic of Minerva – Land of the Rising Atoll – was born.

The principalities of Hutt River and Sealand were founded in defiance of government regulation, and not to further any

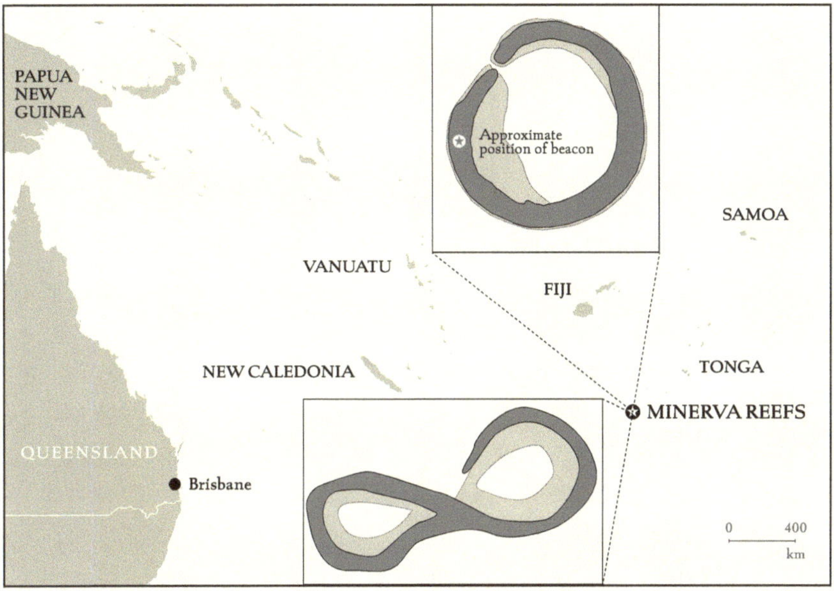

Location of the Republic of Minerva

grand political philosophy. They were a response to what their founders saw as a personal injustice. In the case of Leonard Casley, that was the feeling of being cheated out of his natural right to harvest as much wheat as he could. For Roy Bates, it was the view that the UK radio broadcasting regime unfairly targeted entrepreneurs such as himself. The Republic of Minerva was different. Its chief architect, Michael Oliver, wanted to create his own libertarian paradise.

The Republic of Minerva was just one of the new country projects that Oliver was involved in. For decades he scoured every square inch of the globe, looking for an opportunity to create his own nation. After Minerva, he cast his eyes to the Bahamas and the New Hebrides (Vanuatu). Unfortunately for Oliver, he never realised his dream.

Grand plans

Michael Oliver was born Moses Olitsky in Lithuania in 1928. His early years were incredibly difficult. After spending four years in a Nazi concentration camp and surviving the communist takeover of his homeland, he emigrated to the United States in 1946. He left behind the memories of his parents and four siblings, all of whom had been killed. In his new country he prospered, earning a fortune as a coin dealer, gold speculator and real estate mogul in Nevada.

Despite his newfound prosperity and security, Oliver could not escape his early years. He worried constantly that the United States was becoming a 'fascist-socialist' state because the government controlled the economy and the media. The US Constitution was no better, containing 'enough collectivist clauses to ensure a steady drift toward totalitarianism'. Anxiously, Oliver began to develop ideas for how an ideal society could be organised. Inspired by the libertarian economist Ludwig von Mises, author Ayn Rand and philosopher Andrew Galambos, Oliver drafted a political manifesto for a laissez-faire paradise.

A New Constitution for a New Country became a 'genuine underground bestseller, selling over 20 000 copies'. In it, Oliver outlined his basic theory of government. 'Government, under this constitution, can be *construed* as a private corporation, which is to be hired by participants on a voluntary basis, for the specific purpose of protecting their personal rights,' he wrote. 'Regardless of majority vote, no person, entity, or governmental agency may take away these rights from others.'

Oliver explained further in a 'Statement of Fundamental Principles':

> Only 200 years have elapsed since the idea of the necessity to separate church and state really took root ... Now the time has come to go a step further, to establish a nation based on the principle that not only must government be separated from religion, but also it must be separated from economics and limited in function to an entity hired by persons and other entities to protect and give recourse to their personal rights against force and fraud.

In an interview with the American libertarian magazine *Reason*, Oliver expanded on his utopian paradise:

> The first thing is to limit government *only* to protection against force and fraud. This means that there will be *no* free schools, *no* social security, *no* government welfare, etc. The people will get only court protection, police protection, and external defense from government. Not even internal police protection will be free, although there will be occasions where non-participants will get benefit of the police; if a person is being robbed, a policeman seeing it will stop the crime even if the victim is a non-participant.

Citizens could pay a voluntary annual premium for the ability to initiate court action, like an insurance policy taken out with the state. All laws would automatically expire after five years.

For Oliver, this paradise need not be theoretical. He was committed to making his libertarian utopia a reality. In *A New Constitution for a New Country*, Oliver explained that this would be relatively straightforward:

> A surprising number of nearly uninhabited, yet quite suitable places for establishing a new country still exist ... The exact location of the new country cannot be revealed at this time ... Many such places are scarcely developed colonies whose governmental or other activities are of little or no concern at all to their 'mother' countries. There will be little problem in purchasing the land, or in having the opportunity to conduct affairs on a free enterprise basis from the very beginning.

Drawing on the success of his political manifesto, Oliver established the Ocean Life Research Foundation and secured 2000 investors keen to help him build their libertarian state.

Libertarianism is a branch of political philosophy. Libertarians believe that all people are autonomous individuals of equal moral worth. This means that we have the right to determine what we do with our person and that we are not entitled to do anything to another person without their consent. This can support liberal values such as the right of women to bodily autonomy. It can also support attacks on progressive taxation and other forms of redistribution. Robert Nozick, the prominent libertarian philosopher, infamously described taxation as 'morally on par with forced labor'. Because libertarians place great weight on individual consent, they can regard the exercise of coercive state power as illegitimate.

Some have suggested that the ideal libertarian society involves people relating to each other only on a voluntary and consensual basis. If the state exists, it is minimal and limited to functions like the enforcement and protection of individual rights. It does not provide social welfare, nor does it limit individual freedom in any way. In the words of US anti-tax activist Grover Norquist, the goal is to cut government down to a size where 'it could be drowned in a bathtub'.

For several years, Michael Oliver travelled or sent representatives all over the world in search of a suitable location where he could realise his vision for such a society and escape 'from high taxes, riots, drugs and crime'. The task proved more difficult than he imagined.

Oliver met with representatives from several governments, including the Turks and Caicos Islands, Costa Rica, French Guyana, the Bahamas, Suriname, Curacao, New Caledonia, and the New Hebrides (Vanuatu). Despite initial promise, each ended with disappointment. No government was willing to cede sovereignty over a portion of their territory. *Reason* magazine explained that

> none of these efforts has succeeded, principally due to an incredible unwillingness on the part of established governments to relinquish sovereignty over even the smallest, most worthless piece of land. (Even the worst collectivist bureaucrat is apparently aware of the remarkable power of truly free enterprise to turn barren islands and deserts into centers of commerce – and he's not about to relinquish his 'sovereign right' to move in and tax what the newcomer capitalists might produce.)

Minerva Reefs
Richard Marshall and Michelle Marshall

Oliver decided that to succeed his project needed more than to be housed within an existing country – 'a new libertarian polity needed its own sovereign powers'. Eventually, he settled on the Minerva Reefs.

The Minerva Reefs take their name from a whaling ship from the British colony of New South Wales that ran aground on the southern shoal in 1829. This was not the reefs' first sighting. The area was a traditional fishing ground for the Ono-i-Lau people of Fiji and may have been visited by Tongan fishermen for generations. Of the Europeans, Captain John Nicholson first charted the reefs in 1818. Despite this, no state had asserted sovereignty over the atolls. This may have been because permanent settlement was impossible; at high tide the reefs were half a metre under water. This minor inconvenience would not prevent Oliver from seeking to realise his life's dream.

In the second half of 1971, the Ocean Life Research Foundation ferried sand on barges from Fiji to raise the reefs above sea level and began rudimentary construction. The plans were extensive. Oliver envisioned creating 2500 acres of habitable land (2000 acres for residential development and 500 acres for commercial uses) elevated around 2.5–3 metres above mean high tide. Floating cities and an ocean resort would be established within the lagoon. the *Minerva Times* (a newsletter created by Oliver to update current investors and to seek new ones) announced that the entire project would 'sparkle like a jewel in the blue South Pacific'. A sea wall would be constructed to protect the site from rough weather.

Oliver considered that the state would become a lucrative investment. He imagined that 'the new nation could compete with Liberia and Panama in becoming a "flag of convenience" for owners of merchant ships. In time, multinational companies looking for a tax haven might want to establish a base there'. Although Oliver envisioned a 'new Venice' of perhaps 30 000 settlers, he expected that most citizens would not be residents. Instead, people would be more interested in the tax advantages that citizenship would offer. The residents themselves would largely be Tongan or Fijian labourers, but it is not clear whether they would be offered (or allowed to take up) citizenship. The racism and elitism inherent in the project reflected Oliver's politics, and indeed the politics of some other members of the broader hard-right libertarian movement in America in the 1970s.

Progress proved hard going. By the end of the year, some 15 acres of land had been reclaimed, exhausting the initial US$200 000 capital. Oliver hoped that these efforts could convince additional investors to finance the remaining 2485 acres. However, reports suggested that 'investors showed little interest'.

Oliver and the Ocean Life Research Foundation were undeterred. On 19 January 1972, the Republic of Minerva announced its independence and issued a Declaration of Sovereignty sent to more than 100 countries. In its Declaration, the republic assured the world it would operate under a 'peaceful and free republican system of government in adherence to democratic principles'. It seemed the world was unsure how to respond. News reports suggest that 'only one head of state, His Majesty The Sultan of Occussi-Ambeno ... bothered to reply'.

Reflecting the bizarre environment in which micronations operate, the sultanate itself was a hoax; it was the creation of New Zealand anarchist, artist and stamp collector Bruce Grenville. Beginning in 1968, Grenville produced thousands of stamps for the sultanate, which he sold to collectors to fund his art practice. In the 1970s and '80s he began to sow confusion by attempting to establish diplomatic recognition with other states – including Minerva and the Hutt River Province. Oliver should not have been so upset. Grenville managed to fool journalists all over the world, as well as a European consortium who paid him US$40 000 for the exclusive rights to produce and sell the sultanate's stamps. The sultanate is still going strong today. In addition to his work with Occussi-Ambeno, Grenville serves as a technical adviser for the Republic of Mevu, a micronation based in Antarctica whose primary population is the emperor penguin.

Stamps from the Sultanate of Occussi-Ambeno
Bruce Grenville

The team behind the Republic of Minerva was unaware of the sultanate's true status. Nonetheless, the republic continued to engage in diplomacy, sending an emissary to neighbouring Tonga. The Roving Ambassador for the Republic of Minerva sought an audience with King Tupou IV to 'appraise him of the scheme'. The audience was not granted, but a senior member of the Prime Minister's Department did meet the ambassador. The Minerva ambassador screened a documentary film produced by the Pilkington Glass Company, outlining the feasibility of a 'sea city' of 30 000 people to be constructed on the Dogger Bank in the North Sea. As the ambassador explained, 'this was the model upon which Michael Oliver's organization was basing its plans'.

In February 1972, Morris Davis was appointed provisional president. Davis explained why settlers should join the fledgling republic: 'people will be free to do as they damn well please. Nothing will be illegal so long it does not infringe on the rights of others. If a citizen wishes to open a tavern, set up gambling or make pornographic films, the government will not interfere'.

It seemed that some members of the business community in the United States might be attracted to the new country. Later that year, Carl Gerstacker, the chairman of Dow Chemical Company, remarked:

> I have long dreamed of buying an island owned by no nation and of establishing the World Headquarters of the Dow Company on the truly neutral ground of such an island, beholden to no nation or society. If we were located on such truly neutral ground we could then really operate in the United States as US citizens, in Japan as Japanese citizens and in Brazil as Brazilians rather than being governed in prime by the laws of the United States ... We could even pay any natives handsomely to move elsewhere.

Oliver approached Dow to invite the company to move its world headquarters to Minerva. Gerstacker did not respond.

The search for investors continued. Davis minted 10 500 coins and sold them to raise funds. The silver coins were adorned with an image of the Roman goddess Minerva and the location of the reef republic. Each coin cost US$75 and was worth 35 Minerva dollars. A December 1975 advertisement in the *Libertarian Review* encouraged buyers with the tagline: 'the world's most unusual new country: inspiration for the most unique metal coin ever minted'.

The Minerva dollar
Roger Griffith

The Pacific islands act

The Republic of Minerva faced difficult financial and technical challenges in reclaiming sufficient land. It was also failing to secure recognition of its claim to sovereignty. Soon a much greater problem emerged. The Minerva Reefs may not have been claimed by any recognised state, but this did not mean that neighbouring countries would consent to the presence of the libertarian interlopers.

The Kingdom of Tonga in particular had a connection to the reefs that it wished to preserve. On the evening of 4 July 1962, the *Tuaikaepau* ('Slow But Sure'), a small Tongan vessel carrying 17 people to Auckland, New Zealand, was caught in a storm and struck the south Minerva reef. At dawn, the survivors of the disaster discovered the wreck of a Japanese trawler on the far side of the reef. Abandoning their ship, they took up residence in the much larger vessel. After several weeks, the captain, Tevita Fitita, his son Sateki and another crew member, Tevita

Uaisele, decided to sail for help. They constructed a raft and set sail for Ono-i-Lau, a small Fijian island some 350 kilometres north. Their craft was battered by storms, and Sateki Fifita drowned after eight days at sea without food or water. The two remaining men eventually landed on Fiji's Kadavu Island and raised the alarm.

After 102 days, the remaining *Tuaikaepau* crew and passengers trapped on the reef were rescued by the Royal New Zealand Air Force, save for two people who had passed away in the meantime. Upon the return of the shipwrecked survivors, Tonga held a national celebration in the capital Nuku'alofa. Four years later, Tevita Fifita returned to the south Minerva reef with a group of Tongans. They reburied the remains of those who had died during the shipwreck; placed a copy of Australian journalist Olaf Ruhen's book *Minerva Reef*, coconuts and watermelons on each grave; and raised the Tongan flag. Tonga did not formally claim the Minerva Reefs as part of its sovereign territory, but the *Tuaikaepau* incident 'undoubtedly sealed the Tongans' emotive connection' to the atolls.

The sudden emergence of the upstart Republic of Minerva prompted alarm among Pacific Islands nations. In late January 1972, Fijian prime minister Ratu Sir Kamisese Mara noted that the purported declaration of independence could create a 'dangerous precedent', asking, 'If these people can claim Minerva, what would stop them from doing it here?' Cook Islands premier Albert Henry was similarly concerned, wondering if soon 'all other reefs in the ocean would start announcing themselves as independent nations'. The next month, a Tongan government spokesperson acknowledged that Tonga had never formally asserted sovereignty over the reefs. He explained that the raising of a Tongan flag in 1966 was believed to be in memory of fallen crew rather than a declaration of sovereignty. Nonetheless, he noted that due to the *Tuaikaepau* shipwreck, 'Tonga would always look upon the reefs with special concern and had strong feelings about any claim.'

Larger powers were less interested. The United States maintained a position of 'no position', while New Zealand 'seemed generally too busy to care'. One British diplomat joked to a journalist: 'Heaven forbid for this kind of thing to happen. We'll have every crackpot with an ounce of imagination claiming sovereignty over every last scrap of unclaimed land. The next thing you know, they'll be demanding loans from the World Bank.'

Tonga determined to take action. In February 1972, the Tongan boat *Ekiaki* sailed to the south Minerva reef to establish a refuge station. Tonga's Marine Department subsequently issued a notice to mariners announcing the newly built station and advised Fiji, New Zealand, Australia and the UK of its location. A government spokesperson explained that the refuge station was intended to substantiate Tonga's 'longstanding connection with the reefs'.

Two days later, the issue was considered further at the South Pacific Forum. At this meeting, representatives from Fiji, Tonga, Nauru, Western Samoa, the Cook Islands, Australia and New Zealand resolved to support 'the stand of Tonga in relation to Minerva Reef'. The leaders also agreed to investigate the legal status of the reefs and ask the United States to pressure the Ocean Life Research Foundation to halt their venture. Prince Tuiplehake, the Tongan prime minister, was adamant: 'We can't have people setting up empires on our doorstep.'

Tongan interest intensified. In May, King Tupou IV of Tonga visited the reefs. The king dismissed rumours that he intended to claim the reefs on behalf of Tonga, instead noting that he was simply there to investigate the situation. Nonetheless, he explained to the *Tonga Chronicle* that 'it was in the best interest of Tonga not to allow a group of people, whose objects were to make money and whose activities could be harmful, to become established on the reefs'.

Despite this activity, Tonga still did not assert sovereignty over the atolls. Why did they hesitate? It may have stemmed from ambiguity over the proper legal status of the reefs: could a country claim sovereignty over atolls that were submerged at high tide? After some debate, Tonga's legal adviser concluded that to claim the reefs under international law they would need 'to build a permanent structure above high water'. In early June, Tonga followed that advice.

Ninety convict labourers were sent to the reefs. Their job was to remove any features created by the Americans and construct two artificial islands with permanent structures above the high-tide mark. On 15 June 1972, Tonga formally declared sovereignty over the two artificial islands on the reefs in a royal proclamation:

> WHEREAS the Reefs known as North Minerva Reef and South Minerva Reef have long served as fishing grounds for the Tongan people and have long been regarded as belonging to the Kingdom of Tonga; AND WHEREAS the Kingdom of Tonga has now created on these Reefs islands known as Teleki Tokelau and Teleki Tonga; AND WHEREAS it is expedient that we should now confirm

> the rights of the Kingdom of Tonga to these islands; THEREFORE we do hereby AFFIRM and PROCLAIM that the islands, rocks, reefs, foreshores and waters lying within a radius of twelve miles [19.31 kilometres] thereof are part of our Kingdom of Tonga.

On 26 June, King Tupou IV held a formal ceremony on the north Minerva reef. The Tongan Defence Force tore down the Minervan flag and raised the Tongan flag. The king read the royal proclamation, a band performed a rousing rendition of the Tongan national anthem, and the royal yacht *Olovaha* fired a salute. Some sources suggest that in the middle of the celebration a fight broke out between several of the convict labourers. By the time it was stopped, one man had been killed. Thus, when the Tongans finally sailed for home, they left the former Republic of Minerva with a grim statistic – a murder rate higher than its population.

The Republic of Minerva was caught by surprise. It was, however, optimistic that a resolution could be reached. In an interview with *Reason* magazine, Michael Oliver explained that the syndicate 'had just completed an engineering survey and didn't have anyone at the Reef at that instant. But I think the Tonga problem can be resolved'. He was mistaken.

Morris Davis, the president of Minerva, was in Suva, Fiji, buying supplies when he heard of Tonga's actions. Davis immediately flew to Nuku'alofa, the Tongan capital, seeking an audience with the king, but was snubbed:

> Upon my arrival in Nuku'alofa I was invited to the office of the half-brother of the king, a Mr. Inoke Faletow. Also

> present was the crown solicitor. I was treated very rudely and informed I would not have an audience with the king, and further that any attempt by any of our group to land on the reefs would result in their being removed by force, if necessary, and escorted to Nuku'alofa and brought to trial for trespassing on Tongan territory. I inquired as to how far Tonga was prepared to go to maintain her claim to the reefs and was informed: 'To any extent short of war'.

Davis spoke to the *New York Times*: 'We can't for the life of us understand why the King should suddenly decide he wants the reefs. He never had any use for them before.'

The Ocean Life Research Foundation issued a press release setting out the basis for their claim. They explained that they had complied 'with every conceivable requisite of national sovereignty in establishing' their claim to the reefs and did not pose 'a threat to the peace and security of any nation'. The King of Tonga had violated the Republic of Minerva's territorial sovereignty and had 'threatened the peace and tranquillity of the South Pacific'. Despite these aggressive and dangerous actions, the king 'has refused to discuss the matter' with representatives of the republic. The press release lamented that Tonga 'has no plans to develop the reefs' and concluded with a warning: 'Our rights as individuals and citizens of a sovereign state have been violated; we intend to defend those rights.' Other supporters offered inducements to the king to recognise the Minervan claim, including 'an airline, low-voltage television station, a shipyard and other considerations'.

Unfortunately for Oliver and his supporters, none of Tonga's neighbours would recognise the Republic of Minerva either. In September, the South Pacific Forum issued a communiqué noting that 'Members of the Forum recognised Tonga's historical association with the Minerva Reefs, welcomed the Tongan Government's continuing interest in the area and agreed that there could be no question of recognising other claims, and specifically that of the Ocean Life Research Foundation, to sovereignty over the reefs'.

The communiqué was careful not to recognise Tonga's sovereign claims. Although it made clear that no other claims would be accepted, it merely recognised Tonga's 'historical association' with the atolls. This distinction is important because authority over the reefs remains disputed. In 2005, Fiji lodged a complaint with the International Seabed Authority, claiming the Minerva Reefs as part of their exclusive economic zone. Tonga lodged a counterclaim but the dispute has not been resolved. In the absence of a conclusive resolution, the Fijian navy has reportedly destroyed Tongan navigational equipment on the atoll several times.

Oliver abandoned his republic in late 1972, but several of his followers have attempted to reassert that claim over the years. After Oliver gave up, a memo was issued by a man styling himself 'Major Travers', who may have been involved in a similar libertarian island-building exercise. The memo called for volunteers to return and occupy the reefs for 90 days. Participants would be equipped with arms and supplies and ferried to the location on a vintage World War II–era cargo ship. The participants would continue Oliver's work by building up the site, protecting it from the elements and repelling foreign interference. At the end of the 90 days, the land would be divided among the group. The venture failed for lack of interest.

At least one attempt has made it back to the reefs. In 1982, Davis and another group of American libertarians attempted to reassert the republic. Unfortunately, after spending three weeks moored in the lagoon, they were expelled by the Tongan military. While there is some suggestion that several groups have since tried to re-establish the Republic, none have attempted to take possession of the reefs. Today, while Tonga and Fiji fight over the reefs, they have been 'more or less reclaimed by the sea'.

A libertarian revolution

Oliver did not resile from his dream but adopted another strategy. Instead of creating a new country in the middle of the Pacific Ocean, this time he would build a new libertarian state by supporting rebel movements in already inhabited countries. After his experiences with the Republic of Minerva, perhaps Oliver recognised that the international community would more readily accept the right of a secessionist movement to assert its statehood, rather than an artificial island in international waters settled by wealthy Americans. As luck would have it, Oliver could also attempt this strategy much closer to home.

In the early 1970s, the Bahamas were on the path to gaining independence from the United Kingdom. However, some of the 6500 residents of the Abaco Islands in the north of the territory wanted to stay part of the British Empire. In 1971, when Bahamian prime minister Lynden Pindling announced that he would seek independence, a hastily formed Greater Abaco Council petitioned the Queen to allow them to become a 'completely self-contained and fully self-supporting' territory under British jurisdiction. The UK government refused to consider the petition, and a general election in the Bahamas the following year confirmed clear majority support for parties desiring independence. This was not replicated in the Abaco Islands, where a majority of votes were cast in favour of parties opposing independence.

The Bahamas secured independence on 10 July 1973, leading some Abaco residents to harden their opposition. Although support for British rule had been shared among white and black residents, a new group emerged with a very different motivation. The Abaco Independence Movement was almost entirely white and was driven by its fear of 'the outspoken black nationalism of a few members of the Pindling Government'. Aware of Michael Oliver's politics, wealth and connections, its leaders reached out to him.

Oliver sensed his moment. Funding was provided to prop up the independence movement, manipulate public opinion towards secession and organise a rebellion. Local militias flew to facilities in Florida and Georgia to undergo military training and learn propaganda techniques under the auspices of Mitchell WerBell III, an American millionaire, arms dealer and former adviser to at least one Caribbean dictator. At the same time, Oliver sought to ensure that any rebellion would not lead to British intervention. Robert Hamilton, a member of the scheme and a conservative member of the House of Lords, was able to gain assurances in the UK Parliament that the British would not intervene to prevent the 'harassed' Abaconians from seeking their independence if they so determined.

The first issue of the *Abaco Independent*, the Abaco Independence Movement's newsletter, set out their basic philosophy of government. It would be familiar to those who knew Oliver:

'The purpose of government is to protect the freedom of the individual from force and fraud. Government should be the servant, not the master, of the people.' The new Abaco government would be restricted from doing almost anything:

> The Abaco government would be limited by the proposed constitution to a list of specific functions, and expressly prohibited from carrying out a long list of other activities. For example, under the constitution the government could NOT:
>
> - Issue money
> - Pass or enforce any legal tender laws
> - Restrict trade in any way
> - Establish or aid any school or church
> - Own any business or property
> - Establish or support any form of charity, welfare, or insurance program
> - Grant exclusive franchises
> - Subsidize any business
> - Interfere with wages or prices.

Oliver and WerBell outlined their plans in a briefing to a potential investor. Oliver explained his motivations:

> Abaco is not going to be another banana republic. That's not the point; I wouldn't spend an hour's time just to make some money that way. The point is that the Republic of Abaco will be, first of all, a moral experiment, a place where we'll try to keep individual freedom alive even if it doesn't survive in America.

At the same briefing, WerBell explained how they were sure that the Abaconians would support their libertarian paradise:

> 'Well, we're training quite a few natives with leadership potential,' says WerBell. 'Political indoctrination, and so on. They'll organize a following, maybe half the population, that'll go along with us, vote the way they're supposed to. And Bob here, Colonel Bayard, he's also training some natives with good potential, except he's training his boys how to shoot at a moving target without missing. And we figure the natives who won't buy what we tell 'em – they'll listen to Bob Bayard's boys.'

However, Oliver's plans soon fell apart. In an eye-opening interview with *Esquire* magazine, WerBell and Oliver outed themselves as central players in the planned revolution. The journalist explained:

> The day known as U.D.I. – that is, the date when Abaco breaks away from the Commonwealth of the Bahamas, the Unilateral Declaration of Independence – is tentatively set for New Year's Day of 1975. The operations required to seize control of the island have been disguised as the 'uprising' of an 'autonomous, locally organized independence movement' with such amazing skill that none of the world's major press has spotted what is going on.

Any pretence of operating under the radar ended with the *Esquire* exposé. WerBell soon drew the US Senate's notice as evidence about his apparent connection to targeted assassinations became public. Later suggestions that WerBell may also have been connected to the Watergate break-in forced him to reduce his activities, leading the incipient independence movement to collapse. Half a million 'Hands off Abaco' bumper stickers were left to rot in a southern Florida warehouse.

Undeterred, Oliver and his supporters quickly turned their attention to the New Hebrides (now Vanuatu). Oliver had long been interested in the New Hebrides – he bought about 4000 acres (16 square kilometres) of land there in 1971 and had previously attempted to create a libertarian state from that base. At the time, the territory was governed under a peculiar arrangement called a 'condominium' whereby Britain and France shared sovereignty. There were three separate governments – one British, one French, and one under joint administration. The third – the condominium government – could not act unless both the British and French agreed, meaning that it did little. Those living in the territory were more likely to dub the arrangement the 'pandemonium' as the two substantive administrations simply produced duplication. There were 'two police forces, two education systems, two resident commissioners and their staffs, two district agencies for local government centres, and eventually two post offices'. In 1979, the British and French finally agreed that the New Hebrides could attain independence the following year.

Enter Michael Oliver. In March 1979, he met with a group of Americans, French, Germans and Australians at a house in Melbourne to hatch a plan. The group called themselves the Phoenix Foundation, and were based in the Netherlands for tax purposes. Since 1975 they had been financing a rebel leader in the north of the New Hebrides. The messianic Jimmy Moly Stevens, who called himself Moses, headed a nationalist movement called Na-Griamel that sought the independence of the largest island in the condominium: Espiritu Santo. The Phoenix Foundation provided radios, training and other support to Stevens. At the same time, they were also marketing shares in the Vemarana Development Corporation that was to run the island after it achieved its own independence.

Independence for the entire New Hebrides would complicate their plan, so the group agreed to step up their activities. In May 1980, Stevens seized Espiritu Santo and declared the formation of the new Republic of Vemarana. Stevens' troops were armed with 'spears, bows and arrows and a few submachine guns'. Coins and passports (minted and printed in the United States) were ready to go. Reporters immediately picked up on the connection to Oliver:

> Some reports say Mr Stevens' rebellion was financed by a right-wing United States group, which hopes he will turn the island into a tax-free haven where free enterprise can function unhindered by government regulations. Mr Stevens displayed boxes of khaki uniforms he said he received from Michael Oliver, a Carson City, Nevada, businessman who helped him draw up a constitution for the island.

In response to inquiries about his role, Oliver justified his actions, explaining that he was merely trying to 'stop the Soviet Union taking over a country'. On the Vemarana Constitution, an associate noted, 'It's got a lot of the United States in it. It's got

The Na-Griamel Federation coin
Jansen Molisingi

some state constitutions in it. It's got some British in it. It's very short. Thomas Jefferson would love it.'

Vemarana did not survive for long. Vanuatu appealed for support from Papua New Guinea, which sent troops to put down the rebellion. Thankfully, there were few casualties. The residents of Espiritu Santo generally welcomed the Papua New Guineans as fellow Melanesians. The 'war' concluded after Stevens' son was killed when attempting to break through a Papua New Guinean roadblock. Soon afterwards, Stevens surrendered and was eventually sentenced to 14 years' jail. At his trial it was revealed that the French had secretly supported Stevens in a bid to derail independence for Vanuatu. Oliver was interrogated in the United States over interfering in other countries' internal affairs and was permanently banned from entering Vanuatu.

Oliver was nothing but persistent. Following the Vemarana debacle, he held talks with 'independence-minded' people on the Isle of Man, a semi-autonomous island between Ireland and England. When discussions went nowhere, he turned to the Azores Islands off the coast of Portugal. This too went nowhere.

Recurrent failures to foment rebellion left Oliver looking wistfully once more towards the sea. In the early 1990s, he proposed an artificial floating city off the coat of Panama. As advertised, 'Oceania', as it was called, promised to free residents from governments 'entangled in bureaucracy, corruption, and the free lunch philosophy', declaring that 'In our new country, OCEANIA, we can practice genuine free enterprise, enjoying true freedom in the tradition envisioned by Von Mises, Hayek, and Rand'. Once again, the project failed, this time for lack of funds.

It is unclear what happened to Michael Oliver. He may have failed to build his libertarian paradise, but his efforts inspired others to follow in his footsteps.

5

LIBERTY ON THE HIGH SEAS: REEF REPUBLICS AND SEASTEADS

The idea of building floating structures on the high seas can be alluring. What better way to gain respite from government and create your own model society? But just how easy is it to create a new country on artificial islands or reclaimed land on coral atolls? We have already seen that the Republic of Minerva was laid low by a small Tongan force, but perhaps the problem was that Tonga did not value the spirit of free enterprise ... so, would a libertarian reef republic off the coast of the United States work better? In the 1960s and 1970s, several American businessmen decided to try by building new countries off the coasts of Florida and California. They did not succeed, but they were far from alone. Here we explore the many attempts to build new nations on the high seas.

Reef republics

In 1962, two men attempted to create a new country on a series of reefs several kilometres off the coast of South Florida. The Grand and Triumph Reefs run parallel to the Florida Keys and are 5.5 kilometres from Elliot Key, south of Miami. Miami businessman William Anderson purported to have 'discovered' the reefs. Despite their proximity to the US mainland, it appears that the question of sovereignty had never been raised. Anderson wrote to the Florida state government and the federal government, asking about the status of the reefs.

Everything appeared positive. The Florida government replied that the reefs were 'outside the Constitutional Boundaries of the State of Florida and therefore, not within the jurisdiction' of the state. The federal government was similarly uninterested. The Department of the Interior replied to Anderson, saying that it 'has no jurisdiction over land that is outside the territorial limits of the United States'. A legal adviser with the State Department agreed, noting that 'the areas in question are outside of the jurisdiction of the United States and constitute a part of the high seas. The high seas are open to all nations and no state may validly subject any part of them to its sovereignty'.

Excited, Anderson gave public notice of his discovery in US and British newspapers. His notice recorded his intention 'to hold and own and develop into a Sovereign State subject to the jurisdiction of no State or Nation, and to provide for the government thereof in accordance with the democratic principles and International Law'. He also announced his new country would feature hotels and casinos. It seems that gambling was the primary motivation for the project. Casinos were banned in Florida and Anderson was searching for a suitable site for a casino in easy reach of Miami Beach.

Anderson envisioned a 'new sovereign nation' to be called 'Atlantis, Isle of Gold'. Encouraging 18 Miami Beach millionaires to tour the reefs, he estimated he would need

US$250 million to build an island and construct government buildings. There would be a post office, a stamp department, foreign offices, a government palace and a congress. There would even be a bank 'where people could bank by number just as they do in Switzerland'. Anderson projected a total site of about 2600 acres (10.5 square kilometres), several times the size of Monaco. Journalists joked that the nation could try to get a 'cut of the vast foreign aid programs which are now lining the pockets of new rulers the world over', or that it even might go communist to secure 'a fat loan from ambitious Nikita Khrushchev'.

Around the same time, Louisianan Louis Ray announced a similar plan, proposing the establishment of the 'Grand Capri Republic' on the same group of reefs. Ray's plan involved building an island about 600 metres long and 150 metres wide. He acknowledged that he never obtained 'any kind of permission if it was necessary' but considered the surest approach would be to simply occupy the reefs and take possession. Sailing out to the reefs, he started to pile sand on top of the coral and set up a prefabricated hut. He explained:

> I went out there and I sat on that island and I built these caissons and a house and I was going to put a family in the house and I [was] going to make some semblance of a defense. And don't get me wrong by saying if I am going to attack the Coast Guard or Navy, but I was going to have some semblance of a defense and I was going to build it and claim it and I occupied it, and I was going to defend it to the best of my ability and I was going to own it. Now, am I a nation? Me and four investors?

Neither Atlantis, Isle of Gold, nor the Grand Capri Republic were built. While Ray commenced dredging work, and Anderson constructed four prefabricated buildings on the reefs, financial and technical impediments proved considerable. Ultimately, the US government dashed their ambitions. In April 1965, it charged Ray with trespass and construction without Army Corps of Engineers permit, and sought a permanent injunction against any further development on the reefs. Anderson intervened in the case, claiming superior title to Ray's claim based on his prior discovery. Both Ray and Anderson argued that the reefs were islands outside US jurisdiction and were therefore subject to colonisation under international law.

The US District Court for the Southern District of Florida disagreed. The court ruled that the reefs were not islands because they were submerged at high tide. Instead, they were part of the 'subsoil and seabed' of the outer continental shelf (as defined in the United Nations Convention on the Continental Shelf), and therefore 'subject to [United States] jurisdiction, control, and power of disposition'. As the court explained, national security interests were also front of mind:

> The issues of this case are of great public interest, involving not only the preservation of rare natural resources, but the preservation of our very security as a nation. If these reefs were available for private construction totally outside the control of the United States Government, they could conceivably support not only artificial islands and unpoliced gambling casinos, but even an alien missile base, all within a short distance of the Florida Coast. Congress has seen fit to claim this area

> so that it may be used for the Commonwealth rather than private gain.

On appeal, Ray and Anderson lost again. A journalist remarked poetically, 'The dreams of the separate group for a new nation must perish, like the lost continent Atlantis, beneath the waters of the sea which constantly submerge the reefs.'

Perhaps the problem had been that the Grand and Triumph Reefs were too close to the US mainland. In 1966, one group of entrepreneurs decided to strike out a little further afield. They chose the Cortes Bank, a large, submerged island in the North Pacific Ocean about 170 kilometres west of San Diego. This was an eclectic bunch. Among the group were two abalone canners, a B-movie star famous for his role as comic-book hero Joe Palooka, a professional golfer and an aquatic expert. Together they hatched a plan for a new island nation. First, they bought the SS *Jalisco*, a World War II–era surplus troop ship that was mothballed in Suisun Bay, California. They then towed it out to the Cortes Bank, moored it on a shallow ridge and opened the seacocks to sink the vessel.

The next stage involved hauling rocks and rubbish from the city of Los Angeles to create a base on top of the sunken ship. From this base they would build a habitable structure and a new country. The plans were extensive. 'Lemuria' would include a runway, a refuelling station for ships, a casino and, most importantly, an abalone cannery to harvest the abundant abalone and lobster of the area. One of the abalone canners, Richard Taggart, was optimistic, explaining to the *Pasadena Independent*: 'I know it sounds fantastic. But we've consulted experts in international law and they say there's nothing to

Wreck of the *Jalisco*
Associated Press

prevent us from starting our own country if we want to. The Cortes Bank is international waters off the continental shelf and beyond either U.S. or Mexico.' An incredulous media christened the project 'Abalonia'.

Abalonia never took off. After setting the *Jalisco* in place, the group found that an anchor and a section of the anchor chain were missing, which meant it would be impossible to position the vessel at the correct site. Things then went from bad to worse. Rough seas broke the mooring line and the *Jalisco* crashed into a submerged rock, puncturing its hull. Quickly taking on water, the vessel had to be scuttled in deeper waters. Abalonia was sunk.

Authorities in the United States were watching the spectacle closely. When the chastened group arrived back on dry land, they were threatened with the charge of creating a navigational hazard. The US Department of the Interior agreed not to sue the promoters on the condition that they agreed not to return to the Cortes Bank.

The US had reason to be worried. Two other groups were also interested in building a new country on the Cortes Bank. One, based in Seattle, claimed to have secured US$15 million from investors to fill the bank with rocks and build 'Taluga'. Taluga would be around 1000 acres (4 square kilometres) in size and eventually contain three cities. Attorney Jack England, spokesperson for the Taluga project, rubbished claims that Abalonia had any legal claim to the bank, asserting that 'in 1959, my clients drove the first claim stake' by placing a buoy marker 'on the spot with a legal claim in it'. The other project was more mysterious. 'Aqualandia' also claimed the bank and threatened any interloper with military action. Unfortunately for all three claims, the US held firm. Although the Cortes Bank is located far offshore, it is still part of the continental shelf and is thus part of the United States and under the authority – strangely enough – of the US Department of the Interior.

Unlucky at sea: Operation Atlantis

By this stage, the Department of the Interior must have had a file for people attempting to create their own nations off the US coast. Maybe the key for would-be nation builders was to avoid media and political attention? In 1968, Werner Stiefel, born in Brooklyn, New York, gave it a try. Stiefel's family was originally German. Like Michael Oliver and the Republic of Minerva before him, Stiefel was shaped by World War II and the Cold

War. His family's successful soap- and candle-making company had been taken from them by the Nazis, and he was convinced that the United States was on the same road to socialism that had strangled free enterprise across Europe and Asia. Yet, as with Oliver, the United States had been good to Stiefel. With his father and brother, he had established a new business under the Stiefel name. Stiefel Laboratories was thriving, and by 1968 had made Werner a millionaire. The family business continued to succeed: at Werner Stiefel's death in 2006 it was the largest privately owned dermatological company in the world, employing over 2500 people with offices in more than 100 countries.

Inspired by libertarian author Ayn Rand, Stiefel began to consider alternative models of governance for his new nation. After studying systems from across the world, he found that all were 'prone to follow the same old, tired' path to despotism. Stiefel even considered that Michael Oliver's libertarian paradise was disposed to socialism and totalitarianism on the basis that citizens would have to make regular 'quasi-voluntary payments' to access the courts. True freedom required the prohibition of all forms of regular payments.

After initially growing despondent, Stiefel had a burst of insight: 'Why have a government at all?' Operation Atlantis was born. A carefully sequenced three-stage project, Operation Atlantis would 'test the hypothesis that a free, capitalist society can exist and flourish in today's world'. As Stiefel explained, 'The logic is that we are here in Atlantis because we have concluded that it is hopeless to think in terms of meaningful fundamental reforms in the U.S. To dream of repealing laws like Social Security, federal income tax, and Medicare is just simply not facing up to reality.' This country would have to be developed offshore because 'no unclaimed territory is left'.

The first stage focused on gathering libertarians and other like-minded individuals into a single location so that they could work together to build an integrated community. A wholly voluntary society, the community would be based 'on market-rule, the protection of private property and individual rights'. Stiefel bought the Sawyerkill Motel in Saugerties, New York, near one of his soap-making plants, to serve as a base for the community. Under a pseudonym, he published *The Story of Operation Atlantis*, which set out his manifesto and provided details on his plan. Importantly, the 'only tax-like payment' any person would ever have to pay to the government would be an 'admission fee' of 1000 Decas (Stiefel's currency) if that person chose to become a citizen.

The book attracted 'a sizeable number' of enthusiastic libertarians who flocked to the motel. One supporter described it as 'like John Galt's speech in [Ayn Rand's] *Atlas Shrugged* after a good editor got hold of it and deleted the preachy mumbo-jumbo and redundancy and translated most of the rest from Rand-speak into standard American-English'.

The Sawyerkill Motel proved a good testing ground for the project. Community members were free to hold a job outside and leave at any time. Those who worked part-time on Operation Atlantis were rewarded with free accommodation. It also had the benefit of 'closely simulat[ing] a land-locked ship'. 'Freedom Forums' held every Sunday offered lively and active discussions on libertarianism and promoted a sense of community. The motel also allowed individuals to return home 'with little or no financial loss or personal stigma' if the enterprise failed.

It was only a matter of time before news of the enterprise leaked. A September 1970 issue of *Esquire* magazine reported:

> Operation Atlantis is a real mind-blower, for they're not just interested in a floating community, but an honest-to-god independent *country*. They are reportedly well-financed, well-managed, and *very* serious. How are they going to do it? They're going to build an island, baby, in the middle of the ocean.

Those in residence at the Sawyerkill Motel were working on stage two of Operation Atlantis: building a boat. Under a large geodesic dome situated next to the motel, they built a 12-metre-long ferro-cement vessel. With the help of independent contractors, *Atlantis II* was completed in December 1971. The plan called for the ship to anchor off the coast of the United States and serve as a temporary home for the community while they built their island nation somewhere in the Caribbean. Building the offshore nation was step three. The ship would then be used to supply the new island. It sounds outlandish, but Operation Atlantis was a serious project. It was hoped that the new nation could become a place 'for people to flee to when the United States, like Germany in the 1930s, became a police state'.

With great excitement, *Atlantis II* was launched in the Hudson River at high tide. Here is where the plan began to fall apart. 'The tide went out, and the ship was left lying on its side in the mud,' reported Erwin Strauss, who witnessed the launch. 'A kerosene lantern left in the wheelhouse broke in this process, but the concrete construction of the vessel limited the fire damage. Nevertheless, it was an omen of things to come.'

Liberties had been taken in the design of the vessel. A concrete deckhouse left the boat so top-heavy that it almost capsized again when crossing New York Harbor. The crew managed to right the ship and it continued to sail south, though it broke a propeller near South Carolina. Eventually, it made it to the Bahamas. While anchored in shallow waters near Acklins Island, a hurricane destroyed the hull and *Atlantis II* sank beneath the waves.

The loss of the vessel was not the end of Operation Atlantis. Stiefel bought a new ship and immediately turned his attention to finding land on which he could build his independent nation. After a failed attempt to purchase the Prickly Pear Cays in Anguilla, the group looked towards the Silver Shoals, a submerged reef between Haiti and the Bahamas. With the shoals only a few feet under water at low tide, the site was attractive. However, there were problems. The territory was claimed by both countries, and rumours of shipwrecked Spanish galleons full of treasure meant competition was fierce.

After constructing sea walls around the ship and beginning rudimentary dredging work, the group was approached by gunboats and forced to abandon the site. They relocated to Tortuga Island in the north of Haiti. Stiefel signed a long-term lease with the Haitian government, which was interested in developing the island into a free port. They got as far as using a hydraulic soap press to mint their own currency – the deca – named for the ten grams of sterling silver each coin contained. A ship's wheel adorned the face of the coin with the words 'reason' and 'freedom' inscribed, and a setting sun at sea on the reverse. Unfortunately, the Haitian government learned of Operation Atlantis's grander plans and cancelled the lease.

The Deca coin
Credit unknown

Stiefel was not yet defeated. Several years later he sailed out to the Misteriosa Bank, a 322-square-kilometre submerged atoll in the Caribbean Sea, around 350 kilometres from Mexico, Honduras and Cuba, with the intention of finally founding Atlantis. This time the plan called for an oil rig to be toppled and turned upside down, and residences to be built upon it. Alas, before they could secure the rig, a hurricane swept through and destroyed the site.

While no more was heard of Operation Atlantis, several members involved are adamant that the project continued in a different form. Isabelle Simpson explains that Stiefel bought a 6-acre (24 280-square-metre) island called Hatchet Caye, located around 32 kilometres east of Placencia, Belize. Hoping to transform the island into a free port, he eventually grew tired of bureaucracy and put the island up for sale. It is now a private island resort called Ray Caye, available for the price of

US$9999 per night. Stiefel passed away in 2006, having never realised his dream.

Searching for paradise: New Utopia and Rose Island

Operation Atlantis may have failed, but the Misteriosa Bank would prove popular. On 13 April 1999, American businessman Lazarus Long proclaimed the formation of the Principality of New Utopia, located on the same Misteriosa Bank. Originally named Howard Turney, Long took his new name from a series of science fiction novels by Robert Heinlein. The fictional Lazarus Long was the result of a selective breeding experiment that had given him a life span of well over 2000 years. The name was apt, as the real-life Lazarus Long was a committed advocate for the anti-aging effects of human growth hormones. Long made a fortune selling this treatment in a clinic he owned in Mexico before he was forced to close. That fortune would be used to develop New Utopia.

Long had grand dreams. Sailing to the bank, he anchored a buoy to the seabed and planned to erect a glittering city that would 'out Cayman the Caymans'. New Utopia would be constructed on top of an enormous, pillar-mounted concrete platform. The platform would be designed to create 'Venice-style waterways', dotted with four beautiful public parks '2000 feet long and 600 feet deep' (610 by 180 metres) named in honour of Ayn Rand and Robert Heinlein. New Utopia would have state-of-the-art features: a private hospital, a casino modelled on the famous marble-and-gold casino in Monte Carlo, and 'the ultimate luxury spa'. There would be 642 apartments and condominiums for residents. Funded by a 20 per cent tax on imported goods, there would be no need for personal income taxes. Reflecting Rand's vision, New Utopia would be 'a free-market oasis without government constraints where money can be made and stashed and the taxman never calls'.

Unfortunately for Long, the US Securities and Exchange Commission did call. Although rich himself, Long needed more money to develop New Utopia – around US$350 million to be precise. The Commission believed that Long's citizenship bonds (sold for US$1500 each) were nothing more than a 'classic securities swindle', as they were apparently unconvinced that the city would be constructed. The courts agreed. In 2000, the US District Court for the Northern District of Oklahoma held that in offering and selling securities over the internet to fund the development of New Utopia, Long made material misrepresentations and omissions concerning the status of construction of the project, the safety of the investment, and the status of the Securities and Exchange Commission's investigation into his activities. Long died in 2012.

American libertarians are not the only people interested in establishing nations on the high seas. We have already seen that in 1967 Englishman Roy Bates declared himself the ruler of the Principality of Sealand – an artificial naval installation located just outside the UK's territorial waters. In 1968, an Italian citizen made a similar bid. Setting out from the small city of Rimini, on Italy's east coast, engineer Giorgio Rosa built a 400-square-metre platform just under 300 metres outside Italian territorial waters. Once complete, he announced the formation of a new independent nation named Isola delle Rosa – the Republic of Rose Island.

Top: Republic of Rose Island
Bottom: Republic of Rose Island at the moment of its destruction, February 1969
Courtesy of Comune di Rimini Biblioteca Gambalunga, 'Speciale Isola Delle Rose', 1968-Febbraio 1969

The republic had its own flag, currency and national anthem. It also had its own language – Esperanto, a constructed international auxiliary language created in 1887. Mimicking the actions of real states, the newly formed Council of Government swiftly declared war on Italy, its closest neighbour. While Giorgio Rosa's motivations were not clear, Italian authorities believed that the platform was a ploy to raise money from credulous tourists and avoid taxation. Rumours swirled that the republic would host prostitution, pirate radio and gambling; that it was the centre of an international spy ring; and that 'it was even a Soviet submarine base'. Uninterested in legal wrangling, the harbour office of Rimini issued a demolition order.

Giorgio Rosa, the republic's president, appealed to the Italian Council of State. Rosa's argument was based on the United Nations Convention on the High Seas, which Italy had ratified in 1964. According to Rosa, the Convention 'granted a right to the free use of the high seas both to States and to individuals'. In fact, the Convention does no such thing. The Council of State dismissed his argument, holding that the Convention 'only creates rights and obligations of an international character for the Italian State with respect to other nations of the international community'. One of those obligations was to prevent activities that may obstruct freedom of the high seas.

The platform was demolished, but the republic lived on. As a self-declared government-in-exile, the republic issued several stamps portraying the Italian destruction of its homeland. The story is now the subject of a film, *Rose Island*, on Netflix.

Seasteading: A home on the high seas

Why did Werner Stiefel and Lazarus Long choose a remote reef for their new nations? They must have known that the distance would make it difficult to raise the reef above sea level and construct any buildings. Why did they not try to build closer to the shore, as Giorgio Rosa did?

Stiefel worried that states might start to assert jurisdiction over reefs located near their coast, so he looked further afield. His hunch proved accurate. Developments in international law since the 1960s and 1970s have drastically reduced the possibility of building a nation on the waves.

The 1982 United Nations Convention on the Law of the Sea confirmed the scope of coastal state authority. Entering into force in 1994, the Convention provides for an expansive jurisdiction. All coastal states enjoy a 12-nautical-mile territorial sea within which they may set laws, regulate and use any resource. Coastal states also possess a further 12-nautical-mile contiguous zone, in which they can enforce laws in customs, taxation, immigration and pollution. There is also a 200-nautical-mile exclusive economic zone for coastal states, within which they have sole exploitation rights over natural resources. In addition, they possess exclusive jurisdiction over mineral and non-mineral resources within their continental shelf – an area that may exceed the 200 nautical miles of the exclusive economic zone. The greatly increased authority of coastal states under the Convention means that future micronations seeking to establish themselves on atolls or artificial structures must look far beyond the nearest state.

The failure to build habitable structures on remote coral reefs does not mean that the libertarian dream has ended.

More recently, attention has focused on the California-based Seasteading Institute. Co-founded in 2008 by Wayne Gramlich and Patri Friedman, grandson of Nobel Prize–winning libertarian economist Milton Friedman, and initially financed by Silicon Valley billionaire Peter Thiel, the Seasteading Institute aims to succeed where earlier efforts have failed. Instead of building artificial islands, seasteading involves creating floating structures that are 'arranged into atolls and archipelagos' allowing individuals to settle on the high seas outside national jurisdiction.

The Institute's website suggests that seasteading could offer significant benefits to humanity. Backers are interested in seasteading's potential to 'peacefully test new ideas for government' so that 'the most successful can then inspire change in governments around the world'. Peter Thiel has explained: 'Decades from now, those looking back at the start of the century will understand that Seasteading was an obvious step towards encouraging the development of more efficient, practical public-sector models around the world.'

Patri Friedman concurs: 'Let's think of government as an industry, where countries are firms and citizens are customers!' The underlying idea here is that if you do not like the government that you are living under, you could simply sail away to another seastead operating under a different government. To 'compete' for citizens, floating city-states would be forced to serve 'as incubators for new forms of government'. While nominally agnostic on political systems, the most prominent and vocal proponents of seasteads are zealous libertarians. They are primarily motivated by a quest for profit and material advancement without regulatory burdens.

The Seasteading Institute has a comprehensive page of Frequently Asked Questions. Some of their answers are a little optimistic.

> **What about pirates?**
> Piracy is generally a problem occurring near the coast of failed or poor states. Just as you wouldn't want to build your beach home in a dangerous neighborhood, you wouldn't want to park your cruise ship off their coasts either. Initial seasteads will be hosted in the territorial waters of secure nations who patrol their own waters. Private security firms that protect cargo ships passing through piracy waters right now can also protect seasteads in safe waters.

It is not always clear whether proponents conceive seasteads as entirely new states or as enclaves within existing states. So far, technological and financial challenges have meant that the latter has been prioritised. However, no large-standing seastead has been constructed. Negotiations with French Polynesia for the development of proof-of-concept floating cities within their territorial waters stalled when community pressure forced the government to withdraw from the project. Many were concerned, as one Tahitian local put it, that 'facilitating the tax evasion of the world's greatest fortunes' would offer no benefit to the islands at all.

The first seastead was launched off the coast of Thailand in 2019. Designed and constructed by Ocean Builders, the two-person 'SeaPod' was anchored 12 nautical miles off the Phuket coast in the Andaman Sea. Ocean Builders may have overcome the technological challenges, but political problems soon emerged. The Thai navy claimed that the seastead endangered Thailand's national sovereignty. The couple who occupied the SeaPod avoided capture, but a police complaint alleges they intended to 'deteriorate the independence of the state', an offence punishable by death. Ocean Builders have relocated to Panama, apparently with the support of government officials there.

Similar projects have been considered. In 2011, Silicon Valley company Blueseed announced its plans to lease a decommissioned 1500-passenger cruise ship and moor it 12 nautical miles off the Californian coast. Founded by two ex-Seasteading Institute employees, the idea was to create 'a vibrant workplace for innovative industries to bloom, unencumbered by onerous regulations on new technology-sector businesses'. The cruise ship would be outfitted with 'coworking spaces, high-speed wifi, 24-hour concierge services, and a gym'. It failed for lack of funding.

The group behind Ocean Builders made it one step further. Interested in scaling up their two-person SeaPods, the team purchased the 245-metre cruise ship *Pacific Dawn* in 2020. Designed by the Italian architect Renzo Piano, the ship had been mothballed by the Covid-19 pandemic. Renaming it the MS *Satoshi*, in 'homage to Satoshi Nakamoto, the pseudonym of bitcoin's mysterious inventor (or inventors)', the group planned to anchor it off the coast of Panama and establish a utopian crypto-community. Sophie Elmhirst explains:

> The *Satoshi* ... offered a chance to marry two movements, of crypto-devotees and seasteaders, united by their desire

Artist's rendering of Seapods
Ocean Builders

for freedom – from convention, regulation, tax. Freedom from the state in all its forms. But converting a cruise ship into a new society proved more challenging than envisaged. The high seas, while appearing borderless and free, are, in fact, some of the most tightly regulated places on Earth. The cruise ship industry in particular is bound by intricate rules.

The team could not find insurance for their crypto-utopia. After the project leaked around US$1 million a month in operating costs, the ship was resold in 2021 for cruise operations.

The Seasteading Institute has moved on. Patri Friedman is now looking to buy land in developing nations to establish semi-autonomous cities. In this effort they join a long line of libertarian nation builders.

6

FIGHTING FOR CHANGE: POLITICAL PROTEST AND LAW REFORM

As we have seen, the desire to create a micronation often arises out of an individual grievance. A person may become so frustrated with a law or bureaucrat that they feel they have no other option but to secede and found their own country. Even if they do not become a real state, they can thus register their disgust with what they regard as insensible authority.

Other micronations are established to address broader issues, such as to shine the political and media spotlight on a significant issue affecting many people. These types of micronations are founded to protest government policy and agitate for law reform, and some have proven very effective.

Gay and Lesbian Kingdom of the Coral Sea Islands

In May 2004, Australian attorney-general Philip Ruddock introduced a bill into parliament to affirm that marriage meant 'the union of a man and a woman to the exclusion of all others, voluntarily entered into for life'. The aim was to rule out the recognition of same-sex marriage in Australia, including same-sex marriages legally entered into in other countries. Ruddock claimed the Bill was needed to protect the 'institution of marriage'. The Bill passed and became law in September 2004. Many sections of the community strongly opposed it, labelling the measure the 'Marriage Discrimination Bill'.

The fight was not over. Earlier that year, at the Brisbane Pride festival, a group of activists met to consider how they could put pressure on the Australian government to remove law and policy that discriminated against gay and lesbian people. In June 2004, in the middle of the parliamentary debate on the marriage amendment bill, the activists chartered a yacht. Christening the ship the *Gayflower* (a reference to the *Mayflower*, the ship that transported the Pilgrims from England to North America in 1620), the group landed on the small uninhabited island of Cato in the Coral Sea Islands, 200 nautical miles off the coast of Queensland. There they raised the rainbow flag and declared the independent Gay and Lesbian Kingdom of the Coral Sea Islands.

They then began to set up the institutions of the nation. The leader of the group, Dale Parker Anderson, was declared emperor of the kingdom. Anderson was the perfect choice. He claimed to be a descendant of King Edward II, who ruled England between 1307 and 1327 (although the evidence is uncertain, many historians consider Edward II to have been gay). Their campsite was re-formed as the nation's capital and renamed Heaven after a famous gay nightclub in London. A post box was installed. Gloria Gaynor's 1983 hit 'I Am What I Am', a song originally from the Broadway show *La Cage aux Folles*, was made the national anthem. The Pink Triangle,

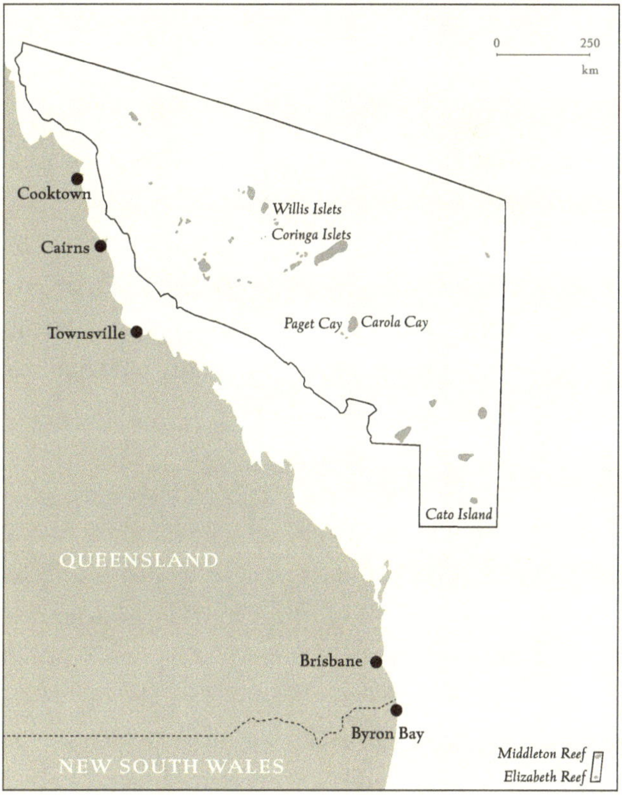

Gay and Lesbian Kingdom of the Coral Sea Islands territory

a symbol used to distinguish gay men in Nazi concentration camps but later reclaimed as a positive symbol of self-identity, was chosen as the kingdom's coat of arms.

Several laws were also enacted. One, similar to Israel's Law of Return, automatically granted any gay or lesbian person permanent resident status and made them eligible for citizenship. A memorial plaque commemorating the founding was placed on the north-eastern tip of Cato Island. It reads:

> On the 14th day of June 2004, at this highest point in the Coral Sea, Emperor Dale Parker Anderson raised the gay rainbow flag and claimed the islands of the Coral Sea in his name as homeland for the gay and lesbian peoples of the world. God Save our King!

The founders also issued a Declaration of Independence explaining their motivations. Declaring that 'discrimination against gay and lesbian people is as morally repugnant as racism or anti-Semitism', they stated:

> Homosexual people have honestly endeavoured everywhere to merge ourselves in the social life of surrounding communities and to be treated equally. We are not permitted to do so. In vain we are loyal patriots, our loyalty in some places running to extremes; in vain do we make the same sacrifices of life and property as our fellow citizens; in vain do we strive to increase the fame of our native land in science and art, or her wealth by trade and commerce. In countries where we have lived for centuries, we are still cried down as strangers ... in the world as it is now and for an indefinite period ... I think we shall not be left in peace.

Signed by Emperor Dale Anderson, the Declaration was promptly sent to every politician in Australia. At least two replies were received. Both were non-committal. John Faulkner, the Leader of the Opposition in the Senate, noted: 'Your letter raises a number of issues of international law on which I am not qualified to comment. I see from your letter that you have forwarded your declaration of independence to the Governor-General and I am sure that it will received [*sic*] due attention.' The chief of staff of the Queensland premier responded similarly: 'Thank you for your letter of 14 June 2004 informing of the declaration of independence from Australia of the Coral Sea Island Territory.' Both letters were addressed to 'Mr Anderson'.

Perhaps Australia should have taken the announcement more seriously. Just a few months later, following the passage of Ruddock's bill banning same-sex marriage, Emperor Anderson declared war on Australia. Adopting the same legally erroneous strategy as the Principality of Hutt River, Anderson claimed that because Australia did not defeat the kingdom – in fact, Australia did not even reply – Australia was bound under the Geneva Convention of August 1949 to recognise the sovereignty of the Gay and Lesbian Kingdom of the Coral Sea Islands.

Hutt River was firmly in the minds of Anderson and his compatriots. Anderson was initially appointed 'administrator' of the government. However, this was quicky changed (and Anderson made emperor) for the same reason that the Hutt River province was restyled as a principality. The kingdom apparently received legal advice explaining that:

> under Australian law (Australia is a Kingdom) a de facto prince trying to claim his crown cannot be charged with treason, this law goes further and states in fact that anyone hindering a de facto prince or his supporters from obtaining his crown can themselves be charged with treason ... Had a republic model of government been chosen all the gay and lesbian activists could have

> been charged with treason and been bought before the Australian courts.

No such law exists.

The legal basis for the kingdom's claim to sovereignty and statehood was also non-existent. The founders identified two legal principles on which they grounded their claim. The first was based on the concept of unjust enrichment, a principle that can be traced to Roman law. It holds that where one person is unfairly or unreasonably enriched at the expense of another person, the first person must give what they gained back to the second person. According to Anderson, Australia was guilty of unjust enrichment because laws discriminating against gay and lesbian people in the fields of marriage, adoption, IVF treatment and spousal benefits, among others, unjustly deprived gay and lesbian people of the right to be treated equally. Rather than financial compensation, Anderson sought 'territorial compensation' by establishing an independent state on Cato Island in the Coral Sea.

The choice of location was made in line with the second legal principle underlying the claim to statehood. First charted in 1803, the Coral Sea Islands are a group of tropical islands and reefs east of the Great Barrier Reef. Stretching over 780 000 square kilometres (most of which is ocean), the absence of a reliable supply of fresh water has prevented long-term habitation. Only Willis Island is permanently inhabited: four people run a meteorological station. In 1969 the Coral Sea Islands were made an Australian external territory.

For Anderson, the combination of the Coral Sea Islands' legal designation as an external 'territory' and its lack of an Indigenous people was perfect. Drawing on a series of international instruments, such as the United Nations Charter and the General Assembly Declaration on the Granting of Independence to Colonial Countries and Peoples, Anderson argued that international law recognised a right of self-determination for 'oppressed people of overseas territories'. As gay and lesbian people were oppressed, they had a right to form their own state in the Coral Sea Islands.

The legal basis for the kingdom's claim to statehood may have been spurious, but its value as a political and moral symbol was clear. The Declaration of Independence outlined the multitude of legal discrimination focused on gay and lesbian Australians.

> As a nation, Australia maintains appalling laws against gay and lesbian people ... We are people, first and foremost. We work, we have lives, we love and have relationships. We are family. Yet despite being citizens, voters and taxpayers, lesbian and gay Australians do not have the same rights – or in many cases have no rights – to those things in life that heterosexual people take for granted. Gay & Lesbian people can be denied access to a hospital to visit their partner if they are sick or injured – because their relationship is not legally recognised as next of kin. Should they die, their partner has no legal claim to their superannuation death benefit, despite the fact that they may have been nominated as a beneficiary.

It also quoted statistics detailing the appalling rates of verbal and physical abuse that gay and lesbian people faced daily in

Border post and post box on Cato Island
Credit unknown

Australia. That abuse, the Declaration continued, contributed to the extremely high rate of suicide among young gay and lesbian people.

By claiming statehood, the Gay and Lesbian Kingdom sought to give 'give gay people a voice' in the United Nations and in international affairs. In an interview, Anderson explained further that:

> only sovereign states and territories can access an international court. So ... we can't as a community take on Iran and say, look, why did you, you know, kill those two teenage boys last month because they were gay ... we thought, if we have a sovereign, if we have some type of sovereignty that could access the courts and give gay people

Stamps of the Gay and Lesbian Kingdom of the Coral Sea Islands
Credit unknown

> a voice on the international stage, whether it be through the UN or [whatever] ... then why not look at doing that?

Anderson was realistic about the prospect of creating a new country, but recognised the value of the kingdom's claim. In a 2008 interview with *Star Observer*, he noted: 'The [Australian] government's obviously not going to recognise it but if we can force them to do something about it [discriminatory legislation], then they can't ignore it.'

In the years after its founding, Anderson and other citizens expanded their visibility. In 2006, they issued postage stamps to raise money and attract attention.

The kingdom attracted international attention and received hundreds of applications for asylum and citizenship from people all over the world desperate to escape persecution in their home countries and move to remote Cato Island. One of the men involved in establishing the micronation, Willoughby Potter de Grimaldi, explained the difficulty that this caused:

> I reached back explaining the problem with that, and how there isn't a residence there. There – there's nowhere specific to go. But, although you can't necessarily seek asylum there on Cato Island, your voice is not lost. We could then connect those people with local organisations, to offer protections for discrimination and things like that.

William Jackson Freeman, who served as lord chancellor, agreed. Freeman noted that requests for asylum from desperate gay and lesbian people placed a lot of pressure on the founders. These requests also forced the group to work out what sort of role the kingdom could play. Some wanted the kingdom to serve as a viral political and media campaign to help push for legal reform. Others wanted it to be a state recognised by the United Nations. Others again thought that the kingdom could be monetised. Some even wanted to genuinely settle on Cato Island. Ultimately, the group could not agree on a vision for the kingdom.

By 2014, Dale Anderson was no longer involved in the project and the kingdom was largely defunct. It was not until 2017 that its existence once again attracted mainstream attention.

At a Senate Estimates hearing in February 2017, Liberal senator Eric Abetz objected to the rainbow flag being displayed in the foyer of the Department of Finance in Canberra. Noting the ongoing debate on whether to legalise same-sex marriage, Abetz argued that government departments should remain politically neutral. He concluded his comments with an observation:

> you realise this particular flag is the flag of the Gay and Lesbian Kingdom of the Coral Sea Islands, which has declared war on Australia. Senator Cormann, you would understand they did the same as Prince Leonard of the Principality of Hutt River and this is now their official flag. It is the flag of a hostile nation, if we are to believe them, having declared war on Australia.

The minister for finance, Senator Mathias Cormann, responded:

> Senator Cormann: It is certainly not the government's intention to fly the flags of hostile nations in any of our official buildings.
>
> Senator Abetz: Very good. That is a start.
>
> Senator Cormann: We will make sure that there are no flags of hostile nations anywhere in any government building.

The situation resolved itself in December 2017 when the Australian Parliament voted to legalise same-sex marriage. That same month, the Gay and Lesbian Kingdom announced that it had dissolved. The Gay and Lesbian Kingdom of the Coral Sea Islands had won.

The Conch Republic: 'We seceded where others failed'

In the 1970s and '80s, the illicit drug trade was a major problem in the United States. Cocaine and marijuana cultivated in Colombia and other South American countries flowed into the US in staggering amounts. As a key gateway, Florida became home to 'the largest narcotics network in America' – some 70 per cent of all cocaine entering the United States passed through South Florida. The trade was lucrative. By 1980 the US Drug Enforcement Agency estimated that the annual Miami marijuana trade brought in about US$12 billion, more than real estate and tourism combined. The cocaine industry was even more profitable: in Miami alone cocaine was an annual US$20 billion business.

The 'War on Drugs' was officially launched in 1971 under president Richard Nixon. However, it was not until Ronald Reagan took office in 1981 that the war really stepped up. Reagan reinforced and expanded many of Nixon's policies, expanding penalties for possession, imposing mandatory minimum sentences and establishing procedures for asset forfeiture. Other measures were also attempted. In early 1982, the US Border Patrol set up a roadblock and inspection point on the only road between the Florida Keys, a string of limestone islands that stretches almost 300 kilometres off the southern tip of Florida, and the mainland to curb drug smuggling and undocumented immigration.

The roadblock upset many of the residents of the small community on the Keys. The inspection point resulted in a 27-kilometre traffic jam, severely inconveniencing residents and hurting the Key's tourism industry. Residents were up in arms.

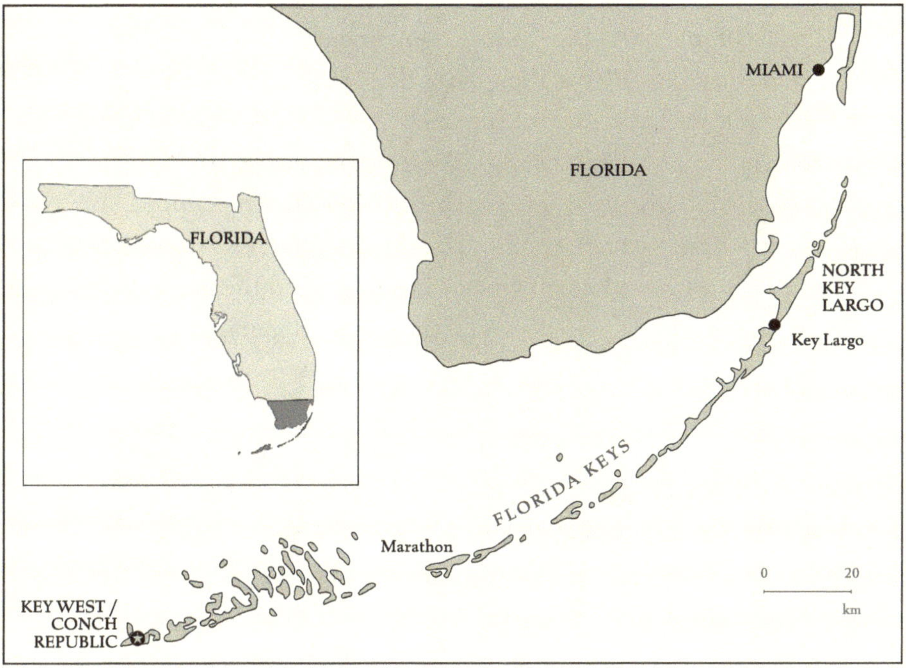

Location of the Conch Republic

While no one 'doubted that drugs were trafficked widely in the Keys by road and by boat', the roadblock was bad for business.

The community fought back. Dennis Wardlow, mayor of Key West – the most populated town on the islands, and the furthest from the mainland – and the city council attempted to persuade the federal government to remove the roadblock. When that was unsuccessful, they went to court seeking an injunction to force the government to take it down. The US government remained firm. According to the Border Patrol, the roadblock was none of the mayor's business. The court agreed.

Determining that the federal government had essentially established a border station as if they were a foreign nation, Wardlow declared to a waiting media pack outside the federal courthouse in Miami that Key West would secede.

The following day, on 23 April 1982, Wardlow stepped up to a hastily constructed podium in Mallory Square, at the centre of Key West. In a booming voice he announced the creation of the newest country in the world: the Conch Republic:

> We're the Conchs and we've had enough. We secede from the United States ... We've raised our flag, given our notice and named our government. We serve notice on the government in Washington to remove the roadblock or get ready to put up a permanent border to a new foreign land.

A large crowd of almost 1000 Conch patriots cheered on Wardlow, the republic's inaugural prime minister. Supporters waived miniature flags – a pink conch shell on a yellow sun against a blue background. Many also held up placards declaring their support for the new Conch Republic with ironic twists on popular American slogans, like 'Remember the Aloe' and 'Don't tread on Conchs'. Other placards announced solidarity with similar island communities: 'Conchland United with Cuba and Falkland and Other Beleaguered Islands'.

Residents of the Keys and surrounding region have long been nicknamed 'Conchs' in honour of the humble conch shell. The name dates to the American War of Independence. Following the rebel victory, many Americans loyal to the British Crown fled to the nearby British colonies of British

North America (Canada) and the Bahamas, just a short boat ride from the Florida Keys. Unfortunately for the new residents, the British Parliament began to levy taxes on imported food. The new Bahamians retorted that they would rather eat the bountiful sea snails that lived in conch shells rather than pay tax. The name stuck.

The US State Department was initially unsure how to react to the Conch Republic's independence announcement. In response to a journalist questioning whether the US had plans to recognise the new country, an official pointed out that if Key West did become a foreign nation there would be a permanent checkpoint, thereby producing an ironic end to the stand-off. Nonetheless, the declaration was well received across the new republic. Key West city commissioner and incoming defence minister of the Conch Republic, Joe Balbontin, exclaimed 'everybody's going bananas. We're getting calls from all over. The switchboard at City Hall has lit up like a clam bake. People think it's great'. The minister added that 'a tremendous amount' of people had volunteered for the Conch Republic militia, including several survivors from the failed 1961 Bay of Pigs invasion of Cuba.

Despite the enthusiasm, it was not immediately clear how the republic would defend itself from its much larger neighbour. Balbontin admitted that the new nation did not have a standing army. Nonetheless, he boasted that the republic's navy was formidable. Playing on the region's connection to the South American drug trade, the minister noted wryly that the navy comprised several vessels including some 'very high speed boats familiar with clandestine night operations'.

The might of the republic's military was going to be critical.

Immediately putting themselves to the test, Wardlow declared war on the United States. Balbontin rushed over to two figures dressed in US naval officer uniforms and whacked one of them on the head with a loaf of stale Cuban bread. The crowd went wild, erupting into cheers, screams and chants. Worried about what might happen next, Wardlow issued a declaration of surrender before requesting US$1 billion in foreign aid to restore the local economy. He wanted to make clear that the republic's intentions were financial rather than militaristic. The Chamber of Commerce president Ed Swift acknowledged, 'We're kind of like the mouse that roared.'

The military conflict between the Conch Republic and the United States may have been short-lived but the republic scored an early victory in a related skirmish. They did not obtain their $1 billion in development aid, but the Conch Republic's national baseball team (Key West High School) defeated the United States' Archbishop Curley-Notre Dame High School 7–1 to win the Florida district high schools title. Wardlow, whose son Joey was a member of the team, declared to a waiting media pack, 'This victory is very sweet for our country'.

The following day, Florida governor Bob Graham became the first foreign dignitary to visit the Conch Republic. Invited to speak at the Florida Keys Community College, Graham poked fun at the republic, joking, 'I enjoyed the [College] chorus singing "Battle Hymn of the Republic". But I wasn't sure which republic they were singing about.' The governor added that president Ronald Reagan and secretary of state Alexander Haig would be pleased by the secession: 'Cuba is no longer 90 miles from the shore of the United States. Now it's 150 miles off the shore of the United States.' Nevertheless, there were reasons to be worried. Reports suggested that the republic might soon be the subject of its own coup. The shadowy Mangrove Liberation Front was preparing to overthrow the Wardlow regime and institute a People's Democratic Republic of the Florida Keys.

As should be clear, the Conch Republic's declaration of secession was tongue in cheek. The goal was not to create a new country but to remove the federal government inspection point and restore the region's vital tourist industry. Independence was a public relations effort to draw national attention to the roadblock and force the government to remove it. Jimmy Mira, a city commissioner and pizza parlour owner who was appointed the republic's commissioner of nutrition and food and drug enforcement, made this motive clear. 'We've had a lot of fun and a lot of publicity, and we got a message across to the federal

Key West Airport, 2007 (aka the Airport of the Conch Republic)
Deror Avi

government,' he said. 'We made fools of the Border Patrol and whoever put them there.'

Bill Smith, executive director of the Greater Key West Chamber of Commerce, agreed, noting 'You just can't buy the kind of advertising that we got with the mock secession'. Over two decades later, Wardlow reminisced that it was 'one of the best publicity stunts and it didn't cost us anything'.

Independence was successful in at least two ways. Although Border Patrol officials maintained that the checkpoint would continue indefinitely, the protests compelled federal officials to modify its operation. Less than a week later, reports indicated that 'patrolmen were making only spot checks of passing vehicles'. More significantly, the Key West community discovered that independence was good for business. Throngs of Conch patriots and tourists did not just hang out in bars; they also purchased hundreds of T-shirts, national flags, blue-and-gold passports, visas and commemorative stamps.

The Conch Republic shows how micronations can drive tourism and how, over time, the idea can take on even greater life. After several years, the organising committee of the annual Independence Day celebrations grew tired of the event and planned to bring it to a close. Enter Peter Anderson, an American who had moved to the republic in the mid-1980s. Appointed secretary-general of the republic in 1990, Anderson 'decided to take the job seriously'.

Anderson prioritised the development of national symbols and re-energised the annual Independence Day celebrations. The Conch Republic now has its own pledge of allegiance:

> I pledge allegiance to the flag
> Of my tiny island nation
> And to the republic
> For which it stands
> One nation under the sun
> Indivincible [*sic*]
> Where the liberty is true
> And the justice divine

Independence celebrations have also expanded. They now stretch for ten days and showcase 'the independent and eccentric spirit that characterises' the republic. Events include drag races, sea battles, a bed race, and the 'world's longest parade' – so named because it starts at the Atlantic Ocean and finishes at the Gulf of Mexico (a mere 2 kilometres in distance). Anderson passed away in 2014 after a battle with cancer, but his drive and enthusiasm has ensured the Republic's longevity. Anderson explained:

> We're keeping alive a tradition, and, of course, exercising our mission – mitigation of world tension through the exercise of humour. The world is in sore need of levity. So it [is] our function to be the joker in the deck. You may not always wish to play with us, but we have to be there, or you're not playing with a full deck.
>
> We are America's only free and independent people, and we're damned proud of it. In a country overladen with bureaucracy, we're the ones who said 'No more. We're out of here'.

As Anderson was fond of noting, 'We seceded where others failed.'

Anderson's efforts also led to several international incidents. In December 1994, leaders from North America and South America met for the first 'Summit of the Americas' in Miami, Florida. The high-level meeting was intended to foster discussion on issues affecting the Americas. All 34 countries, except Cuba – and the Conch Republic – were invited to participate. When the republic discovered that they had been snubbed, they sent a formal letter of complaint. A summit official noted to a reporter, 'I got a letter from the Conch Republic. They are very offended at not having been asked to participate.' When no formal response was received, Anderson crashed the summit.

A few months later tensions flared again. In September 1995, a local radio station reported that the US Army's 478th Civil Affairs Battalion was planning to conduct a mock invasion and occupation of an island in the Florida Keys. The army had not notified the Conch Republic, or Key West officials, about the operation, who took it as a slight on their status. Anderson wrote to president Bill Clinton, and the heads of the army and navy, advising them that the Conch Republic opposed the 'invasion' and would mobilise residents to defend the nation. Later that month, the republic's navy – consisting of a few private vessels – attacked the US navy with water balloons and stale Cuban bread. As Darien Cavanaugh explains, the attack 'caught the naval command off guard, at least from a public relations perspective'. A similar fate befell the army, who were attempting to enter the island by a bridge. Around 200 locals blocked their path and refused to allow them to pass. The stand-off ended without a shot being fired, though the army did send a letter playfully stating that the exercises 'in no way meant to challenge or impugn the sovereignty of the Conch Republic'.

Two months later, Anderson and the Conch Republic were again in the news. In December 1995, tensions between Democrat president Bill Clinton and the Republican-controlled Congress led to a federal government shutdown. The failure of the presidency and Congress to agree on a long-term budget to fund the government meant that hundreds of thousands of public sector workers had to be furloughed. The national park service was not spared. Fort Jefferson in the Dry Tortugas National Park on the Florida Keys was closed.

Anderson was worried that the closure was financially crushing tour operators in the Keys. Discovering that it cost $1600 a day to run the park, Anderson initially tried to keep the park open through private funding. However, he could not speak to anyone in Washington, DC, about his plan: 'There was nobody home in Washington to ask. They were either furloughed, or on vacation for the holidays.' Although the state of Florida was sympathetic, they were unable to enter into a private agreement as the park was a federal responsibility.

As the shutdown continued, tour operators were growing increasingly desperate and the republic increasingly indignant. Anderson decided to invade the national park and declare it open in the name of the Conch Republic. Three seaplanes filled with Conch dignitaries planned to descend on the park, bombing the fort with the republic's customary weapons – stale Cuban bread. After landing, Anderson would present a cheque to the park service to cover the cost of running the national park for one day. Anderson explained that 'what we're hoping to accomplish is to thoroughly embarrass the federal government and elected officials who are responsible for this awful situation'. While the bombing was cancelled on environmental grounds after park rangers explained that the island had a serious rat problem and the bread would only encourage them, Anderson did land. He received a ticket for trespassing. Thankfully, the shutdown ended a few days later and the Dry Tortugas National Park reopened.

The Conch Republic did not actively seek sovereignty, but throughout this period it continued to engage in the rituals of statehood, including issuing passports. Estimates suggest that more than 10 000 passports were sold in the 1990s: regular blue passports retailed for around $100, and red 'diplomatic' passports for up to $1200. Although of no legal value, the passports looked realistic – perhaps enough to fool immigration authorities. Anderson claimed that he and others had entered the United States on Conch Republic passports many times: 'You get a lot of scrutiny. We had a "diplomat" go into Russia with his passport.'

This steady stream of income was affected by the September 11 terrorist attacks. In 2001, the FBI announced that Mohamed Atta, one of the September 11 hijackers, may have been granted a Conch Republic passport in 2000. Anderson was defensive, explaining to journalists, 'All I know is what we've been told, that we did issue a passport to a Mohamed Atta.' It was not clear whether Atta used the Conch Republic passport to illegally enter the United States, but the republic had seen a surge of applicants in autumn 2000. Around that time, the Discovery Channel began replaying a segment on the

Conch Republic passports across its international broadcasts. After that, 'We started receiving a lot of requests from people all over the world and from people who were in the U.S. who we had reason to believe may not have been in the U.S. legally.' Anderson contacted the Immigration and Naturalization Service but never received a follow-up call.

The next major incident involved the republic's two closest neighbours: the United States and Cuba. Following the Cuban Revolution in 1959, the United States adopted a policy to accept any Cuban citizen who had emigrated and entered US territory. In 1995, after talks with Fidel Castro's regime, the Clinton administration revised that policy. Any Cuban citizen intercepted on the waters between the two countries would be returned to Cuba or sent to a third country, while any citizen who made it to shore would be allowed to remain in the US and eventually receive citizenship. In 2006, 15 Cuban refugees landed at the base of Seven Mile Bridge in Key West. Originally constructed in 1982, the bridge had been abandoned for several years. In fact, a significant 3.5-kilometre section no longer connected to any land. It was here that the 15 refugees landed.

The US Border Patrol and Coast Guard ordered that the Cubans be returned. Because the span was not connected to the US mainland, they determined that it did not constitute 'shore'. The quick-thinking Anderson led a small party of Conch Republic citizens to the bridge and raised their flag, claiming the territory: 'Since the federal government decided in its infinite wisdom that the old Seven Mile Bridge is not territory of the United States, the Conch Republic is very interested.' Anderson met no resistance, remarking that the federal government 'chose not to defend it'. A spokesperson for Florida governor Jeb Bush

Old Seven Mile Bridge, Pigeon Key
Ebyabe

replied, 'With all due respect to the Conch Republic, the bridge belongs to all the people of Florida, and we're not currently in negotiations to sell it.'

Anderson had hoped that the Seven Mile Bridge site could resolve housing affordability issues for residents of the Key West. As this suggests, while the Conch Republic was initially created to promote tourism to the region, Anderson recognised that the media attention gained by eccentric performance art could promote other causes. Under Anderson's leadership, the Conch Republic raised hundreds of thousands of dollars for charitable causes. Following the 2010 Haiti earthquake, for example, the Conch Republic navy delivered medical and food supplies to the devastated community. The republic's navy also conducted humanitarian missions to Jamaica following Hurricane Gilbert in 1988 and Honduras after it was struck by Hurricane Mitch in 1998.

The Conch Republic is still going strong today. In 2022, it celebrated its fortieth anniversary with the longest and largest independence celebrations yet. Many real countries have not survived for half as long.

Frestonia: 'We are all one family'

In 1977, residents of Freston Road in west London voted to secede and created the Free and Independent Republic of Frestonia. The neighbourhood around Freston Road on the border of North Kensington and Notting Hill was primarily composed of public housing. Residents frequently complained about the poor state of their shelter, but the local government failed to rectify significant problems. After many years of deteriorating conditions, the council decided instead to redevelop the area. An elevated motorway, bisecting the community, was constructed in the late 1960s, but recurrent delays meant that no further progress was made for many years. Rows of terrace houses were left to rot.

Over the course of the 1970s, an eclectic mix of squatters moved into the abandoned area. Some were attracted by the free (if deficient) housing, others by the ideal of communal life. Even so, life was not easy. The Greater London Council (GLC) had adopted a scorched earth policy to deter squatters by 'destroying roofs, ripping out wiring, cutting off water, and replacing windows with corrugated iron sheets'.

The GLC finally got its act together in September 1977. Two

Location of Frestonia in west London

residents of Freston Road saw a man from the council walking up and down the road with a clipboard. He explained that the local government was preparing to transform the area into an industrial estate. The squatters quickly organised a public meeting to discuss the development. At this meeting, Nicholas Albery proposed that the residents declare the community independent of the United Kingdom. Albery had been inspired by the 1950s comedy film *Passport to Pimlico*, in which a small section of the London suburb Pimlico is found to be legally a part of Burgundy – and thus not subject to World War II–

era restrictions. Albery had also previously visited the semi-independent intentional community of Freetown Christiania in Copenhagen.

Albery's suggestion was accepted. In a referendum the following month, 94 per cent of the residents supported the plan, and a further 73 per cent voted to join the European Economic Community. A flag was designed, border guards installed, passports and visas issued, and an application for membership in the United Nations posted (complete with request for a peacekeeping force):

> We appeal to the United Nations, in particular to other small, emerging and non-aligned nations, to treat our application with the utmost seriousness and urgency. If delay in processing our application occurs, an invasion into Frestonia and eviction by the GLC may occur, in which case there will exist a crisis with international ramifications.
>
> The necessity may arise for Frestonia to require the UN to send a token peace-keeping force. These are developments which we must at all costs avoid.

The residents claimed that they had a right to self-determination and self-governance because of the 'neglect' and 'mismanagement' of the Greater London Council and the UK government:

> The G.L.C. and the British Government [have] demonstrated their lack of concern for the area and their unfitness to remain as its rulers and to plan for its future.
>
> Over the last 4 years, the present inhabitants of Frestonia moved in and took over the empty houses as

Frestonia, Freston Road
Tony Sleep 1978 / 'Welcome To Frestonia', Frestonian Gallery

Visa stamp for the Free and Independent Republic of Frestonia
Rob Kerr

> caretakers and pioneer homesteaders, and have renovated their homes to a remarkable extent, including putting roofs on houses which lacked roofs. Our architect's report confirms that, if the present period of uncertainty could be ended, it would be possible for the residents to give their buildings a long lease of life – and eventually of course to rebuild.

The Frestonian government was staunchly egalitarian. Ministers were appointed for a three-month rotating period. A national bill of rights modelled on the UN's Universal Declaration of Human Rights was also adopted. Anticipating concern over its small size, Frestonia turned this potential problem into a virtue. As Nicholas Albery explained, 'the ideal size for a nation is about 100 to 200 citizens – any bigger and one's not likely to know all the ministers or have easy access to them'.

Independence was seen as critical to ensure that the community could remain together. That ideal also lay behind the motto chosen for the Free State: 'Nos Sumus Una Familia – We Are All One Family'. It also lay behind the decision for all residents to change their names. Exploiting a loophole which provided that local government authorities could not split up families when providing public housing, all 120 residents adopted the same surname – Bramley – after one of the streets within the site. If independence failed, perhaps the community would still have to be rehoused as a single-family unit.

Frestonia caught international attention, with newspapers across Europe reporting on the development. The spotlight was largely favourable. London's *Daily Mirror* splashed a headline, 'All Hail, Frestonia'. The shadow chancellor of the exchequer, Sir Geoffrey Howe, even expressed his support. The following year, Sir Geoffrey wrote to Albery (who had renamed himself Nicholas Exelby-Bramley):

> As one who had a childhood enthusiasm for the Napoleon of Notting Hill Gate, I can hardly fail to be moved by your letter of 11th July – and am only surprised that I had not previously heard of the aspirations (and anguish) which led you and your colleagues to establish a Free Independent Republic of Frestonia.
>
> On the other hand, my training as an international lawyer (and a former Law Officer of the Crown) is bound to induce a degree of scepticism about your aspirations for international status!
>
> Even so, I shall certainly make some enquiries about

> the attitude of the GLC towards your particular plans. I shall, of course, be in touch with you again.

The Greater London Council were less moved. Sir Horace Cutler, the leader of the council, replied tersely: 'All I can say is were you not to exist it would be necessary to invent you.' Nicholas Albery retorted: 'Since we do exist, why is it necessary to destroy us?'

Independence paid off. As photographer and Freston Road squatter Tony Sleep explained,

> it was a snowball that started rolling, and getting bigger. Normally, squatters had terrible, terrible press. But journalists found this really amusing. The tabloids loved it. They came down here and starting interviewing people, and before you knew it, it was a big story. Then as word got around, the streets started filling up with Japanese and Danish TV crews.
>
> The great thing about Frestonia being a joke was that it was non-threatening ... If we'd turned it into a riot, we'd just have got beaten over the head and thrown out. But the Greater London Council found it hugely embarrassing: 'Why the hell have you got all these people living in all these ridiculously empty houses that you've done nothing with, and why do you now want to turn it into a load of rubble and make all these people homeless?'

The Greater London Council decided to negotiate. In 1982, Frestonia rejoined the UK as the residents formed the Bramleys Housing Co-operative. The Co-op partnered with the Notting

Hill Housing Trust to redevelop the site. The decrepit houses were replaced with safe and liveable homes. Today many of the residents of the site are descendants of the original Frestonians – a testament to the way that micronations can build communities and promote reform.

7

ENVIRONMENTAL MICRONATIONS: CREATING A COUNTRY TO SAVE THE PLANET

Founding and running a country is a big deal. Drafting a Declaration of Independence and raising a flag can attract significant media attention. So long as you play it right, this can be turned into a larger political campaign, as the micronations created for political protest and law reform have shown. Community groups and environmentalists have also recognised this. Creating a micronation can draw attention to local and global problems and excite interest in a way that would otherwise be impossible. Here, we explore some of the prominent efforts to create a country as part of an environmental campaign.

Waveland: No new oil

Late in the evening of 10 June 1997, three Greenpeace activists clambered out of a small inflatable dinghy onto a slimy, barnacle-encrusted, guano-covered rock jutting out in the North Atlantic Ocean. With no obvious path, it took ten minutes for Al Baker, Meike Huelsman and Peter Morris to scramble to the top of the rocky crag. Years later John Vidal, who had been invited

Location of Rockall

to accompany the team, recalled his first moments: 'Knuckles grazed and still in an extreme state of fear, I reached the top, and was violently sick'.

Still, there was work to be done. Baker, Huelsman and Morris raised a flag and declared the uninhabitable granite outcrop the capital of the new Global State of Waveland. Vidal called his mother on a satellite phone:

> 'Hello Mum, I'm on Rockall.'
> 'Where?'

'Rockall. In the Atlantic.'

'I know where it is. Are you quite mad?'

Vidal's mother had a point.

The uninhabitable outcrop known as Rockall is located more than 300 kilometres west of Scotland's St Kilda archipelago and around 420 kilometres north-west of Ireland. Rockall is remote; in fact, it may be 'the most isolated small rock in the oceans of the world'. Stretching about 25 metres wide, 31 metres in length and a touch over 21 metres above sea level at its highest point, the rocky atoll is only around 780 square metres in size. It is also covered in guano and often washed over by large storm waves, particularly in winter. There is no soil or fresh water, there are no trees or bushes; 'just moss, seaweeds and one black lichen'.

The atoll was known to the Vikings and has been documented in written records since the late 16th century. However, because of its steep, smooth granite surface, constant swell and frequent violent storms, very few people have ever set foot on Rockall. In fact, there are suggestions that 'more people have landed on the moon than have landed on Rockall by sea'. In 1971, Lord Kennet of the UK House of Lords described Rockall as 'a dreadful place', noting that '[t]here could be no place more desolate, more despairing and more awful to see in the whole world'. Yet in 1955, it was formally claimed for the United Kingdom in what proved to be the final 'territorial expansion of the British empire'.

At the peak of its dominance, the British Empire was a truly global power. In 1821, the *Caledonian Mercury*, a Scottish newspaper, described the scope of the British Empire at the time, from Canada to India and Australia and beyond. 'On her dominions the sun never sets,' the paper asserted. '[B]efore his evening rays leave the spires of Quebec, his morning beams have shone three hours on Port Jackson [Sydney], and while sinking from the waters of Lake Superior, his eye opens upon the Mouth of the Ganges.' In the early 20th century, the Empire covered around one-quarter of the globe's total land area and about 23 per cent of the world's population. Over the course of that century, British control dimmed as former colonies gained independence and the empire was gradually dismantled. However, in several regions the empire continued to grow.

Rockall may be a lonely, windswept island incapable of sustaining life, but it had value. After competing claims by Iceland, Ireland and Denmark, the UK formally annexed the tiny islet on 18 September 1955. That morning, a four-person British expedition team was winched onto the islet by helicopter. The team cemented a brass plaque onto the site and hoisted the Union Jack to stake the British claim. The plaque specified that 'in Accordance with Her Majesty's Instructions dated 14.9.55 a landing was effected on this day upon the Island of Rockall from H.M.S. *Vidal*. The Union Flag was hoisted and possession of the Island was taken in the Name of Her Majesty'.

Many people in England were bemused. Satirists Michael Flanders and Donald Swann captured the public feelings in their song 'Rockall':

> The fleet set sail for Rockall
> Rockall
> Rockall
> To free the isle of Rockall

Rockall
Andy Strangeway

From fear of foreign foe.
We sped across the planet
To find this lump of granite
One rather startled gannet
In fact, we found Rockall.
So praise the bold bell-bottoms
Bottoms
Bottoms
Who saw Britannia's peril
And answered to her call.
Though we're thrown out of Malta,
Though Spain should take Gibraltar,
Why should we flinch or falter
When England's got Rockall.

Donald Swann noted that while the lyrics 'looked innocent enough', when sung it was a bit more daring – 'Rockall' sounds a lot like 'fuck all'.

The decision to annex Rockall was motivated by the desire to prevent the Soviet Union from using it to monitor British missile testing. The UK were planning on launching their first guided nuclear missile over the North Atlantic from South Uist in Scotland. As declassified NATO reports later revealed, the Ministry of Defence was worried that 'hostile agents' might install 'themselves on the island in order to observe the effects of the tests on the South Uist range'.

At least one formal protest was made to the UK government. However, the protest was not made by a foreign state, but by a member of the Clan Mackay of the Scottish Highlands. Eighty-four-year-old J. Abrach Mackay declared: 'My old father, God rest his soul, claimed that island for the Clan of Mackay in 1846 and I now demand that the Admiralty hand it back. It's no' theirs.' Another member of the Clan remarked, 'It wouldn't surprise me to see a battleship appearing off Rockall any day. You can't afford to underestimate the Mackays'. The House of Lords later debated whether another clan might claim Rockall, namely 'the MacLeods of the Western Isles'. It is not clear if the British government replied to the Mackays, but they dismissed any private interests that Clan MacLeod might have had.

A second motivation lay behind the sudden UK interest in Rockall – government was attracted by the idea of using the islet to further their exclusive economic zone. An exclusive economic zone is a legal concept. It is the area in which a state has special rights to explore and use marine resources, such as fisheries or energy production. By claiming Rockall, the UK would gain secure access to the rich fisheries in the surrounding seas. This could be a substantial windfall so, under the Fisheries Act, the UK claimed a 200-nautical-mile exclusive economic zone surrounding Rockall.

Soon it became an even bigger deal. Geological surveys in the early 1970s suggested that substantial oil fields might lie within the undersea Rockall plateau – valued at up to US$160 billion. In 1971, a second British expedition landed on Rockall to install a light beacon and further ground the UK's claim to the rock – and its surrounding resources. The following year, the UK formally incorporated Rockall into the Shire of Inverness.

Ireland, Iceland and Denmark were not happy with these developments. All three sent formal diplomatic missives stating that they did not recognise the British claim. In the public sphere, the Wolfe Tones – an Irish nationalist band named for the leader of a 1798 uprising against the British – penned a song, 'Rock on Rockall', promoting Irish claims to the rock:

> Oh the Empire, it is finished,
> No foreign lands to seize.
> So the greedy eye of England
> Is turning t'wards the seas.
> Two hundred miles from Donegal
> There's a place that's called Rockall
> And the groping hands of Whitehall
> Are grabbing at its walls.
> Oh the seas will not be silent
> While Britannia grabs the waves.
> And remember that the Irish
> Will no longer be your slaves

And remember that Britannia, well
She rules the waves no more,
So keep your hands off Rockall
It's Irish to the core.

In the middle of this spat, the British made a bizarre attempt to demonstrate sovereignty, in 1974 installing a sentry box on Rockall and placing two royal marines in full dress uniform to guard this 'mere speck in the surface of the waters'. It may have been just for a laugh, but photos were taken and distributed to other governments.

Alas, the sentry box was unsuccessful, and the situation soon became more difficult for the UK. In 1982, the United Nations Convention on the Law of the Sea entered into force for nations that had agreed to its terms. Article 121 provided that uninhabitable rocks do not possess an exclusive economic zone. Although UK legislation referred to Rockall as an 'island' rather than a rock, it was not at all clear that the island could sustain human life. In 1985, former SAS member Tom McLean attempted to prove that the rock was habitable and 'reaffirm British rights to the islet'. After climbing to the summit and raising the Union Jack, McLean lived in a tiny survival unit a little bigger than a wardrobe for 40 days and nights. Conditions were tough. 'You get a lot of wind, a lot [of] spray,' he recalled. 'In the winter the sea goes right over the top – you'd get wiped off the thing. But I was bolted down. I had the radios, I was talking to the fishermen. It was wild and wet.'

Unfortunately for McLean and the UK, 'staying in an accommodation pod strapped to a rock and eating food brought to that rock cannot really demonstrate habitability'. When the

UK signed the Convention on the Law of the Sea in 1997, it finally acknowledged that Rockall could not sustain human habitation. The UK therefore lost its claim to a 200-nautical-mile exclusive economic zone. It could only retain control over a 12-nautical-mile area around the rock.

Throughout this period, Greenpeace was increasingly focusing on oil exploration projects in the North Atlantic. In the early 1990s, the Shell oil company announced plans to dispose of Brent Spar, a disused oil storage and tanker-loading buoy in the Brent oilfield off the coast of the Shetland Islands. In 1995, after the British government declared their support for Shell's plan to sink the buoy in the deep Atlantic some 250 kilometres from Scotland, Greenpeace launched into action. In April 1995, around 25 activists, photographers and journalists occupied Brent Spar. The energetic political and media campaign succeeded. In June that year Shell withdrew its plans; Brent Spar was relocated to Norway where it was mothballed.

In May 1997, Greenpeace launched its Atlantic Frontier Campaign. Drawing on alarming data revealing the consequences of unabated climate change, the campaign called on the UK government to abandon its plans to develop oil extraction projects in the Atlantic and to phase out the use of fossil fuels. The campaign also drew attention to the vulnerability of biodiversity in the Atlantic from oil exploitation and deep-sea fishing. Greenpeace believed that – appropriately used – the small islet of Rockall might help propel political and media attention for their campaign. This time, however, their plans involved more than simple occupation.

Greenpeace sought permission from the UK to land on Rockall. No doubt unaware of Greenpeace's true motives, the

UK government agreed, believing that it might be a good opportunity to further demonstrate British authority and sovereignty over the islet. However, after scaling the summit the Greenpeace group announced that they rejected British sovereignty, raised their flag and declared the creation of the world's newest country: the Global State of Waveland. They unscrewed the British plaque, turned it back to front and reattached it. Next to that plaque they installed their own: 'Let the sun and wind do their work. Leave the oil beneath the waves.'

In their declaration, the activists explained their motivations:

> We reject the governance of a country which permits new oil exploration despite professed concern for the climate. Waveland is a new kind of country designed to protect the global commons rather than to exploit it. We hope this is the start of a peaceful revolution. Waveland expresses every person's right to oust destructive governance and replace it with a new one, to put the climate before profits from oil.

Rockall had been chosen carefully. Although the UK had formally claimed the islet in 1955, British control had never been accepted by its neighbours. 'The seas around Rockall, potentially rich in oil, are fought over by four nations – Britain, Denmark, Iceland and Ireland,' one of the activists noted. 'By seizing Rockall, Greenpeace claims these seas for the planet and all its peoples.'

Waveland citizenship was immediately offered to anyone willing to take the pledge: 'Without violence and by bearing

Greenpeace occupies Rockall, 1 June 1997
Greenpeace / David Sims

witness, to defend nature, to protect the global commons, to reform industrialism, and to secure peace, believing in action, rather than words.' Around 15 000 people across the world registered as citizens, attracted by its founders' stated aspiration to manage the earth's resources for the common good.

The activists stayed on Rockall for 42 days. They hoped that outlasting Tom McLean's visit would give them a stronger 'territorial claim' than that of the UK and thus prevent oil exploration. However, the length of each visit is of no legal significance as the rock cannot sustain human life. From an egg-shaped solar-powered survival capsule, barely 3.5 metres by 2 metres in size, they sent regular bulletins describing life on Waveland. At one point, the Western Isles Council – the Scottish local government area responsible for the rock – contacted Greenpeace explaining that they would need to apply for planning permission to live there. The council also threatened to charge a tax based on their unlicensed dwelling.

Despite claiming Rockall as the new capital of Waveland, Greenpeace clarified that they did not want to permanently control the outcrop. Rather, they said that they would borrow the rock until it was 'freed from the threat of development'. The distinction was not appreciated by the UK government. In a short response, a government official noted that 'Rockall is British territory. It is part of Scotland and anyone is free to go there and can stay as long as they please'. Competing oil companies were more upset.

They need not have worried. Greenpeace's occupation ended after 42 days, and Waveland has since ceased to exist. Writing many years later, Peter Morris, one of the Greenpeace occupiers, lamented that their activism was before its time. 'No New Oil was our slogan, and we called for 20% cuts of CO_2, (compared to 1990 levels) by 2005,' he wrote. 'Ahh, if only people had listened – but back then most didn't believe in climate change, didn't see an urgency, and didn't believe our carbon addiction was to blame.'

Their record has also been surpassed. In 2014, Scottish adventurer Nick Hancock survived alone on Rockall for 45 days. Even so, Waveland has been successful in other ways. As Stephen Royle notes, 'although it may not be down to the Greenpeace campaign, no oil has yet been pumped from the waters close to Rockall'. Or, in the words of Peter Morris, 'the fools are still wasting time and money looking for oil out there in the deep, dark, wild ocean'.

Today, the lucrative waters surrounding the outcrop remain the site of contestation between the UK, Denmark, Ireland

and Iceland. Although the UK continues to assert jurisdiction over the islet, Ireland maintains that no country can own the rocky atoll and its waters should be shared by all EU member states. Every now and again these competing positions can lead to conflict. In 2019, for example, Scotland warned that it would board any Irish vessels caught fishing within Rockall's 12-nautical-mile radius. Ireland pushed back. Negotiations are ongoing.

The Glacier Republic: An icy home

The success of Waveland inspired more environmental micronations. In March 2014, Greenpeace activists planted a flag in a Chilean glacier and announced the creation of the new Glacier Republic. The formation of the republic was also proclaimed in a full-page advertisement in the *New York Times*. Claiming all 23 000 square kilometres of Chilean glaciers, the republic aims to 'draw attention to glacier retreat and global warming' and encourage Chile to enact environmental laws protecting glaciers. The issue is critical, as Chile is home to around 82 per cent of South America's glaciers. The republic has pledged to maintain its assertion of sovereignty until all mining near glaciated areas is abandoned.

There is no legal basis for the formation of the Glacier Republic. This has not stopped activists attempting to justify their position. They argue that the glaciers 'were in no man's land' because neither the Constitution of Chile nor the Chilean Water Code specifies that glaciers are part of the national territory. On this basis, the executive director of Greenpeace Chile, Matías Asún, explained, 'We took possession of the entire surface area of glaciers in Chile and declared ourselves an independent republic.' But the glaciers are subject to Chilean control, along with all other parts of the natural environment, because they are located within that nation's territory. It is irrelevant whether glaciers are mentioned in the Chilean Constitution or Water Code.

The republic's founders have encouraged people from all over the world to take up citizenship. So far, the republic boasts over 165 000 citizens – considerably more than many recognised countries like Tonga (99 000), Liechtenstein (39 000) and Vatican City (800). The republic has also solemnised a marriage on the El Morado glacier near Santiago and set up embassies (operating out of Greenpeace offices) with more than 40 countries. No country has yet recognised the Glacier Republic.

Aramoana: Defeating a prime minister

Local communities have also embraced the idea of creating micronations to further their environmental goals. In the 1970s, an aluminium smelter was proposed at the small coastal settlement of Aramoana, near Dunedin, in New Zealand's South Island. The plan required the destruction of the villages of Aramoana and nearby Te Ngaru. It also threatened a local wildlife reserve. In 1974, residents and supporters formed the Save Aramoana Campaign to oppose the smelter. The group was successful, and the plan abandoned.

Later that decade, the smelter proposal was revived. In 1977, the government of New Zealand under prime minister Robert Muldoon announced its 'Think Big' economic policy.

Stamps and postmark of the Independent State of Aramoana
The estate of Don Binney / Alexander Turnbull Library, Wellington, New Zealand

The interventionist plan called for the government to borrow heavily and use the funds for large-scale industrial projects. A smelter at Aramoana was central to this strategy. With support from a consortium of multinational companies, the government determined to move ahead. The Save Aramoana Campaign was re-formed, and opposition intensified.

In December 1980, following several years of community activism, the residents struck upon a new plan. They announced their secession from New Zealand and declared the creation of the new Independent State of Aramoana. Their aim was to raise funds, and to generate publicity to build a national campaign opposing the smelter. The campaign also wanted the government to declare the area a scientific and recreational reserve to protect it from future development.

The Aramoana activists established a border post and a travelling embassy, and they printed citizenship certificates, passports and stamps. The micronation raised considerable funds. One estimate suggests that the sale of stamps, passports, citizenship, T-shirts and bumper stickers netted the campaign NZ$500 000. It also focused public attention on opposition to the smelter. Public support soon rallied to the cause. Celebrated Māori artist Ralph Hotere, who lived and worked near Aramoana, produced a series of paintings to protest against the smelter.

The small community enjoyed the theatrics of nationhood. They established roadblocks and manned the border post every weekend over summer. Border patrol guards would stop entrants and check the contents of their car, saying, 'Welcome to the Independent State of Aramoana. We have declared this area independent to stop a smelter being built here. Do you have any smelters concealed in your car?' While amusing, the roadblocks had another purpose. They would allow the community to quickly 'seal the area if construction work was attempted'.

The campaign was successful. Public pressure led one of the companies involved in the smelter project to withdraw. Unable to secure financing, the government was forced to back down. The failure of the smelter plan eventually paved the way for the Independent State of Aramoana to reintegrate with New Zealand. Almost two decades later, the campaign achieved its final goal. In 1998, the area was gazetted as an area of national scientific and natural importance, providing it with status similar to a national park.

Wendland: Campaigning against nuclear waste

Other environmental micronations have been less successful. On 3 May 1980, at the same time that the Independent State of Aramoana was operating, protesters campaigning against the establishment of a nuclear waste dump in the town of Gorleben, West Germany, created their own micronation.

The Free Republic of Wendland adopted the normal state symbols, including a flag and coat of arms, and issued a Declaration of Independence. Border checkpoints were established (non-citizens could enter for 10 deutschmarks), and passports issued. The Wendlandians assured a reporter that their passports were good 'for the entire universe ... so long as its owner could still laugh'. The community chose the name Wendland in honour of a Slavic tribe from the Middle Ages that was famous for resisting Christianisation. These modern-day Wends fought against environmental harm.

The Free Republic of Wendland drew political and media attention, but it did not prevent the construction of the waste station. After a 33-day sit-in, during which West Germany's minister of the interior decried the purported declaration of independence as an act of high treason, 3500 police evicted the 2000 non-violent Wendlandians. The Free Republic was no more.

Westarctica: A country you can't visit

Not all leaders can live in their own micronation. The Duchy of Westarctica claims sovereignty over a 1.6-million-square-kilometre portion of one of the most remote lands on Earth. As the coldest, driest and windiest continent, Antarctica may

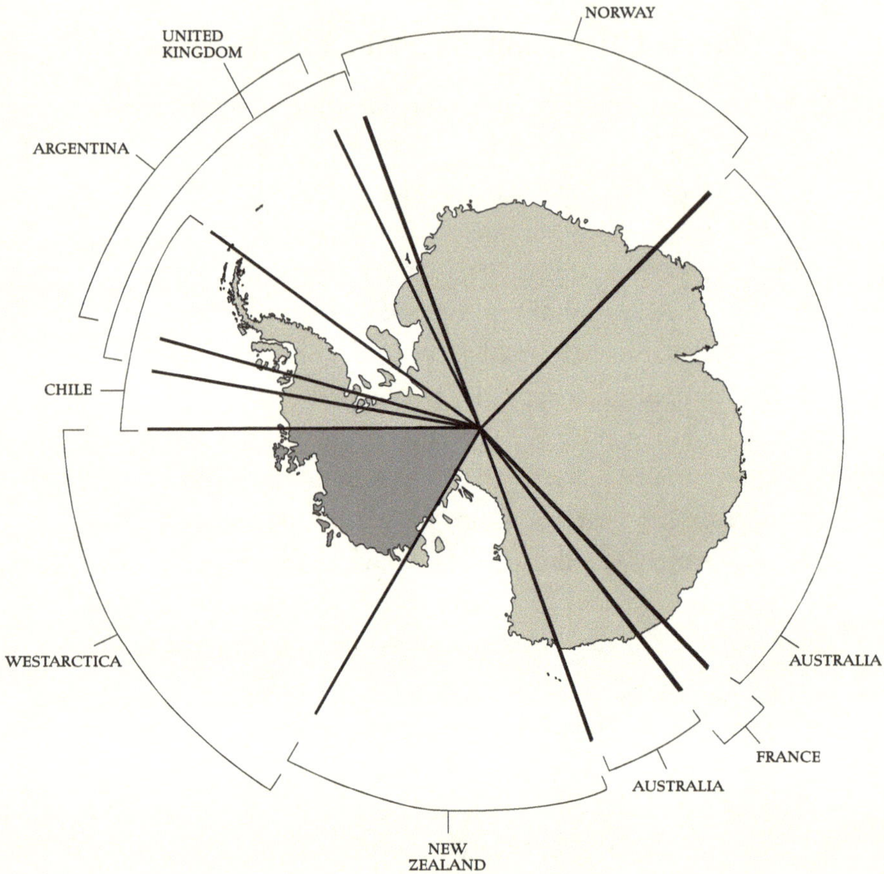

Antarctic territories, including Westarctica

appear to be a strange territory to host a nation. However, its hostile environment, lack of easily accessible resources and isolation are alluring to the right person. Covering 14.2 million square kilometres, Antarctica is the only substantial territory on Earth without indigenous human inhabitants.

This does not mean that it was entirely unknown to humans. Polynesian sailors may have first sighted the region in the early

600s. The first western sighting occurred over a thousand years later, when in 1820 a Russian expedition sighted the Fimbul Ice Shelf. Today, around 4000 scientists and staff live in Antarctica during the summer months, with the population falling to about 1000 over winter. In fact, the continent is not only extremely lightly populated but much of it is unclaimed; where claims have been made, they have not always been recognised.

This is due to the Antarctic Treaty of 1959. Several countries claim territory in Antarctica, but the Antarctic Treaty was designed to prevent these from being enlarged and other claims from being made. The Treaty provides that no state can assert, support or deny a claim to territorial sovereignty in Antarctica or create any rights of sovereignty in Antarctica. It also prevents new claims being asserted, or existing claims to territorial sovereignty being enlarged. The Treaty sometimes causes complications. For example, Japan continues to operate whaling fleets within the Australian Antarctic Territory, despite an Australian court finding such practices a violation of Australian law. Japan does so by refusing to recognise Australian sovereignty in Antarctica.

The Antarctic Treaty also left large portions of the continent unclaimed. This includes the 1.6-million-square-kilometre Marie Byrd Land, which remains the largest unclaimed territory on Earth. Unclaimed by *recognised* states, that is. Several micronations assert their sovereignty over Marie Byrd Land, and other parts of Antarctica, based on a supposed loophole in the Antarctic Treaty first discovered by American Travis McHenry.

In August 2001, McHenry was serving in the US Navy as an intelligence specialist. During his downtime aboard the USS *Kearsarge*, he spent many hours reading about the countries of the world in the classified version of the CIA's *World Factbook*. In the course of his research, he found that Marie Byrd Land had not been claimed by any state. Over the rest of the month, he studied the 'complicated political situation surrounding Antarctica and read the entire text of the Antarctic Treaty multiple times'. He soon believed he had found a loophole. According to McHenry, while the Treaty precludes states from making territorial claims, it does not prohibit claims made by individuals. Discovering that Marie Byrd Land had not been claimed by any state, McHenry claimed it for himself – and then established a state to rule over the land. As McHenry considered, 'If no one had bothered to claim that large swath of Western Antarctica known as Marie Byrd Land ... why not take the opportunity to do it himself?'

On 2 November 2001, McHenry wrote letters to each of the twelve original signatories to the Antarctic Treaty – Argentina, Australia, Belgium, Chile, France, Japan, New Zealand, Norway, Russia, South Africa, the United Kingdom and the United States – announcing his formal claim and the creation of a new country:

> I have been heavily studying the continent of Antarctica, and I have come to several conclusions. There are very few places on earth where a man can be truly alone. Antarctica is one of those places. It's [sic] vast ice fields hold more than just frozen water, the entire continent holds the potential to unlock the secrets of our past.
>
> Therefore, at this time, I deem it necessary to formally claim for myself all land between 90 degrees west and

> 150 degrees west and south of 60 degrees south to include all seas and ice shelves. The area will henceforth be known as 'The Achaean Territory of Antarctica.' The purpose of this acquisition is to secure the territory for research and development and future colonization. Also, to protect it from those parties who would exploit the territory with misdeeds.

His letters were ignored but McHenry continued. In 2004, he renamed and restyled his country 'Westarctica' and invested himself as grand duke. He designed a new flag and issued new currency. Although a grand duke, McHenry's day job was in the US Navy. When officials from the Pentagon discovered that he was communicating with foreign governments, they interrogated him and threatened to revoke his security clearance. McHenry recused himself from his throne during the remainder of his time in the armed services.

McHenry left the military in 2008, but he did not formally resume command of Westarctica until 2010. When he did so, he changed its focus. No longer interested in developing a research station or planning a colony, Westarctica would become a not-for-profit organisation focused on advocating for western Antarctica and fighting climate change. As McHenry explains:

> Western Antarctica is one of the most fragile ecosystems on the planet, yet there is no single organization dedicated to studying and preserving this vast, magnificent, desolate region. It falls under the political dominion of no government, thus Western Antarctica has no voice in the international community.

Grand Duke Travis McHenry of Westarctica
Gabriela Alvarez

Westarctica seeks to change that by acting as Western Antarctica's advocate to the world. In line with our mission, we have established ourselves as an independent nation with self-granted sovereignty, free from restrictions or obligations imposed by other countries.

In 2018, Westarctica was granted tax-exempt status by the US Internal Revenue Service as a charitable organisation. Since then, a small but steady stream of donations has trickled in, from $14 000 in 2018 to more than $20 000 in 2020, but down to $4000 in 2021.

Westarctica is making a small but real contribution. Many of its 2300 citizens donate, participate in letter-writing drives, attend climate change rallies and join public campaigns to stop whaling operations in the Antarctic region. In 2018, Westarctica was 'an official partner with the People's Climate Movement to help organize the Rise For Climate protests'. The duchy also offers a US$500 grant for early-career researchers working in climate change science. It is not a lot, but it helps. As McHenry explains, 'Westarctica has gone from an ego project to being of service to the environment. The work that I do is not for my own benefit or aggrandizement anymore.'

Many other micronations have followed McHenry's lead. The Grand Duchy of Flandrensis asserts authority over five Antarctic islands. Grand Duke Niels Vermeersch has explained what drove him towards micronationalism: 'I wanted it to be useful. I learned of micronations proclaiming territories in Antarctica so I did it, but as an ecological venture, to raise awareness on ice melting. Flandrensis is the only country that does not want citizens on its territory.'

Other micronations with environmental goals claim even more remote territory. The Angyalistan Empire asserts sovereignty over the Great Pacific Garbage Patch and other garbage vortexes, making it the only country in the world 'that seeks its own destruction'.

8

HUMOUR AND BOREDOM: PLAYING A KING

Micronations are not always serious. For many people, creating your own country is the perfect way to poke fun at the symbols of statehood or simply to have a laugh. They enjoy investing themselves with regal titles, dabbling in European-inspired heraldry and pinning made-up military medals on their chests. Creating a country can also be a good way to pass the time. And it can certainly take some time. King Robert of Talossa, a micronation based in the US state of Wisconsin, once estimated that he spent up to eight hours a week serving as king. Here we examine three micronations established for fun and to relieve boredom: the Principality of Outer Baldonia, the Republic of Molossia, and the Great Bitter Lake Association – a micronation created when 14 ships were stranded in the Suez Canal as a result of the 1967 Six-Day War.

Outer Baldonia: Tuna and the Cold War

For 13 days in October 1962, the world waited with bated breath. When the United States deployed nuclear-armed ballistic missiles in Italy and Turkey, the Soviet Union responded by placing its own missiles in Cuba. With the world seemingly on the brink of nuclear war, only frantic negotiations between the White House and the Kremlin averted a catastrophe and ensured a peaceful resolution.

The Cuban Missile Crisis saw the United States and Russia come closer than ever before to nuclear conflict. But a little-known incident a decade earlier could also have spiralled out of control. In the 1950s, the small Principality of Outer Baldonia – a rocky, 3-acre (12,140-square-metre) island off the coast of Nova Scotia, Canada, whose population consisted of 'mewing gulls, a few hardy sheep [and] untamed beach grass' – declared war on the Soviet Union. How would the Russians respond?

In the 1930s, the Acadian fishing community of Wedgeport in Nova Scotia became host to the world's largest international sport tuna fishing tournament. The event's status grew throughout the decade as politicians, businessmen and celebrities from across North America rushed to the small town. Prominent attendees included US president Franklin D. Roosevelt, aviator Amelia Earhart and Chicago mobster Tony 'Big Tuna' Accardo. In the mid-1940s, Russell Arundel, an American businessman, lobbyist and keen sportsman, began to compete.

Arundel worked in Washington, DC, as the founder and chairman of a company that bottled Pepsi-Cola in Long Island, New York. He also owned several Pepsi bottling facilities in Virginia, where he lived on a large fox-hunting estate. Arundel was well known in Washington. Initially working as a journalist, he had been appointed to the Mount Rushmore National Memorial Commission by President Roosevelt in the 1930s.

Later, as a lobbyist, he gained a reputation for hosting wild parties. In 1953, he was implicated in a major bribery scandal: he had offered senator Joseph McCarthy $20 000 to pay off some of the senator's debts at a time when McCarthy was waging a political campaign against the government's policy of sugar rationing. Arundel, as a prominent soft-drink businessman, denied any wrongdoing, stating that the transaction for his 'friend' was unconnected to the subject of sugar.

In 1948, Arundel was competing in the International Tuna Cup. The waters around Wedgeport were often rough, leaving many anglers seasick. To allow the competitors to regain their composure, their guides often set them ashore for a few hours on one of the many small islands surrounding the town. During this event, Arundel and his guide landed on Outer Bald Tusket Island, a small, treeless, rocky isle about 20 kilometres south of Wedgeport. Arundel's guide noted that it was a shame that there was no shelter. On an impulse, Arundel volunteered to buy the island and provide materials for a small clubhouse on the condition that the tuna guides would contribute their labour and build it. The guides agreed and Arundel bought the island for US$750. Initially intending to use the clubhouse as a base during the sport-fishing season, Arundel soon had a better idea: 'Back in Washington, the deed in my pocket and a drink in my hand, the Principality of Outer Baldonia began to take shape.'

Declaring himself the Prince of Princes, Arundel began to create the institutions of his new nation. He first appointed his friend and tax attorney Prew Savoy as 'Prince Regent, Minister of State, and Ambassador to the United States without Portfolio or Credentials'. In July 1949, Arundel issued a Declaration of

Fishermen competing in the Wedgeport tuna fishing tornament,
Outer Bald Tusket Island in background, 1940s
Credit unknown

Independence for his new principality:

> Let these facts be submitted to a candid world. That fishermen are a race alone. That fishermen are endowed with the following inalienable rights. The right of freedom from question, nagging, shaving, interruption, women, taxes, politics, war, monologues, cant and inhibitions. The right to applause, vanity, flattery, praise, and self-inflation. The right to swear, lie, drink and gamble. The right to be noisy, boisterous, quiet, pensive, expansive, and hilarious. The right to sleep all day and stay up all night.
>
> Now, therefore, we bond ourselves to a new nation, forever independent of all other nations, and do establish on the islands and waters of Outer Bald [Tusket] Island

> a new government which shall forever be respected and recognized as the Principality of Outer Baldonia.

The Declaration of Independence was printed on parchment paper, signed by Arundel and sealed with an official royal seal. Arundel also drafted an accompanying Charter of Outer Baldonia, which set out the obligations and privileges of citizenship – anyone who caught a bluefin tuna and paid a US$50 fee was named a prince of the realm. He established trade and industrial policy (Outer Baldonia's primary export was listed as empty beer and rum bottles) and created a national currency. The 'Tunar' came in two denominations: a $1 gold coin bearing Arundel's image, underneath a banner that read 'Principality of Outer Baldonia' and above an inscription that read 'War on Poverty'; and a $25 000 note. He also drew up a coat of arms, consisting of a tuna tail and a rod, and designed a flag for his new nation: a tuna tail in a circle of white on a sea-green background. Reflecting the blokey and exclusionary language of the Declaration of Independence, women were banned from the island and prevented from taking up citizenship.

Prince Russell and Prince Prew next sought to find citizens for their country. Seeking only the most renowned and capable individuals, they approached several colleagues they considered of impeccable character and invested them as princes. Among the group was former US vice president Alben W. Barkley, who requested to serve as secretary of the treasury; Barkley 'wanted to handle a treasury with no money, no assets, no debits, just a blank piece of paper and a few speeches'. Arundel and Savoy also drew from the ranks of the Nova Scotia Guides Association – the men who helped the competitors during the

Outer Bald Tusket Island
Credit unknown

tuna tournament. They commissioned 69 eight-star admirals in the Outer Baldonian Navy, and one nine-star admiral.

Prew Savoy contacted the Canadian government to announce that the new principality officially recognised their nearest neighbour. After some discussion, Arundel and Frew chose not to recognise the United States. 'The principality is only three acres in all,' Savoy explained, 'and where the hell would we put all of the bags of money, Point IV experts, ECA and Mutual Security Administration missions the United States would insist on sending if we extended recognition?'

Canada did not reply, but Arundel was having too much fun to be concerned. The first semi-official recognition of his principality occurred when Arundel convinced the Chesapeake and Potomac Telephone Company to formally list the Outer Baldonian Legation in the Washington telephone directory – under the same number as his office. In due course, the National Geographic Society called asking for the exact latitude and longitude of Outer Baldonia. Soon a low-level State Department official inquired about the chief exports of the country. Arundel's secretary answered: 'I listed sheep, seal, lobster, and beer. After all, I couldn't tell him that the only thing we have plenty of is guano.'

Relying on the good faith of other actors, Arundel increased his activity. He persuaded mapmakers Rand McNally to include Outer Baldonia on their maps. He warmly entertained a journalist preparing a feature on Washington's embassies, and accepted literature from the US Office of Defense Mobilization on 'what to do in the event of an atomic attack'. Arundel soon began receiving routine US State Department calls that went to all diplomatic missions inviting him to attend functions. In time, he began issuing press releases on the major international affairs of the day, including the Cold War.

Arundel never seriously sought to garner international recognition of his principality, but he enjoyed the attention that he received. Newspaper articles across North America announced the formation of the Principality of Outer Baldonia and examined its peculiar laws. In one syndicated column that appeared in papers from Edmonton to Los Angeles, a journalist noted: 'The world's newest state may never be eligible for the United Nations. It would be hard to find it on a map, and its population is sometimes non-existent. But it has one distinction – it allows no women to enter its boundaries.' Perhaps recognising the project for what it was – an elaborate man cave – no one bothered to inquire further.

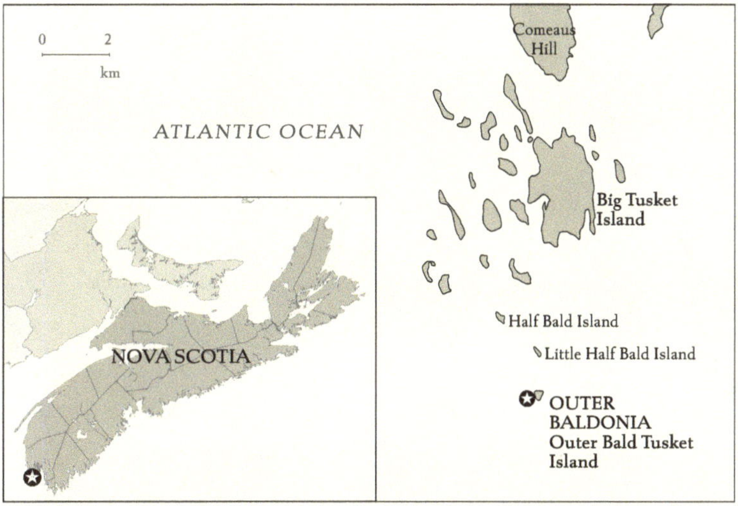

Location of Outer Baldonia

Other journalists questioned the geopolitical factors behind the sudden emergence of this new country on Canada's doorstep. An article in the *Ottawa Citizen* mischievously speculated:

> Did the late Liberal government let the U.S. set up a satellite regime on Canadian soil, right under Nova Scotia's Bluenoses? There has been no word as to whether Prime Minister [John] Diefenbaker intends to look into this question, though on other matters he has adopted a sturdily nationalistic attitude towards Washington.

North American papers understood the principality was not a real nation, but it may not have been so clear to everyone. It appears that one of the feature stories on Outer Baldonia made its way to West Germany. There the story was picked up by the weekly paper *Industrikurier* and printed as if it was real. This story was noticed in Moscow – leading to a diplomatic showdown with the Soviets a decade before the Cuban Missile Crisis.

In 1952, the Soviet literary magazine *Literaturnaya Gazeta* published a scathing critique of the 'sovereign capitalist state' of Baldonia. The magazine's writer 'L. Chernaya' explained that their report was drawn from the 'thoroughly respectable bourgeois newspaper *Industrikurier*, an organ of the West German industrialists'. 'From immemorial times', Chernaya wrote, the small island had been inhabited by tuna fishermen who 'lived quietly and peacefully and, evidently thanked God that their [catch] was not an important strategic material, and that the island itself was too small to be turned into a US military base'. However, 'the modest mackerel fishers rejoiced too soon', as Mr Arundel, 'the future *Fuehrer* of Baldonia', landed on the island and declared himself its new ruler. Chernaya continued:

> Mr. Arundel has set himself the aim of turning his 'subjects' into savages. In the 'constitution' which he has devised, the master of Baldonia, as *Industrikurier* reports, 'granted his subjects the "unrestricted right" to tell lies, to be rude, the right not to answer questions, the freedom to go unshaved,' etc. In a word, the 'right' not to adhere to the ethical and moral laws which have been established by mankind!

The author also sketched parallels between Baldonia and American capitalism and imperialism. As Chernaya explained, many of Arundel's 'comrades' were trying to establish similar morally depraved capitalist extractive states 'over the territory of the whole world':

> Of course, Mr. Arundel will not succeed in turning the peaceful fishermen into cannibals. For much bigger adventures of a similar kind have ended in utter failure. There is no doubt that the mackerel fishers will not become savages. But the American businessman himself, of whom the newspaper of the West German militarists writes with unconcealed respect even when he stands out in the role of chief 'Baldonian,' has he not reached the completest degree of savagery?

It took a little while, but by January 1953 the Soviet story had been translated into English and published in full in several North American newspapers. The papers had a field day. The *Calgary Herald* lampooned the caricature painted by Chernaya, playfully describing Arundel as 'a capitalistic cannibal preparing to gobble up the humble fishermen of the island'. *Esquire* magazine commissioned a cartoon imagining how the Soviet readership saw the Prince of Princes: in the image, Arundel held a spike club, a placard with a dollar sign and a holstered gun.

Unsurprisingly, the papers jumped to Baldonia's defence. A headline on the front page of the Virginia-based *Fauquier Democrat* published on 29 January 1953 joked, 'Russians Rise to Defend Poor Islanders from Fauquier Ruler' (Arundel lived in Fauquier County, Virginia). The *Ottawa Citizen* reminded its readers that the 'so-called principality exists only in the playful minds of a group of sportsmen'. The paper remarked further that the Soviet author had been disqualified from ever obtaining Outer Baldonian citizenship, for 'one of the constitutional crimes for which a man can be permanently expelled from outer baldonia [*sic*] is "lack of a sense of humor"'. Others encouraged Baldonia to 'break off diplomatic relations with the Soviets'. After all, 'Who do these Russians think they're pushing around?'

The principality's neighbours soon promised to assist. The Royal Yacht Club of Halifax (the capital city of Nova Scotia) offered to contribute its vessels to the defence of Outer Baldonia. One of the members of the yacht club was also a member of the Nova Scotia Parliament. The member 'made a speech excoriating Russia and moved that the government legally recognize the independence of the island principality, and it did', wrote journalist Nancy Coe. 'Its only condition: the Baldonians must continue to pay the equivalent of their real-estate taxes into the Nova Scotia treasury each year.' The governments of the United States and Canada also apparently each issued a statement ridiculing Russia for missing the joke. Arundel was not impressed: 'We didn't ask the United States to recognize our independence. We haven't recognized their independence.'

In an interview with Prince Prew for *Esquire* magazine, the motivations of Chernaya were explored. He explained: 'We have been able to determine that L. Chernaya, author of the diatribe, is really a woman. We figure that she is bitter towards us because we ban all women from the Principality.'

Nonetheless, Arundel recognised his advantage. He wrote to Soviet leaders, threatening to withdraw recognition of the USSR unless the magazine apologised. He also demanded that the Soviets keep their fishing trawlers out of Baldonia's waters – 'a rod-and-reel guy, he massively disapproved of their fishing practices involving nets and electroshocking'. Later in the year, 'filled with the spirit of Christmas', Arundel invited Chernaya to the principality to attend the next Outer Baldonia tuna tournament – 'Getting out of Russia will be her own problem.'

The Soviet government never responded to Arundel's letters and Chernaya never visited his nation. Insulted, Arundel declared war on the USSR. The Soviets again did not respond, and Arundel claimed victory. As *Esquire* magazine surmised, 'One thing is sure – when the Soviets attack Outer Baldonia our only reaction is to feel sorry for them. I'm positive they never ran into anything like Outer Baldonia before, and it has them utterly baffled.'

After the war with the Soviet Union, Arundel began to visit the principality less frequently. In 1959, the Washington phone number was disconnected. Arundel explained that 'We just couldn't handle the number of phone calls'. In 1973, Arundel sold the island to the Nova Scotia Bird Society for $1 and retired.

The principality may have lost its territory, but it continued to exist in the minds of many people across the globe – and, after all, Arundel enjoyed the attention. In 1975, he claimed that Baldonia had ambassadors in 22 countries and was looking for more. In 1977, the year before his death, Arundel noted that he still received two or three letters a week from people all over the world wanting to become citizens. The Wedgeport

Tuna Museum holds a letter sent in 1997 from an employee of a German real estate company asking about diplomatic positions and noble titles.

Why were people seeking citizenship in a defunct micronation? Arundel was uncertain, but he knew who was to blame: 'The Russians caused all the fun by taking everything seriously.' Ron Wallace, Baldonian Ambassador Extraordinary and Plenipotentiary to Canada, and later a Halifax member of the Nova Scotia Parliament, had a different view. 'There was just a little sense in the message he [Arundel] was trying to tell – the idea of a country free from interference from outside and a minimum of government involvement in personal lives,' Wallace suggested.

Some journalists saw another reason. 'In the midst of international snarling, consider today the good news from the principality of Outer Baldonia,' advised the *Arizona Republic*. 'There all is calm, peaceful, the Russian threat has diminished. The farm problem has been solved – no farms. Not even a royal wedding disturbs its pleasant days.'

During the height of the Cold War, where better to spend one's days than a small clubhouse on a little island in the Canadian summer drinking rum? Or, at least pretending to do so. Wendy Arundel, Russell's granddaughter, claims that he 'spent only one uncomfortable night there, blaming the mosquitoes and relentless cold wind'.

Molossia: A benevolent dictator

The Republic of Molossia was also created for comedic value. The growth of the internet has allowed this micronation to prosper and the republic to play 'an unparalleled role in micronational development'. It inaugurated the Intermicronational Olympic Movement in 2000 and established MicroCon, a biennial convention of micronation governments held since 2015 that brings together 25 to 50 micronations. These activities allow the leaders of micronations to meet, discuss and learn from each other. It also creates opportunities for other state-like behaviour, including signing bilateral friendship treaties and engaging in trading relationships. The Republic of Molossia illustrates the depth and breadth of activities that are possible when pretending to run a country.

Molossia was initially founded by two teenage friends as the Grand Republic of Vuldstein in 1977, inspired by the Peter Sellers film adaptation of *The Mouse That Roared*. After several years of dormancy, name changes and drastic shifts in systems of government (from republic to communist state, and back again), the nation began to take shape when its original prime minister, Kevin Baugh, bought property in the US state of Nevada. After spending several years in the US military stationed in Europe, Baugh became fascinated with the 'idea of tiny nations like Monaco and Liechtenstein'. Baugh explains: 'It kind of really stuck with me this is something I would like to do and continue to do ... when I got property in Northern Nevada that became the home for the Republic of Molossia.'

On 3 September 1999, the Republic of Molossia was formally declared, with Baugh becoming president. Baugh explains that the name 'Molossia' was drawn from the Hawaiian word *maluhia* meaning 'harmony in the world'. It is not related to the ancient Greek nation of the same name, which is a perfect example of, Baugh says, 'why you should probably Google things before you use them'.

President Baugh argues that Molossia is a 'sovereign nation'. It certainly looks like a real country. It has a post office, stamps, a railway and a national flag – the Grand Triune, a horizontal tricolour of blue, white and green (essentially the inverse of the flag of Sierra Leone).

It has a navy, a movie theatre, and a national anthem, 'Fair Molossia is Our Home':

> There's a place beneath the western sun,
> A country proud, a nation next to none,
> An oasis amid the desert sand,
> Standing tall in this uncommon land.
> From the mountains high down to the valleys wide,
> Our flag of blue and white and green it ever flies,
> Where hawks and mustangs roam,
> Fair Molossia is our home.
> Treasured land of wind and sage and mighty dreams,
> Our country strong and free and proud, it reigns supreme,
> Fair Molossia is our home,
> Fair Molossia is our home.

It has a space program (consisting of model rocket launches several times a year), a population of around 30 (only three of whom actually live in the republic) and a growing territorial empire. While the capital, Baughston, is located near Dayton,

His Excellency President Kevin Baugh of the Republic of Molossia
Kevin Baugh

Nevada, Molossia claims two colonies: Desert Homestead Province in southern California, and the Farfella colony in northern California. It also has a constitution that establishes three arms of government – a national assembly, a president and a supreme court. However, owing to the 'ever-present foreign menace from over the border', the constitution has been suspended. The republic has operated under a state of martial law for many years, allowing President Baugh to exercise 'absolute, enlightened and benevolent leadership over Molossia'.

President Baugh acknowledges that not many micronations are military dictatorships:

> Most have kings or dukes and queens and emperors – you would never believe how many emperors there are out there. I just wasn't feeling the whole royalty thing, so I declared Molossia to be a military dictatorship. Of course, a cool uniform is required when you're a military dictator, you know a sash and medals and a big hat. I get more medals every year. You've gotta have the sunglasses and the whole nine yards.

The republic also has its own currency: the valora. One valor is equivalent to 100 futtrus, and the valora is pegged to the relative value of chocolate-chip cookie dough. Baugh explains, 'we don't go with a silver standard – nothing worthless like that'. Cookie dough is stored in the Bank of Molossia, from which valora coins made from gambling chips and printed banknotes are sold. It also has its own system of dates.

As is clear, Molossia reflects the vision and eccentricities of its president. 'It's an expression of personal sovereignty, creativity, imagination, and political satire ... It's a nice way to look around the world,' Baugh explains. 'You can see what countries are doing and say, "I can do that".' At the same time, he is realistic: 'Can I lower the drinking age? ... Well no, I can't. Come on, let's get real. We all want to think we have our own country, but you know the U.S. is a lot bigger.'

Molossia's small size has not prevented it defending its honour when action is needed. The republic has been at war with a much larger adversary since the 1980s. In 1983, Baugh was stationed in West Germany while serving in the US Army. Military exercises conducted by East Germany often kept him awake at night, which he considered a declaration of war. Although East Germany ceased to exist when it was reintegrated into Germany in 1990, Baugh claims that the war is ongoing. The negotiations that led to the reintegration of East and West Germany did not mention Ernst Thälmann Island, a Cuban possession which Fidel Castro promised to donate to East Germany in the 1970s. While both Cuba and Germany maintain that the gift was merely symbolic, Baugh asserts that it remains East German land and so the war continues. After all, 'it's good to have an eternal enemy that you can blame all your ills and woes on'.

In 2000, Baugh created the Intermicronational Olympic Games to run alongside the Sydney Olympics. Aimed at building friendship and partnership between all micronations, the Games were designed 'to allow micronations not recognised by the macronational Olympic Committee to participate in an international sporting event'. Baugh wanted to bring people together: 'I believe that all micronations should exist as much as possible in the real world, doing real things in real places with real people.' The Olympiad welcomed six micronations whose athletes competed in a range of mental and physical events, including chess, shot-put (with a tennis ball), and the 100-metre sprint. Kevin Baugh's son, Mark, won gold in the 100 metres with a time of 19.20 seconds. The principalities of Hutt River and Sealand did not take part. A spokesperson for Hutt River explained that they send their athletes to compete in mainstream sporting events: 'We are not here as part of a game or because we thought it was a fun idea.'

Strangely enough, it was not the first micronational Olympics. Popular fiction launched a micronation boom in Japan in the 1980s. Drawing on reports of New Atlantis, a micronation established on a bamboo raft off the coast of Jamaica by Leicester Hemingway (Ernest's younger brother), novelist Hisashi Inoue authored *Kirikirijin*, a satirical tale that centred on a secluded village in rural northern Japan that seceded, made their regional dialect an official language and fought a war of independence.

The success of the book sparked much excitement; within a few years, more than 200 communities had declared their own independence. Most were primarily concerned with attracting tourists to promote revenue and counter the effects of young people leaving rural towns. However, some did engage in performative assertions of statehood. The Nikoniko Republic established Nikoniko Standard Time (set at one hour behind Tokyo), constructed welcome signs at their border, minted their own currency and renamed the local tofu shop the National Protein Research Institute. The Japanese minister of internal trade and industry even signed a satirical treaty of friendship between the nation of Japan and the Kingdom of Inobhutan.

Several of these nations established their own Olympic Games, which received prime-time television coverage, and a micro-United Nations, which held summit talks between 1983 and 1985. However, when the Japanese asset price bubble burst in 1991, many villages were forced to merge with neighbouring larger cities and the micronations they established dissolved.

Reflecting his desire to connect micronations in the real world, Baugh inaugurated the first convention of micronation governments in 2015, which he called MicroCon. The event opened with a keynote address on micronational history and concepts, then attendees gave presentations that discussed their own countries. It concluded with a semi-formal ball. The most recent MicroCon was hosted by the Duchy of Westarctica and held in Las Vegas, Nevada, in August 2022. Baugh notes, 'It's fun to get together and exchange ideas. It's fun to see what other people think what a country can be. From traditional to totally non-traditional.'

Despite its best efforts, the Republic of Molossia is not recognised by any country. Nonetheless, because it makes a claim for sovereignty and is prominent online, it attracts people desperate for safety and security:

> About two or three times a week, we do get enquiries from folks who would like to come move to our country. They're actually serious; most of them are frankly from the Middle East and they want to move anywhere. By now, I estimate that our population would have zoomed up to somewhere around 5,000 or so. It's actually kind of unfortunate and sad that so many folks are living in a situation where they just happen to see this random place on the Internet and they think 'Man, I want to move there,' without even really knowing anything about us.

Playing a state can lead to unexpected complications.

The Great Bitter Lake Association: Stranded in the Suez

In October 1968, the eyes of the world were on Mexico City, the host of the games of the 19th Olympiad. However, half a world away another Olympics was in full flight. The crews of

14 ships stranded in the middle of the Suez Canal were preparing to compete in a series of events. Of course, modifications would have to be made to the vessels to turn them into sporting arenas. Polish sailors on the MS *Djakarta* took the lead; they

> produced bows and arrows, and targets. They padded obstructions on their foredecks to make running and jumping courses, and swung out derricks to support the goals of a water polo pitch ... They made weights for weightlifting, certificates and even winners' medals: gold, silver and bronze.

In all, around 200 competitors competed in 14 sports. Participant George Wharton described his experience: 'the atmosphere during the games was fantastic with everyone playing their part to make it the success it really was', he noted. 'It was open to everyone – you could put your name down to any sport you felt you were good at, and then the captain of each sport would select his best team.' The Polish delegation came in first, securing gold medals in swimming, rowing, running and triathlon.

These lesser known Olympics secured media attention. Film crews from Sweden, France, Germany and Britain attended several of the events. The UK's *Daily Express* newspaper decided to sponsor the teams, 'sending out strips and footballs, and providing a trophy'. Their support was worthwhile; the paper was pleased to report another 'world cup victory for Britain' in the soccer tournament – a repeat of England's success in the 1966 World Cup.

But how did these Olympics get started? And what were ships doing stranded in the Suez Canal? On the morning of 5 June

1967, Israel launched a series of air strikes against Egyptian airfields and a simultaneous ground invasion into the Egyptian-controlled Sinai Peninsula and Gaza Strip. The offensive came after several months of simmering hostilities between the two countries, culminating with Egyptian president Gamal Abdel Nasser's May 1967 decision to close the Straits of Tiran to Israeli vessels. The blockade could have been devastating for Israel, as around 90 per cent of its oil passed through the narrow sea passage separating the Arabian and Sinai peninsulas. The Six-Day War ended in a dramatic and overwhelming victory for Israel. By 11 June 1967, it had crippled the Egyptian, Jordanian and Syrian militaries and its forces occupied the Sinai Peninsula, the Gaza Strip, the West Bank and the Golan Heights.

The 193-kilometre-long Suez Canal connects the Mediterranean Sea to the Red Sea, separating Africa and Asia. In making possible a passage between the North Atlantic and Indian Oceans, the canal reduces the journey from the Arabian Sea to London by approximately 8900 kilometres – a canal trip that, in 1966, an average of 57 ships took each day. International law provides that the Suez Canal 'shall always be free and open, in time of war as in time of peace, to every vessel of commerce or of war, without distinction of flag'. However, Israeli occupation of the Sinai Peninsula left Israel in control of the canal's east bank. Nasser would not countenance sharing the canal with Israel and ordered his troops to scuttle ships and install sea mines at both ends to prevent its use by Israel. Fifteen ships travelling through the canal were suddenly trapped. They would remain so until the Suez was reopened eight years later, in June 1975.

Initially the crew were worried about being caught up in

the conflict. Sean Dring on the MS *Port Invercargill* recalled his anxieties: 'We don't know if the Israelis are going to push further, from where they'd stopped on the Sinai side, further into Egypt.' John Hughes, on the MS *Melampus*, agreed: 'Obviously when you see a conflict like that and you watch it on the television war looks glorious, but to be honest it is not, it is completely horrific.' Peter Richmond of the MS *Agapenor* was especially worried: 'the first week was a very anxious one ... we had loaded a lot of ammunition (former British Forces arms from Singapore) in holds one and two. Had we been hit the probability is that the ship would have suffered catastrophic damage'.

Blockading the canal was a financial disaster. It is estimated that Egypt lost around US$300 million annually in canal revenues, the Indian iron ore trade to Europe became uneconomical, and European countries spent an extra US$1 billion in the first 12 months alone because of the increased cost of sending tankers around Africa. The canal also failed in its remaining function as 'a moat between enemies': Israeli and Egyptian commandos sometimes slipped over the border to conduct raids. Fourteen of the ships were bunched together in Great Bitter Lake, a 194-square-kilometre saltwater lake in the middle of the canal. An American freighter, the *Observer*, was cut off by scuttled ships and forced to anchor in Lake Timsah several kilometres north. A reporter for *Time* magazine noted that while 'the crews have a grandstand view of the military fireworks, their biggest enemy is boredom'.

There was little the stranded sailors could do except wait and play cards. Negotiations between Egypt, Israel, the United Nations and the shipping companies dragged on with no obvious resolution in sight. Captain Mirosław Proskurnicki of

Stranded in the Great Bitter Lake
George Wharton

the Polish ship MS *Djakarta* gave an insight into how his crew were handling the situation. 'The first month was like a holiday. The second month was very hard. By the end of the third month, it was terrible.' The ships became known as the Yellow Fleet because the region's sandstorms had stained the hulls. Although some crew had been able to leave, the geopolitical situation made relief difficult. Finally, after three months a compromise was reached. Egypt would not allow the canal to be reopened, but the shipping companies could relieve their crews. Replacements were hired (at double pay because of the ongoing threat of conflict – though in reality, most were paid much less) to keep the ships in working condition. As soon as the canal was open, the ships would be able to leave.

The 14 ships came from eight different countries: the UK, the US, West Germany, France, Sweden, Poland, Bulgaria and

Czechoslovakia. Although Egyptian authorities had initially banned the sailors from using radio to communicate with each other, almost immediately the crews hopped on lifeboats to meet and trade: some ships had too much frozen meat, while others were full of canned fruit. An unofficial marketplace soon emerged, and trading graduated to movie reels, wine and spirits. Concerned about excessive partying, the officers attempted to bring some order to the community. In October 1967, a note was fixed to the message board of each ship:

> At a recent meeting attended by personnel from all the ships at present in the Bitter Lake, it was decided to from an association to be called 'The Great Bitter Lake Association', membership will be open to anyone who has been serving on any of the vessels during the closure of the Canal. The main aim of the Association is to maintain and foster the many friendships that we have, and no doubt you have, formed with the people of the other ships and nationalities whilst here.

The Great Bitter Lake Association was a means to provide mutual support among the group of Western and Eastern Bloc members. They shared food, met weekly for church services (described by members of the Association as beer-drinking sessions), and attended social events hosted by a different vessel. As noted, they also held the Bitter Lake Olympic Games in 1968: football matches were held on the deck of the largest ship, the MS *Port Invercargill*, and lifeboat races were conducted in the lake. Although the Association was formed to curb excessive drinking, this does not appear to have worked. Captain Arthur

High jump competition, Great Bitter Lake Olympics
George Wharton

Kensett of the *Port Invercargill* estimated that around 1.5 million empty beer bottles were dumped in the lake: 'One wonders what future archaeologists in a few thousand years' time will think of this'.

And yet, the Association was more than just a drinking club. It was an attempt to provide 'a sense of stability in an incredibly unstable place. They weren't just individuals on a ship, but members of a society'. They even had a uniform. Members wore a Great Bitter Lake Association tie and were given official badges. The badge was in the shape of a shield, with a large anchor across the centre. At the top were the letters GBLA and at the bottom was the number 14 for the 14 ships

Great Bitter Lake Association stamp

in the lake. A thin blue strip running diagonally behind the anchor represented the Suez Canal.

Over time, relationships between members of the Association grew even stronger. Members started to feel that they were part of 'their own little autonomous community'. As a nation, they reasoned that 'they should have their own postage stamp'. Some of these 'were drawn by hand, and printed using inks, crayons or even coffee grounds for colour. Other stamps were produced from potato cuts or carved from linoleum, and then coloured with inks'. Most letters were posted with both a Great Bitter Lake Association and an Egyptian stamp. However, Egyptian postal authorities sometimes allowed the stamps to be used by themselves, and they have become a collector's item.

Despite the war's quick conclusion, political impasse prevented any attempt to reopen the Suez Canal. Looking at lowering their costs, the shipping companies opted to employ skeleton crews to deal with basic maintenance, leaving only around 50 members of the Great Bitter Lake Association on the lake at any one time. This proved fortuitous. In 1973, Egyptian and Syrian forces led a coalition of Arab states into a surprise war against Israel. Egypt hoped to seize the eastern bank of the Suez Canal and press for the return of the Sinai Peninsula. In what became known as the Yom Kippur War, Israeli forces again succeeded. During the fighting a stray Israeli missile hit one of the ships in the Great Bitter Lake. While the *African Glen*, a US ship, was sunk, no crew members were on board at the time.

Following the ceasefire in October 1973, Egypt decided to reopen the canal. With the support of the United States, the UK and France, scuttled ships, destroyed bridges, 686 000 mines and 13,500 pieces of unexploded ordnance were removed. After 14 months, the canal was cleared, and the Yellow Fleet could continue its journey. In all, more than 2000 men and one woman served on the Great Bitter Lake.

Only two West German ships could leave under their own steam – after eight long years the other vessels were no longer seaworthy, suffering significant salt corrosion – but the delay proved valuable. These two ships were carrying non-perishable raw materials such as wool, steel, lead, and ore sand for sandpaper. The goods had increased in value since 1967 and were 'a thousand percent more profitable'. Around 30 000 spectators welcomed the ships when they docked in Hamburg, having completed the world's longest sea shipping voyage in history: eight years, three months and five days.

The Great Bitter Lake Association illustrates how a group of people can evolve into a micronation and how acting as a state can in turn strengthen the bonds between them so that they become a more tightly knit community. Members of the association continued 'to keep in touch after their service', and many remained firm friends. Their story nonetheless fell out of public consciousness – until, that is, the 20 000-tonne *Ever Given* wedged itself within the Suez Canal for six days in 2021 and revived memories of what had occurred decades before.

9

FRAUDS AND SCAMS: THE GREAT MICRONATION RIP-OFFS

Micronations are not states, but because they look a lot like states they can be used to fool unsuspecting people. Fraudsters and scammers might create a country and sell passports to desperate people, falsely holding them out as legitimate documents. Others might promise victims a wonderful new life in a safe and prosperous country, and sell titles to land they have no legitimate claim over. Here we look at four micronations created to defraud unsuspecting people: Poyais, a fictional nation supposedly located in Central America; Aeterna Lucina in Australia; the Kingdoms of Papaala and Me'ekamui on Bougainville Island; and the Dominion of Melchizedek, based in the United States but apparently located in very remote areas of the globe.

Poyais: The largest fraud in history

In 1822, in a 355-page leather-bound guidebook called *A Sketch of the Mosquito Shore*, an optimistic 'Captain Thomas Strangeways' introduced the English and Scottish public to the 'delightful and most valuable' Central American territory of Poyais:

Location of the fictional nation of Poyais

Enough has been said to prove the great encouragement, and manifold advantages, which must be derived from commercial establishments in the Territory of Poyais: and now that the well known political circumstances are removed, which have hitherto retarded the advancement of this fine country, in civilization and in the scale of independent states, there seems no reason whatever to doubt, that, protected by the wise and vigorous administration, sound policy, and comprehensive view of His Highness the Cazique of Poyais, this beautiful country will rapidly advance in prosperity and civilization, and will become, in every point of view, and within a very short period, not the least considerable of those 'radiant realms beyond the Atlantic wave'.

Rich in fertile soils, overflowing in game and abundant marine resources; covered by virgin forests of fine mahogany, cedar and redwood; and littered with gold deposits, Poyais was an attractive site. It was also blessed with a mild and healthy climate, quite unlike other settlements in the New World. There was also no need to worry about the name of the shoreline. The 'Mosquito' Coast did not refer to the insect but the cluster of tiny islands offshore.

The geopolitical situation was equally promising. Protected by an inaccessible mountain range, the land had never fallen under rapacious Spanish dominion. In fact, the natives were Anglophiles, desperate to invite British settlers to their paradise on Earth. Only opaque political reasons had prevented the UK from accepting the several offers over the years by Poyaisian kings 'to attach their country to the Empire'. Sporadic British settlement had nonetheless occurred. As Captain Strangeways explained, nestled beneath Sugarloaf Mountain and alongside the mighty Black River sat St Joseph, the flourishing capital of this fledgling land. Built in the European style, its broad tree-lined boulevards and grand colonnades fanned out in all directions from a magnificent domed cathedral. It also housed a royal palace, a parliament and opera house, among several stately mansions – testament to the riches that could be made by enterprising individuals. An engraving of the Port of Black River, a small community just a short distance from St Joseph, provided further insight into the picturesque and bustling Poyais.

The guidebook was accompanied by a major publicity tour led by His Royal Highness the Cazique of Poyais. The cazique (prince) was in London to attend the coronation of King George

Port of Black River, Republic of Poyais from Thomas Strangeways, *A Sketch of the Mosquito Shore* (1822)
Thomas Strangeways

IV on behalf of his subjects. While there, he decided to seek investment and immigrants for Poyais. A natural charmer and boasting an impressive list of military achievements, the cazique arrived unknown and unheralded but soon became 'a great adornment for the dinner tables and ballrooms of sophisticated London'. By the end of 1821, Major William Richardson had provided Oak Hall, his Essex estate, as a British base for the Poyaisian royal family, and for his hospitality was rewarded with the Poyaisian Order of the Green Cross and appointed the top representative of Poyais in Britain. Richardson was grateful, and presented his letter of credence to King George IV.

An engaging and gregarious speaker, the cazique was keen to describe Poyais to all who would listen. The cazique was a reformer. The territory was governed by a tricameral parliament with intricate and complicated constitutional arrangements.

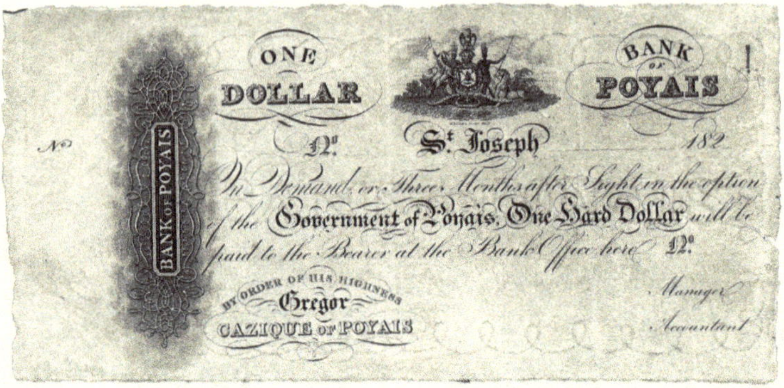

One dollar, Bank of Poyais, Republic of Poyais
National Numismatic Collection, National Museum of American History

His Highness had taken it upon himself to devise commercial and banking mechanisms, design distinctive uniforms for each regiment of the army, and develop the country's own honours system, coat of arms, titles and flag – a green cross of St George on a white background.

The cazique aggressively drummed up attention. In addition to the guidebook, he gave interviews in national newspapers and paid for Poyais ballads to be sung on the streets of London, Edinburgh and Glasgow. The climate suited him. The British economy was booming following the defeat of Napoleon, and falling interest rates caused many people to look for higher returns on riskier investments. The collapse of the Spanish Empire meant that there were a range of new Latin American countries one could invest in at attractive rates: Mexican bonds paid 6 per cent, double the rate of the British government bond. With the support of a respectable City of London bank, the cazique floated £200,000 in bonds at 6 per cent – the equivalent of £3.6 billion today.

Investment was important, but the cazique also needed settlers. Handsome hand-printed land certificates were initially issued at 2 shillings and threepence per acre, roughly equivalent to a working man's daily wage. Demand was strong and the price rose steadily to 4 shillings per acre. Around 500 people sold their possessions and invested their life savings, excited by the prospect of immigrating to 'one of the most healthy and beautiful spots in the world', where 'Europeans do not suffer by any of those disorders so dangerous in the West Indies; and live to a very old age'.

In 1822 and 1823, two ships and 250 colonists set out from London and Edinburgh. The group had exchanged their pounds and shillings into Poyais dollars and spent the trip dreaming of a safe and secure life. Upon arriving just under two months later they assumed that they were in the wrong place. There was no port, no bustling town and no roads – just a dense, mosquito-infested jungle, 'a sinister coast of disillusion'. Over the following months, two-thirds of the settlers died: some of yellow fever, malaria or exhaustion, and others by suicide. Fewer than 50 ever returned to Britain. What happened to Poyais and its bustling towns?

The Cazique of Poyais was Gregor MacGregor, a serial fabulist. A member of the Scottish Highland Clan MacGregor, he enlisted in the British Army as an officer in 1803 at age 16. Following several years' service in Gibraltar he was sent to Portugal to serve in the Peninsular War between Spain and France. There he saw little action. After developing an obsession with dress, rank and insignia that put many of his colleagues offside, a 'trivial' dispute with a superior officer that intensified forced him to request an honourable discharge in

General Gregor MacGregor
Print made by Samuel William Reynolds

1810. Returning to Edinburgh, MacGregor assumed the title of colonel and wore the badge of a Portuguese knightly order.

The ruse did not achieve its goal. Failing to attain the high social status he felt he deserved, MacGregor travelled south to London. In the capital he styled himself Sir Gregor and claimed to have succeeded to the MacGregor clan chieftainship. As David Sinclair notes, this was all nonsense, but it provided MacGregor with an air of respectability in London. It would not last for long. In December 1811, his wealthy wife passed away, leaving MacGregor without his main source of income (her family). Unable to return to the British Army and with limited options to seek fame and fortune, he decided to try his luck in South America, where several colonies were in the midst of wars of independence against the Spanish Empire. MacGregor believed that exotic adventures in the New World might earn him the celebrity status in London that he craved.

Arriving in Venezuela in 1812, MacGregor assisted republican forces in the Venezuelan War of Independence. Drawing on an embellished and exaggerated account of his experience in the Peninsular War, he was able to obtain a commission under revolutionary general Francisco de Miranda and, later, Simón Bolívar. MacGregor enjoyed some success but he rubbed many of his men the wrong way. One official expressed his contempt for the Scotsman: 'I am sick and tired of this bluffer, or Quixote, or the devil knows what,' the official wrote in a letter to a friend. 'This man can hardly serve us in New Granada without heaping ten thousand embarrassments upon us.' Even so, Bolívar was suitably impressed, appointing him a divisional general and awarding him the Order of the Liberators.

MacGregor's main aim was to secure fame and fortune, rather than Venezuelan independence. In 1817 he left Bolívar's command and stumbled upon an idea that he would later perfect in his Poyais scam. It began with a plan to invade Spanish Florida.

Touring the United States, MacGregor raised US$160 000 from investors by selling titles to land in Florida, which was then a Spanish colony. With this money he raised a small force and in June 1817 captured the tiny Amelia Island on the border with the US state of Georgia. Raising a white flag emblazoned with a green cross of St George, MacGregor proclaimed the new 'Republic of the Floridas'. MacGregor was not concerned with establishing republican institutions or invading Florida to make good on his promise to his investors. Instead, he attempted to engage in lucrative privateering and smuggling. Over the following months, MacGregor and his associates smuggled up to US$500 000 worth of contraband, mainly African slaves who had been taken from Spanish slave ships. Citing this slave-smuggling ring and the presence of a 'body of [armed] Blacks from St Domingo' near the country's border, US president James Monroe ordered troops to occupy the island in December 1817. By this stage, MacGregor had escaped to the Bahamas, where he had medallions struck bearing the Green Cross motif and two Latin inscriptions:

> *Amalia Veni Vidi Vici* (Amelia, I Came, I Saw, I Conquered)
> *Duce Mac Gregorio Libertas Floridarium* (Liberty for the Floridas under the leadership of MacGregor)

He made no attempt to repay his investors. Further debacles at Portobelo in Panama and Riohacha in Colombia – where MacGregor began to refer to himself as 'His Majesty the Inca of New Granada' – led to a split between the Scotsman and the Venezuelan revolutionaries. In 1819, Bolívar accused MacGregor of treason and ordered his death by hanging if he ever again set foot on the South American mainland. Wanted for piracy in Jamaica and hounded by disappointed and angry investors in the United States, Haiti and England, MacGregor escaped to the Mosquito Coast, in present-day Nicaragua. There he put the finishing touches on his next plan.

When MacGregor returned to Britain in mid-1821, he claimed that King George Frederic Augustus of the Mosquito Coast in the Gulf of Honduras had invested him Cazique of Poyais. Armed with a series of beautiful-looking fabricated documents, MacGregor announced that he intended to seek investment and immigrants for the new colony. As Sinclair notes, MacGregor 'understood the value of the printed word and the official-looking document. Thus, when he needed tangible evidence to support the concept of his fraud, he merely produced the documents himself, knowing that, no matter how implausible, they were likely to be accepted at face value'.

By the time his surviving would-be colonists arrived back in London, MacGregor had left England. Many of those who returned defended MacGregor, believing that His Highness had been failed by those in his employ. Perhaps they could not admit to themselves they had been duped. In any event, MacGregor had not given up on Poyais. Basing himself in Paris, MacGregor tried to raise £800,000 for another scheme. Although he persuaded 60 would-be colonists, Parisian authorities were alerted when no one could prove the country existed. Arrested but acquitted, MacGregor returned to Edinburgh before emigrating to Venezuela to escape disappointed investors. MacGregor was awarded a military pension for his participation in Venezuela's war of independence, and after his death in 1845 was buried with full military honours in Caracas Cathedral. Today, he is better known as the founding father of securities fraud.

Aeterna Lucina: A promised land

Gregor MacGregor's Poyais scam seems unbelievable today, but the promise of a utopian community was also key to the fraud allegedly perpetrated by German-Australian Paul Neuman. Neuman claimed to have received the title Baron Neuman of Kara Bagh from the exiled former King Hassan III of Afghanistan. He certainly dressed the part, sporting several gigantic medals on his chest.

In January 1978, Baron Neuman founded the Sovereign State of Aeterna Lucina (also known as the Sovereign Humanitarian Mission State of Aeterna Lucina). Neumann designed a flag and devised a series of military medals and chivalric orders. He also wrote letters announcing the formation of a new sovereign state within Australia to leaders all over the world, seeking recognition. In April that year David Passage, a member of the US State Department, wrote to his counterparts in the Australian Department of Foreign Affairs:

> Dear Ed,
>
> First the Hutt River Province, and now the Sovereign State of Aeterna Lucina. Surely there must be one or two Federationists left in Australia!
>
> You will appreciate, I know, that for the time being we have decided not to take action on this ...

The counsellor to the Yugoslav Embassy was blunt: he asked why the Australian authorities had not yet arrested Neuman.

Initially located in Byron Bay in northern New South Wales, Aeterna Lucina moved with Neuman to Curl Curl in Sydney, and later Cooma at the foothills of the Snowy Mountains in the southern part of the state. In a pamphlet entitled *A Promised Land*, Neuman sought to attract members to his new country. Aeterna Lucina was a land of 'unspoiled mountain character' where citizens would 'enjoy the purity of true fruit juices, mineral water, ice cream made from fresh cream and fruit, bread baked in brick ovens ... [and] butter churned in the dairies of our alpine meadows'. Coca-Cola, blue ice cream and cars were all banned. His advertisements were successful; individuals from as far as West Germany bought blocks of land in quarter-acre, 1-acre and 10-acre lots, and became members of the community.

Many did so for idealistic reasons. West German computer technician Gunter Frick paid A$50 000 to move to Aeterna Lucina because he was 'sick of hearing about nuclear missiles, the daily poisoning of the environment and ruthless corporations'.

Unfortunately, Aeterna Lucina soon ran into trouble. Neuman had allegedly told members that because Aeterna Lucina was independent, Australian laws did not apply and land transactions could be completed internally by his government. This was not true. Aeterna Lucina had no basis for its existence and Australia did not recognise its independence. Australian law also did not recognise any land conveyances; the entirety of the 14-square-kilometre Cooma property remained registered in the name of Neuman and his wife. Neuman was charged with obtaining A$144 000 by deception, but after a jury failed to reach a verdict the case was abandoned. The dream of Aeterna Lucina died when Neuman passed away in the 1990s.

Papaala and Me'ekamui: Pyramid scheme

Running a micronation can be a great way to commit financial crimes. Noah Musingku created a country to facilitate a pyramid scheme. Musingku is a Pentecostal Christian who, under the name King David Peii II, claims to rule the twin Kingdoms of Papaala and Me'ekamui on Bougainville Island.

Political and economic strife on Bougainville created space for Musingku to develop his fraud. The island of Bougainville is part of the Solomon Islands archipelago, but has been administered as part of neighbouring Papua New Guinea since 1949 when the island was incorporated into the Australian Territory of Papua to form the United Nations Trust Territory of Papua and New Guinea. This territory was administered by Australia until Papua New Guinea attained independence in 1975. Bougainville became part of the new state.

Political tensions between Bougainville and the rest of Papua New Guinea have long been a feature of the relationship. A brief secessionist attempt in 1975 failed, but a decades-long conflict over independence and autonomy raged between 1988 and 1997. In 1998, hostilities concluded with the Bougainville Peace Agreement, under which the Papua New Guinea government agreed to the founding of the Autonomous Bougainville Government. The peace agreement also required a referendum on Bougainville's political status to be held within two decades. In 2019, a non-binding referendum on independence was held, with an overwhelming majority voting in favour of independence. In July 2021, the governments of Papua New Guinea and Bougainville reached agreement on a deal that will lead to Bougainville gaining independence in 2027.

Noah Musingku's financial scams emerged during the

conflict in the 1990s. In 1997, he established U-Vistract Financial Systems, promoting it as a 'Bank for Bougainvilleans' and 'drawing on Bougainville's sense of having been exploited by international capital'. Initially, U-Vistract attracted praise and support from prominent Bougainvilleans in Papua New Guinea excited about the prospect of 'Bougainville's first international financier'. U-Vistract was popular. Promising to double investors' money over a few months, it enticed thousands of people from across Papua New Guinea, including members of the political elite, to invest. Musingku also attracted around A$500 000 from church groups in Australia 'before the Australian Securities and Investments Commission compelled him to return money to the investors'. This action prompted authorities in Papua New Guinea to take a closer look. Within two years, the scheme had collapsed after failing to meet the government's demand that Musingku present its financial records.

Undeterred by several failed attempts to relaunch his plan in Port Moresby (in Papua New Guinea) and in Honiara (in the Solomon Islands), Musingku returned to his family village in South Bougainville in 2003. Once there he sought an alliance with the Bougainville separatist leader Francis Ona. Ona had proclaimed his own independent Republic of Me'ekamui (meaning sacred or holy island) in 1990 as part of the ongoing civil tensions in the region. In 2004, Ona restyled the republic a kingdom, and declared himself King Francis Dominic Dateransy Domanaa, head of state of the Royal Kingdom of Me'ekamui. Around the same time, Musingku crowned himself ruler of the separate Kingdom of Papaala.

The Kingdom of Me'ekamui was essentially a rival rebel movement on the island hoping to form a government. The

King Musingku of the Kingdoms of Papaala and Me'ekamui
David Lornie

Kingdom of Papaala, in contrast, was a personality cult focused entirely around Musingku and built on the money he had made defrauding people. However, the alliance with Ona led Musingku to reshape U-Vistract and present it as 'the financial foundation of a new state'. Musingku explained in his newsletter, the *Papaala Chronicles*:

> We had to set up our own home-grown international government, monetary and banking system with the capability of resolving the crisis once and for all. At Bougainville national level we had Me'ekamui government as our hardware whilst Papua government provided the software. Internationally we established RAONK (Royal

> Assembly of Nations & Kingdoms) as our hardware whilst U-Vistract System provided the software. We then invited other nations, governments and kingdoms to seek affiliations with us.

When Ona passed away from malaria in 2005, Musingku merged the two kingdoms. He now rules the Kingdoms of Papaala and Me'ekamui as King David Peii II. The twin kingdoms are located within the village of Tonu in the Siwai district of South Bougainville. As king, Musingku wears a brass crown and carries a sceptre.

The Bougainville government is unable to project authority across the entire island without risking inflaming tensions. The Bougainville Peace Agreement also prevents the government from sending in armed troops. Musingku has used this situation to his advantage. Protected by a Fijian militia of between 30 and 100 men, Musingku continues to operate his kingdom, defrauding millions of dollars from unsuspecting people in Papua New Guinea, Fiji and the Solomon Islands from his base in the southern part of the island.

The twin kingdoms possess the trappings of a state. Several members of the militia patrol the borders beside a large sign declaring the kingdom to be a sovereign nation. Musingku has renamed the months of the year after minerals named in the Bible. He has also created his own currency – the Bougainville Kina – graced with the faces of Jesus, Francis Ona and Musingku himself. Reports note than even in 2020 'people are still visiting him to invest more money, or to ask for their promised returns'.

As Bougainville moves slowly towards independence, it is not clear what will happen to Musingku's twin kingdoms.

Entering the Kingdoms of Papaala and Me'ekamui
David Lornie

The United Nations has repeatedly explained to residents that the only recognised states are Papua New Guinea and the Autonomous Bougainville Government. In 2021, the president of the Bougainville government met with Musingku, perhaps seeking a rapprochement. Given the delicate security situation, the leader of a micronation created to defraud unsuspecting people might yet secure a position of authority within the government of a real country.

Melchizedek: Where mysticism meets money making

The possibility of cloaking illegal actions in the veneer of statehood has proven enticing to swindlers. One of the more bizarre, long-running scams committed by someone pretending to run a country was organised by the father-and-son team of convicted American fraudsters David and Mark Pedley.

It took a little while before the Pedleys hit upon the idea of creating a country. In the 1970s, they ran a real-estate scam, then graduated to money laundering, operating a fake bank out of California that they used to assist American tax dodgers move their money to Mexico. Laundering around US$14 million in total, the Pedleys skimmed at least US$6 million for themselves. Following a stint in a Mexican jail, David Pedley became interested in Christian Science. With the help of his son Mark, David rewrote the King James Bible, filling the text with 'idiosyncratic metaphysics', such as referring to the Holy Ghost as a 'Scientific Being'. The Pedleys named their text 'The Melchizedek Bible', after an elusive king and priest introduced in the Book of Genesis. Little is known of this figure, but in the New Testament's Epistle to the Hebrews, Jesus is described as a 'priest forever according to the order of Melchizedek'.

David Pedley may have died in Mexico in 1987. A casket purportedly containing his remains arrived in California that year. Yet some US government officials have their doubts. The Pedley family denied an FBI request to fingerprint David Pedley's body, and reports suggested that he was still alive in 1999. In any event, in 1990, after being paroled from a prison in Washington state, Mark – either on his own or with his father's help – set about creating a country. Drawing on his interest in mysticism, he named his new state the Dominion of Melchizedek. He also developed a curious and intricate government. Its website explained:

> The Dominion of Melchizedek is an Ecclesiastical, Sovereign, Independent society, based on the rule of law and fundamental principles of brotherly love and peaceful co-existence with all Societies within the Family of Nations and its peoples. The People of the Dominion of Melchizedek seek to enhance its integration and recognition across the globe as well as continue cooperative efforts to work with all societies as we move into the future.

For Pedley, the Dominion of Melchizedek is similar to Vatican City. It serves as a territorial seat for followers of the Melchizedek Bible, and operates under its own religion and laws.

Mark began to develop state symbols and institutions for his country. He created a fake currency, 'the Equicurrency', and designed a seal that incorporated religious iconography. The seal consists of a white dove of peace and an infinity sign sitting above the three symbols of Islam, Christianity and Judaism, 'the great three monotheistic religions'. These symbols are encased in a shield upon which sits a gold crown. Mark also created a flag, consisting of the seal of Melchizedek on a white background. He then appointed his wife, Elvira Gamboa, president of the dominion. An alleged 'serial scammer' herself, Gamboa claims to have been made a princess of an unidentified Indigenous Philippines tribe.

Together, Pedley and Gamboa sought land for their nation. Melchizedek was said to be located in several remote places. These included the small island of Malpelo, 500 kilometres off the coast of Colombia; the submerged Karitane Shoal in the South Pacific; and the French possession of Clipperton Island lying more than 1000 kilometres south-west of Mexico. Today its website notes that it claims sovereignty over Taongi, an uninhabited Micronesian atoll administered by the Marshall Islands. It also claims some 14 million square kilometres of land in Antarctica. These locations were no doubt chosen to make it more difficult for unsuspecting victims to disprove Pedley and Gamboa's claims.

How does creating a fake country help one engage in financial crimes? Pedley recognised that by pretending to be a nation he could issue currency, license banks and incorporate companies all under the name of the Dominion of Melchizedek. After the building blocks of his state were set up, he – and a group of 'like-minded fraudsters' – got to work.

For a small monthly fee, Pedley paid for the Dominion's pretend currency to be listed in several financial databases, and the financial tables of the *International Herald Tribune*. Backed by fake bonds, Robert Tillman notes that 'with the wave of his financial wand', Pedley 'created billions of dollars in assets for his mythical country'.

In 1991, a man calling himself Branch Vinedresser (later found to be a pseudonym used by Pedley) chartered several fake banks in Washington, DC. The banks were subsidiaries of a Melchizedekian company that was used to attempt to secure loans from real banks based on fake Dominion of Melchizedek securities. In 1995, an Austrian man named Gerhard Bacher was sentenced to six months in prison in Hong Kong for using cheques issued by fake Melchizedek banks to open accounts in legitimate Hong Kong banks. Bacher had used his Melchizedek 'diplomatic passport' to visit several countries in Asia under the pseudonym of His Serene Highness Gerald-Dennis Sayn-Wittgenstein-Hohenstein.

That same year, Bank of England officials raided the London premises of Inner Sanctum, a company that offered get-rich-quick investment schemes backed by another Melchizedekian bank. Investors discovered that the bank's assets were not backed by US Treasury bonds as they had been led to believe but were worthless instruments issued by the German Weimar Republic – a state that existed between 1918 and 1933.

In 1996, Jeffrey Reynolds, the Dominion of Melchizedek's supposed secretary of commerce, pleaded guilty to insurance fraud in Texas. Reynolds had sold nearly US$47 million worth of bogus policies through a company purportedly based in Melchizedek. In the late 1990s, French citizen Roger Rosemount convinced at least 1400 people to invest over US$4 million in the Melchizedek-chartered Credit Bank International. In what turned out to be a Ponzi scheme, the US Securities and Exchange Commission warned potential investors that 'Credit Bank is not a bank, Melchizedek is not a country and Rosemount is not an ambassador'.

People connected to the Dominion of Melchizedek have also sold passports to their fake country misrepresenting them as legitimate. In 1998, three men were arrested in the Philippines selling Melchizedek passports for up to US$3500 each. By the time they were caught they had allegedly made US$1 million from the scam. Among the men was Australian John Gillespie, who had previously been convicted in the Fine Cotton scandal, in which a syndicate attempted to fix a horse race by painting a horse so that they could pass it off as another. It appears that the Dominion of Melchizedek is based 'more on tax laws than territory' and 'exist[s] mainly so that money can be whisked through shell banks'.

Seal of the Dominion of Melchizedek
Dominion of Melchizedek

Despite all this evidence, Pedley and Gamboa continued to maintain the illusion that the Dominion of Melchizedek was a legitimate state. Sometimes they had help from unsuspecting officials. In 1995, for example, the US Immigration and Naturalization Service sent a letter to the Melchizedek embassy (in reality, Pedley's Washington home) requesting 'some item of uniform insignia from your country's law enforcement services' to be displayed in an exhibition of global law enforcement badges at the Atlanta airport for the 1996 Olympics. That same year, the dominion faxed a press release to journalists announcing that it had declared war on France in retaliation for nuclear testing in the South Pacific. When answering follow-up questions over the legal status of Melchizedek, ambassador to the US, Tzemach Ben David Netzer Korem (another pseudonym of Pedley's), pointed to a copy of the Washington phone book listing the embassy's number.

The Dominion of Melchizedek has been active in officially recognising other countries, hoping that doing so will encourage those countries to mistakenly offer recognition in turn. After its formation, individuals purporting to be members of the Dominion government wrote to hundreds of sovereign states and the United Nations seeking recognition. The responses are proudly displayed on the Dominion's website. In most cases, these are simply letters acknowledging receipt and requesting more information 'especially with regard to its location, economic and political data, and the counties with which it has diplomatic relations and other information about the country which may be pertinent in the establishing of formal ties'. However, a letter from the Central African Republic appears genuine:

> This letter has been drawn to set forth the Central African Republic's official and formal recognition of the government of the Dominion of Melchizedek, an Ecclesiastical Sovereignty.
>
> Therefore, the Dominion of Melchizedek is hereby invited to establish a Diplomatic Mission in our Republic and will be granted all the consummate and traditional rights and privileges delineated in the Vienna Convention on Diplomatic Relations. ...
>
> Finally, any Real Estate purchased by the Dominion of Melchizedek from our Republic shall be treated as Sovereign Territory of the Dominion of Melchizedek.

It had other successes. In 1998, the Republic of Kosovo, a self-declared state seeking independence from the Federal Republic of Yugoslavia, received a message from the Dominion. In a difficult political and military situation, Kosovo needed any support it could receive. The president of Kosovo quickly announced that it had been formally recognised by the Dominion of Melchizedek and that Kosovo 'will soon exchange ambassadors with this country'. It is not clear when the president realised his mistake.

The Dominion of Melchizedek appears to still exist. On 30 August 2021, the Dominion's website reported that the government had appointed 'the Honorable Mike Sonpon as Emissary Extraordinaire to the Republic of Liberia'. Other appointments to 'the African Region' and Honduras were also made in 2021.

No country has ever officially recognised the Dominion, and it remains a non-state. However, it seems that several people connected to the micronation are genuinely interested in statehood and keen to distance themselves from Mark Pedley. In 2012, Pedley stepped away from any involvement with the dominion, explaining in an email to the prime minister, David Williams, 'As you know I no longer take an active role in the DoM [Dominion of Melchizedek] aside from spiritual work mostly involving the Melchizedek Bible and putting out sporadic uplifting tweets from King of Salem.' The prime minister responded forcefully:

> While the Dominion of Melchizedek cannot control the actions of the former founder of the DoM regarding his spiritual beliefs and his activities relating to such beliefs, we do not condone his spiritual work and such work does

> not reflect the beliefs of the current standing Members of the Dominion of Melchizedek.
>
> The Dominion of Melchizedek hereby denounce the 'Melchizedek Bible' and hereby declare it has no bearing to the functions of administration or philosophy of the current standing sovereign Members of the Dominion of Melchizedek. Mr. Korem [Pedley] can choose to believe and profess what he likes. However, in relation to the Dominion of Melchizedek, his beliefs have no bearing on the functions of the State and are separate and apart from how We conduct ourselves as Members of the Family of Nations.

The dominion's website notes cryptically:

> More Information Will be added as we move forward in clearing up allegations and assumptions about the State's assorted history with an update to a more accurate historical perspective of the individuals that have been involved with the DoM, their departure from any association with the DoM, and the New Sovereign Members of the DoM who are dedicated to being a fully recognized Member of the Family of Nations and devoted to adhering to the Principles espoused within the LAW OF NATIONS.

We should not hold our breath.

AFTERWORD

It seems strange to conclude our story by looking at the dark side of micronationalism. It is important to remember that the four micronations discussed in our final chapter are outliers. Micronations are usually founded as creative attempts to build something new. What they look like depends on the person behind the nation. It could be an effort to create a utopian paradise where you can be a king or queen. It may be a way to build a connection with others and create a community. It might be an opportunity to push for political or legal change. It could also be an opportunity to make art. Micronations are incredibly diverse – even if their founders seem to be almost universally male.

There are exceptions. Ladonia, located on a reserve near the Swedish town of Skåne, is ruled by a queen. In fact, succession is matrilineal. As Queen Carolyn explains, 'Historically, women have gotten the short end of the stick when it comes to being rulers, so Ladonia's founders wanted to reverse that trend. It was also thought that ensuring the throne is occupied by a woman serves as a peaceful and stabilising force for the monarchy.' The Kingdom of Ruritania, based in the US state of Georgia but claiming land in Central Europe, is also led by a queen.

Grand Marshal (right) and First Lady (left) wave to guests at an event marking the fifth anniversary of Obsidia
Ambulatory Free States of Obsidia

Of course, not every micronation operates under a monarchy. The Ambulatory Free States of Obsidia, led by American artist Carolyn Yagjian, is a fitting micronation to close our story. Founded on International Women's Day in 2015, Obsidia describes itself as 'the world's only feminist micronation'. Located at the 'confluence of feminism and geography', the Ambulatory Free States of Obsidia is 'a tiny, matriarchal micronation'. Its 'humble' territory comprises a 900-gram chunk of obsidian rock 'liberated' from the house of a former lover. The micronation has an open border; however, it notes that 'due to size limitations and fragility, humans cannot physically enter the landmass'. As Yagjian explains, 'I've always been attracted to the idea of statehood. And this is an opportunity to question a lot of things people accept as normal about national identity.'

The unusual nature of the micronation serves the purpose of attracting attention to Yagjian's political ideals. Obsidia works with Women on Waves, a Dutch organisation that provides sex education, contraceptives and safe abortion services in international waters off the coast of states where abortion is illegal. 'Borders are the enemy of mutual aid, of autonomy, of feminism, and, indeed, freedom,' Yagjian explains. 'Obsidia wants an international sisterhood, where the only boundaries for women are the ones they mandate over their own bodies.' It is through the weird and wonderful world of micronations that people like Grand Marshal Carolyn Yagjian of the Ambulatory Free States of Obsidia hope to realise their vision for a better future.

NOTES

1 The weird and wonderful world of micronations

Page 1 'Having been cut off from Mosman …': Paul Delprat, 'On micronations' [unpublished conference presentation], PoliNation Conference, Dangar Island, Sydney, 17 April 2010, <https://principalityofwy.com/a-paper-on-the-subject-of-micronations-by-prince-paul-of-wy/>.

Page 2 'I look at it with a degree of wry amusement …': AP, 'Don't like the country you live in? Start your own', *Otago Daily Times*, 6 May 2010, <www.odt.co.nz/lifestyle/magazine/dont-country-you-live-start-your-own>.

Page 2 'somewhat embarrassed': Kelly Burke, '"Why, Willoughby begins with a W, Wy begins with a W, it's all quite wonderful my dear!"', *Daily Telegraph* (Sydney), 14 April 2017, <www.dailytelegraph.com.au/news/nsw/prince-paul-vs-mosman-council-maintaining-a-right-royal-rage/news-story/6f3204a38a81f431e2b0eb9b0a8dc9ef>.

Page 2 'as a beacon of hope …': Matthew Benns, 'Urban prince poised for win over council', *Sun-Herald*, 6 May 2007, <www.smh.com.au/national/urban-prince-poised-for-win-over-council-20070506-gdq2n3.html>.

Page 3 'Unless immediate action is taken on your part …': Azzura Lalani, 'Rebellious "Republic of Rathnelly" celebrates 50 years', *Toronto Star*, 12 June 2017, <www.thestar.com/news/gta/2017/06/12/rebellious-republic-of-rathnelly-celebrates-50-years.html>.

Page 5 'Rathnally we will faithful be …': Rathnelly Republic, *Rathnally the Brave*, Rathnelly Republic website, n.d., <www.rathnellyrepublic.com/history>.

Page 6 Lennon then used the tissue to blow his nose: Laurie Johnston, 'Lennon sees a wide impact in ouster', *New York Times*, 3 April 1973, p. 40.

Page 6 'For countless millennia our planet …': Kingdom of North Sudan, *Declaration of Sovereignty*, Kingdom of North Sudan website, 2014, <www.kingdomsudan.org/page/declaration-of-sovereignty/>.

Page 8 'could offer the world's great innovators …': Jack Shenker, 'Welcome to the land that no country wants', *The Guardian*, 3 March 2016, <www.theguardian.com/world/2016/mar/03/welcome-to-the-land-that-no-country-wants-bir-tawil>.

Page 10 In the 1940s, the International Law Commission … : Material from this paragraph appears in United Nations, *Yearbook of the International Law Commission 1949*, 1st sess, 8th mtg, 22 April 1949, pp. 65 [21], 68 [71], and

Report to the General Assembly, p. 289 [49]; United Nations, *Yearbook of the International Law Commission 1950*, 2nd sess, 52nd mtg, 22 June 1950, p. 84 [22].

Page 11 On the face of it, the list seems clear ... : Quotes from this and the following paragraph appear in James Crawford, *The creation of states in international law*, 2nd edn, Oxford University Press, Oxford, 2007, pp. 197, 63.

Page 13 'the only legitimate representative of China to the United Nations': United Nations General Assembly Resolution 2758, UN Doc A/RES/2758 (25 October 1971).

Page 13 an 'illegal racist minority regime': United Nations Security Council Resolution 216, UN Doc S/RES/216 (12 November 1965) [2].

Page 14 an 'error at birth': Christian Hillgruber, *Die Aufnahme neuer Staaten in die Völkerrechtsgemeinschaft*, Peter Lang GmbH, Frankfurt am Main, 1998, p. 601.

Page 14 In his ground-breaking examination ... : Material from this paragraph appears in Crawford, *The creation of states*, pp. 56, 59.

Page 14 not 'under the legal authority of another state': *Austro-German Customs Union Case* [1931] PCIJ (ser A/B) No 41, 57–8 (Anzilotti J).

Page 15 'states are not innate or physical truths': Tom Sparks, 'State', in Jean d'Aspremont and Sahib Singh (eds), *Concepts for international law: Contributions to disciplinary thought*, Edward Elgar, Cheltenham, UK, 2019, p. 840.

Page 15 a 'state is not a fact in the sense that a chair is a fact': Crawford, *The creation of states*, p. 5.

Page 17 'In an age where people increasingly are unified ...': George Cruickshank, *Atlantium Global Sovereign State*, Empire of Atlantium website, 2020, <www.atlantium.org>.

Page 18 'It's an expression of personal sovereignty': Carmen Machado, 'The imaginary Republic of Molossia', *Vice*, 27 April 2013, <www.vice.com/en_us/article/vdywxm/the-imaginary-republic-of-molossia>.

Page 19 'most audacious fraud in history': David Sinclair, *The land that never was: Sir Gregor MacGregor and the most audacious fraud in history*, Review, London, 2003.

Page 20 Micronations World Map: *Micronations world map*, Google My Maps website, n.d., <www.google.com/maps/d/viewer?msa=0&mid=1VzMWnhHJbOWfCFkaEtTSw_3cNO4&ll=-10.102620343996707%2C-100.46428450000002&z=2>.

Page 20 'a list on Wikipedia ...': Wikipedia, *List of micronations*, Wikimedia Foundation, 2022, <https://en.wikipedia.org/wiki/List_of_micronations>.

Page 20 'online map created by Matthew Hubbard': Matthew Hubbard, *Micronations world map*, Google Earth, n.d., <https://earth.google.com/web/@-1.99921679,0.00000001,63.91320881a,14045213.08685379d,30y,0h,0.00000106t,0r/data=MicKJQojCiExQTB1NDRoSS0tMW5Eb1lIOWVnMWdqeHRqMmtZWmhxTkM>.

Page 21 Some estimates suggest that one-third of all micronations ... : Matt Siegel, 'The royal me: What's with Australia's secession obsession?', *The Atlantic*, April 2012, <www.theatlantic.com/magazine/archive/2012/04/the-royal-me/308912/>.

Page 22 'stigma of convict origins': John Rickard, 'Lovable larrikins and awful ockers', *Journal of Australian Studies*, 1998, 22(56): 78.

Page 22 'the rejection of received opinion ...': Manning Clark, 'Larrikins – the context', in Clem Gorman (ed.), *The larrikin streak: Australian writers look at the legend*, Pan Macmillan, Sydney, 1990, pp. 37, 39.

Page 22 'almost archly self-conscious ...': Clem Gorman, 'Round up the usual suspects', in Gorman (ed.), *The larrikin streak*, p. xiii.

Page 22 'very obedient': John Hirst, *Sense and nonsense in Australian history*, Black Inc., Melbourne, 2009, p. 306.

Page 22 highly sceptical of hierarchy: Geert Hofstede, *Culture's consequences: Comparing values, behaviors, institutions, and organizations across nations*, 2nd edn, Sage, Thousand Oaks, CA, 2001, p. 500.

Page 23 'a romantic and rebellious aspect ...': Bruce Tranter and Jed Donoghue, 'Bushrangers: Ned Kelly and Australian identity', *Journal of Sociology*, 2008, 44(4): 386.

Page 23 'historical embodiment of Australian larrikinism': Catherine Austin and Farida Fozdar, 'Australian national identity: Empirical research since 1998', *National Identities*, 2018, 20(3): 281.

Page 23 'Deep in the psyche of Australians ...': James Gorman, 'Australia's hidden micronations: It's not the size of the country but how you rule it', *9News*, 1 July 2017, <www.9news.com.au/national/australias-hidden-micronations-its-not-the-size-of-the-country-but-how-you-rule-it/59a3a943-3d89-4191-befc-3e864e66f7c9>.

Page 23 'from our convict heritage and disrespect for authority': Justin Norrie, 'His Majesty George II: The boy from Hurstville who now rules a big flat', *Sydney Morning Herald*, 7 May 2004, p. 3.

Page 23 'sustained performance art project': This quote and the next appear in Ewan Gilbert, 'Empire of Atlantium: Take a glimpse into Australia's smallest micronation', *ABC News*, 18 October 2015, <www.abc.net.au/news/2015-10-18/micronation-the-empire-atlantium-boorowa-nsw/6856468>.

Page 25 In 1989, the Duke was elected ...: Parliament of Tasmania, *John Charlton His Grace the Most Noble the Duke of Avram*, Parliament of Tasmania website, 2020, <www.parliament.tas.gov.au/history/members/avram676.html>.

Page 25 There is simply no right to secede: Gregory Craven, *Secession: The ultimate states right*, Melbourne University Press, Melbourne, 1986, p. 81.

Page 27 'examine the option of Western Australia becoming a financially independent state': Eliza Laschon, 'WA Liberal Party votes for watered-down secession motion', *ABC News*, 3 September 2017, <www.abc.net.au/news/2017-09-03/wa-liberal-party-to-form-wa-exit-committee/8867918>.

Page 27 according to one 2020 survey ...: Alexis Carey, 'WAxit: Western Australia Premier Mark McGowan says secession referendum "won't be happening"', *News.com.au*, 8 October 2020, <www.news.com.au/finance/work/leaders/waxit-west-australian-premier-mark-mcgowan-says-secession-referendum-wont-be-happening/news-story/c208f2e54f32c1984fb4bce00d49b31b>.

Page 27 'an essentially ceremonial challenge ...': Craven, *Secession*, p. 9.

Page 27 'We did fully expect the response ...': Siegel, 'The royal me'.

Page 28 'affirmed the Murrawarri Republic ...': Murrawarri Republic, *Queen recognises Murrawarri Republic* [media release], Murrawarri Republic, 10 May 2013, <http://nationalunitygovernment.org/pdf/2013/MurrawarriRepublicMediaRelease10May13.pdf>.

Page 28 'because "there are no constitutional means available ..."': Ian Lloyd Neubauer, 'Australia's Aborigines launch a bold legal push for independence', *TIME*, 30 May 2013, <https://world.time.com/2013/05/30/australias-aborigines-launch-a-bold-legal-push-for-independence/>.

Page 29 Population density figures are complicated ...: Material from this paragraph comes from United Nations, Department of Economic and Social Affairs, Population Dynamics, *World urbanization prospects 2018*, United Nations website, 2018, <https://population.un.org/wup/Country-Profiles/>; Australian Bureau of Statistics, 'How many people live in Australia's coastal areas?', *1301.0 – Year Book Australia, 2004*, ABS website, 27 February 2004, <www.abs.gov.au/Ausstats/abs@.nsf/Previousproducts/1301.0Feature%20Article32004>; Australian Bureau of Statistics, *Population by age and sex, regions of Australia, 2015*, ABS website, 18 August 2016, <www.abs.gov.au/ausstats/abs@.nsf/Previousproducts/3235.0Main%20Features102015?opendocument&tabname=Summary&prodno=3235.0&issue=2015&num=&view=>.

2 'While I Breathe, I Hope': The Principality of Hutt River

Page 30 'Confirming my letter ...': Prince Leonard Casley, telegram to Sir John Kerr, 2 December 1977.

Page 31 'the state of war between our countries has now ceased': Prince Leonard Casley, telegram to Sir John Kerr, 4 December 1977.

Page 31 'pondering its predicament': R.C. Hyslop, *The man: His Royal Highness Prince Leonard Sovereign of the Hutt River Province Principality (an independent sovereign state)*, Hutt River Province Principality, Hutt River, WA, n.d., p. 44.

Page 32 The Australian wheat industry had lurched from one problem to another: Material in this paragraph comes from Wendy Way, *A new idea each morning: How food and agriculture came together in one international organisation*, ANU Press, Canberra, 2013, p. 140; Edgars Dunsdorfs, *The Australian wheat growing industry 1788–1948*, Melbourne University Press, Melbourne, 1956, pp. 270–275.

Page 33 Perhaps it was there where he refined his independent streak: Material in this paragraph appears in Norimitsu Onishi, 'Rewards for rebellion: Tiny nation and crown for life', *New York Times*, 1 February 2011, <www.nytimes.com/2011/02/02/world/asia/02australia.html>.

Page 35 'This Quota will not pay the interest ...': Leonard Casley, letter to the Wheat Quotas Committee of Western Australia, 3 November 1969.

Page 35 'Our families in receiving a quota ...': Leonard Casley, letter to Sir Douglas Kendrew, 3 November 1969.

Page 36 'I will not have my family reduced to a state of begging': Leonard Casley, letter to the Minister for Agriculture, 14 November 1969.

Page 36 'of a basic minimum income depending on season ...': Leonard Casley, letter to Sir Douglas Kendrew, 3 November 1969.

Page 36 Considering that 'a claim of compensation is justified': Leonard Casley, letter to Sir David Brand, 3 November 1969.

Page 36 'The land we would propose is a reserve and station country ...': Leonard Casley, letter to Sir Douglas Kendrew, 3 November 1969.

Page 37 'that was the real catalyst': AAP, 'Hutt River Province "prince" Leonard Casley to abdicate', *PerthNow*, 1 February 2017, <www.perthnow.com.au/news/wa/hutt-river-province-prince-leonard-casley-to-abdicate-ng-372efb2cf22dccd8fdfed3b3c598ad08>.

Page 37 'We seceded to protect our lands ...': Andrew Heaton, 'Prince of the outback', *Reason*, June 2013, <https://reason.com/2013/05/14/prince-of-the-outback/>.

Page 37 'Fate Accompli ...': Leonard Casley, letter to Sir David Brand, 21 April 1970.

Page 38 'give formal recognition to our independence ...': Leonard Casley, letter to John Gorton, 23 April 1970; Leonard Casley, letter to Sir Paul Hasluck, 23 April 1970.

Page 38 'I would rather that a position of mutual co-operation ...': Leonard Casley, letter to Sir David Brand, 23 April 1970.

Page 40 'Mr. Casley has written to the Prime Minister ...': R.N. Townsend, letter to Mr Ryan, director-general of the Postmaster-General's Department, 6 August 1970.

Page 40 'with interest': D.R.M. Thompson, letter to Leonard Casley, 19 June 1970.

Page 40 'Administrator, Hutt River Province': John Tonkin, letter to Leonard Casley, 5 October 1970.

Page 40 'Your comments on the constitutional aspects...': Ian Thompson, letter to Leonard Casley, 21 October 1971.

Page 41 'I would like to make it quite clear that the Commonwealth Government ...': William McMahon, letter to John Tonkin, 10 December 1971.

Page 41 'The Commonwealth Government has removed ...': Western Australia Premier's Department, *Hutt River* [media release], A71/324, WA Government, 17 December 1971.

Page 41 'Mr. Casley's land is just as much a part of the State of Western Australia ...': Western Australia Premier's Department, [untitled media release], P73/284, WA Government, 6 July 1973.

Page 41 'The State's jurisdiction is beyond ...': Western Australia, *Parliamentary Debates*, Legislative Assembly, 9 April 1975, p. 672 (Sir Charles Court, premier).

Page 42 'I should like to make perfectly clear to you ...': Gough Whitlam, letter to Leonard Casley, 10 March 1975.

Page 42 'There is a giant lying in the sun...': Reproduced in Jane Cadzow, 'Prince and the pawpaws: At the court of Prince Kevin', *Sydney Morning Herald*, 20 February 1993, p. 162.

Page 46 Menadue asked each department ...: John Menadue, letter to all permanent heads of department, 12 January 1976.

Page 46 the 'economic embargo': 'Australia is "belligerent" to province', *Sunday Times*, 6 January 1974, p. 27.

Page 46 Australia Post officials were forced to explain ...: W.A. Johnston, General Manager, Marketing Services Department, Australia Post, letter to State Manager, Australia Post Western Australia, 10 June 1976.

Page 47 a 'crank' and 'eccentric': Director Posts and Telegraphs, memorandum to ministerial representatives, 3 July 1970.

Page 48 The Premier sought advice as to how this could be shut down: John Tonkin, letter to William McMahon, 31 August 1971.

Page 48 'Broken Serenity: The Ballad of Hutt River': Composed by 'R.M. Müller/Newton' – the recording's liner notes mention 'Rita Pope' as the writer, and 'Newton' is possibly Ranting Lads' member Dobe Newton – and recorded by The Ranting Lads, produced by Warren Gillespie, Frog Gruntwell Recordings, FG-0585, date unknown, <www.45cat.com/record/fg0585>. All efforts have been made to contact the copyright holder for permission to reproduce the lyrics.

Page 51 'Here there are no peasants, serfs or even a middle class': Richard Palfreyman, 'The House of Casley', *Weekend Magazine*, ABC TV, 13 May 1973.

Page 51 'Andorra has been having legal arguments ...': Peter Argo, 'Our Prince Leonard of Hutt hands out visa', *The Australian*, 23 October 1973.

Page 51 'the government was trying to make ... a pauper': 'Australia: The Prince of Hutt River', *Time*, 16 June 1975, <http://content.time.com/time/subscriber/article/0,33009,917529,00.html>.

Page 51 the 'farming Don Quixote': Material in this paragraph is translated from 'Der selbsternannte "Prinz Leonard": "Unabhängigkeitserklärung" eines australischen Farmers', *Neue Zürcher Zeitung*, 10 September 1976.

Page 52 'Who among us in Tasmania ...': This quote and the next appear in Lionel Miller, 'Secede becomes more than word – Achievement is a reality', *The Mercury*, 13 April 1976.

Page 53 transform the 'tiny independent state' from a 'backwater': Charles Westberg, 'Hongkong aid sought: Prince's big plans', *South China Sunday Post-Herald*, 21 July 1974, p. 2.

Page 54 'a State visit': Phil Ackman, 'The second biggest country in Australia: Hutt River Province', *Australian Penthouse*, August 1982, p. 83.

Page 54 The Thirtyniners' Association : Thos H. Parker, federal secretary, Thirtyniners Association, letter to William McMahon, 24 November 1972; Parker, letter to Gough Whitlam, 19 January 1973.

Page 54 In 1979, Michael Hodgman ...: Michael Hodgman, letter to Malcolm Fraser, 6 September 1979.

Page 54 'There has never been a "Hutt River Province" ...': P.F. McDonald, letter to J. Atkinson, secretary, Department of Prime Minister and Cabinet, 21 September 1979.

Page 55 'the issue of these "passports" ...': International Criminal Police Organisation, letter to Secretary, Department of Foreign Affairs, 17 June 1977.

Page 55 The Bolivian government was 'puzzled': J.R. Kelso, Australian ambassador to Bolivia, letter to Secretary, Department of Foreign Affairs, 10 November 1976; Kelso, letter to Roberto Pacheco Herztog, director-general of Ceremonial, Bolivian Ministry of Foreign Affairs and Worship, 10 November 1976.

Page 56 The Swiss Government was 'genuinely puzzled': This quote and the following block quote appear in John Mallett, General Legal Section, Department of Foreign Affairs, memorandum to Mr Vincent and Mr Matthews, Department of Foreign Affairs, 21 May 1976.

Page 57 'I think some people are misled': Western Australia, *Parliamentary Debates*, Legislative Assembly, 9 April 1975, p. 672 (Sir Charles Court, premier).

Page 57 the Australian public may have seen this as mean-spirited and unnecessary: Memorandum from W.H. Bray, assistant secretary general, Legal and Treaties Branch, Department of Foreign Affairs, 29 July 1977.

Page 57 'the Government may look stupid, while he exists …': Patrick O'Neill, *This Day Tonight*, ABC TV, 1 July 1976.

Page 57 A Canadian newspaper dedicated an entire page …: Jack Spearman, 'Meet Hutt's Alberta Consul', publication unknown.

Page 58 the 'response was incredible': Cadzow, 'Prince and the pawpaws', p. 162.

Page 58 '"Hutt River Province?" …': Ackman, 'The second biggest country in Australia', p. 83.

Page 59 the Shah of Iran: 'Iran sends greetings', *The Sunday Times*, 27 January 1974.

Page 59 'Her Majesty's good wishes to you …': Sonia Bonici, senior correspondence officer, Buckingham Palace, letter to Prince Leonard, 16 April 2016.

Page 59 'finally received an official nod': See, for example, Chris Pash, 'This 46-year-old Australian micronation has finally been recognised by Buckingham Palace', *Business Insider*, 21 April 2016, <www.businessinsider.com.au/australias-oldest-micronation-finally-gets-recognition-from-buckingham-palace-2016-4>.

Page 59 In at least one instance, Prince Leonard did manage to successfully fool a state: Tony Walker, 'Hong Kong accolade for Hutt River', *Sydney Morning Herald*, 16 March 1982, p. 10.

Page 60 At another time, Prince Leonard himself was fooled: 'Salaam to Hutt River', *Sunday Times*, 20 January 1974.

Page 61 Over the years, Leonard Casley and his family appeared in Australian courts: Material in this paragraph appears in Hugh Schmitt, 'Talk of war: "Prince" and the council', *Sydney Morning Herald*, 25 February 1973, p. 73; 'Hutt River huff over fines', *Sydney Morning Herald*, 25 May 1974, p. 3.

Page 62 A few years later Casley had his first successful court battle: Material in this and the following paragraph appears in '"Prince" is taxable', *Sydney Morning Herald*, 16 February 1977, p. 3; Hugh Schmitt, 'The Prince of Hutt gets tough', *Sydney Morning Herald*, 22 January 1978; Marilyn Duff, 'The "prince" shows a profit for his principles', *Sydney Morning Herald*, 1 February 1980, p. 15; *Casley v Commonwealth* [1980] WASC 3 (11 January 1980) (Wickham J).

Page 62 Graciously, Leonard Casley wrote to prime minister Malcolm Fraser: R.C. Hyslop, *The man: His Royal Highness Prince Leonard Sovereign of the Hutt River Province Principality (an independent sovereign state)*, Hutt River Province Principality, Hutt River, WA, n.d., p. 45.

Page 63 around 40 000 tourists: Sean Murphy, 'The mouse that roared', *ABC Landline*, ABC TV, 18 April 2010, <www.abc.net.au/landline/the-mouse-that-roared/400444>.

Page 63 Justice Dyson Heydon found …: *Casley v Commissioner of Taxation* [2007] HCATrans 590 (4 October 2007) (Heydon J).

Page 63 Justice Rene Le Miere ...: *Deputy Commissioner of Taxation v Casley* [2017] WASC 161, [15] and [5] (16 June 2017) (Le Miere J).

Page 64 'One day someone will do something about him': O'Neill, *This Day Tonight*.

Page 64 'stuck his nose up, even his finger, at the Federal Government ...': Laura Meachim and Glenn Barndon, 'Hutt River Province celebrates its 50th Anniversary as Western Australia's micronation', *ABC News*, 21 April 2020, <www.abc.net.au/news/2020-04-21/hutt-river-marks-fifty-years-but-is-the-micronation-dream-over/12166302>.

Page 64 he challenged the bureaucracy of the day: Natasha Harradine, 'Prince Leonard, who founded Hutt River Province after stoush with WA Government, dies aged 93', *ABC News*, 13 February 2019, <www.abc.net.au/news/2019-02-13/prince-leonard-who-founded-hutt-river-province-dies-aged-93/10808236>.

3 'From the Sea, Freedom': The Principality of Sealand

This chapter draws on material from Dylan Taylor-Lehman, *Sealand: The true story of the world's most stubborn micronation*, Icon Books, London, 2020, pp. 5–13; James Grimmelmann, 'Sealand, HavenCo, and the rule of law', *University of Illinois Law Review*, 2012, 2: 405; and Adrian Johns, *Death of a pirate: British radio and the making of the information age*, W.W. Norton & Co, New York/London, 2011.

Page 67 'to interests other than the Ministry': 'Army blows up pirate fort', *The Times* (London), 22 August 1967, p. 1.

Page 67 The demolition crew sailed past Roughs Tower: Taylor-Lehman, *Sealand*, p. 44.

Page 67 'Meet Roy Bates ...': Roy Bates' biography draws on Taylor-Lehman, *Sealand*, ch. 1; 'Prince Roy of Sealand', *The Telegraph* (London), 11 October 2012; Martin Wainwright, 'Major Roy Bates's obituary', *The Guardian*, 13 October 2012.

Page 70 'cultural improvement': Johns, *Death of a pirate*, ch. 1; Taylor-Lehman, *Sealand*, p. 3.

Page 70 Despite being a 'technical failure' ...: Johns, *Death of a pirate*, p. 38.

Page 70 'thousands of people' flocked to hear the 'musical yacht': 'Musical yacht', *Daily Mail*, 13 July 1928; 'The musical yacht: Look out for the Ceto', *Daily Mail*, 4 July 1928.

Page 71 'some stations were said to individually bring in upwards of £20,000 each month': This quote and the following quote appear in Taylor-Lehman, *Sealand*, p. 27.

Page 71 'they are beyond territorial waters ...': Bernard Jordan, 'I go aboard the pirate pop ship', *Daily Mail*, 31 March 1964, cited in John Venmore-Rowland, *Radio Caroline: The story of the first British off-shore radio station*, Landmark Press, Lavenham, UK, 1967, p. 37.

Page 71 'mumbling Ministers', 'the fort squatters', 'the forts are a scandal ...': A.P. Herbert, 'The pirate forts' [letter to the editor], *The Times* (London), 13 July 1966, p. 13.

Page 71 'a kind of mild anarchy ruled the airwaves': Grimmelmann, 'Sealand, HavenCo, and the rule of law', p. 415.

Page 72 'a disc jockey has to be many things ...': Taylor-Lehman, *Sealand*, p. 28.

Page 72 His appeal was dismissed the following year: *R v Kent Justices, Ex parte Lye* [1967] 2 QB 153.

Page 74 'Mr. Bates said that Tuesday night's raid ...': 'Sea fort repels boarders: Raiders faced flamethrower', *The Times* (London), 30 June 1967, p. 2.

Page 74 'one man was left hanging over the North Sea ...': 'Struggle for sea fort', *The Times* (London), 28 June 1967, p. 1; '100GNS health trips to sea fort', *The Times* (London), 29 June 1967, p. 2; 'Commandos set to seize fort', *The Times* (London), 8 August 1967, p. 1.

Page 74 'getting himself a bit of reputation...': Michael Bates, *Holding the fort: The extraordinary true story of piracy and violence starting our own country on a fortress island in international waters* [Kindle], Principality of Sealand, 2015.

Page 74 'to end gang warfare on pirate radio stations': United Kingdom, *Parliamentary Debates*, House of Commons, 3 July 1967, vol. 749, col. 191.

Page 74 Advertisers abandoned the pirates: See Taylor-Lehman, *Sealand*, p. 44.

Page 75 'Now you have your very own island': This quote and the next appear in Ian Urbina, 'The pint-size nation off the English coast', *The Atlantic*, 15 August 2019, <www.theatlantic.com/international/archive/2019/08/sealand-outlaw-ocean-tiniest-nation/596074/>.

Page 75 'My solicitors are studying the legal aspects ...': 'Sea fort repels boarders'.

Page 75 Life was hard on Sealand ...: Material and quotes in this section are drawn from Bates, *Holding the fort*; Taylor-Lehman, *Sealand*, pp. 51–53.

Page 75 'like hell on Earth ...': Taylor-Lehman, *Sealand*, p. 51.

Page 76 'It was hours and hours from Paglesham ...': Taylor-Lehman, *Sealand*, p. 52.

Page 77 'ludicrous. Mr. Bates is trespassing ...': 'Independent isle "ludicrous"', *The Times* (London), 4 September 1967, p. 3.

Page 77 'to prevent it falling into the hands of foreign interests': Grimmelmann, 'Sealand, HavenCo, and the rule of law', p. 420; 'Commandos set to seize fort', *The Times* (London), 8 August 1967, p. 1.

Page 78 'implausible', 'prepared to take the Fort over': Grimmelmann, 'Sealand, HavenCo, and the rule of law', p. 422; Taylor-Lehman, *Sealand*, pp. 57–58.

Page 79 Bates jumped on the news, leaking the story: Kenneth Clarke and James Allan, 'Ministry planned to seize sea fort', *Daily Telegraph* (London), 30 May 1968.

Page 79 the matter was raised in parliament: United Kingdom, *Parliamentary Debates*, House of Commons, 18 December 1968, vol. 775, col. 377.

Page 79 'marooned' his children: 'Radio man's children "marooned", *The Times* (London), 7 March 1968, p. 3.

Page 79 Bates had merely to 'hire another boat': 'Children "not marooned", *The Times* (London), 8 March 1968, p. 3.

Page 79 'huge undertaking for a relatively small purpose …': Taylor-Lehman, *Sealand*, p. 40.

Page 80 'It was decided not to take advantage of Mr Bates' attendance in Court …': Grimmelmann, 'Sealand, HavenCo, and the rule of law', p. 423.

Page 80 The government had missed its opportunity: Quotes from the court decision appear in *R v Bates*, The Shire Hall, Chelmsford (25 October 1968).

Page 81 'the beautiful Princess Joan of Sealand': Quotes in this paragraph appear in Gordon McGill, 'The princess on sentry go', *Sunday Mirror*, 27 October 1968, p. 11.

Page 81 'doing no actual harm …': UK Government, Cabinet Office, *Minutes of Meeting Re: Roughs Tower*, 5 November 1968, cited in Grimmelmann, 'Sealand, HavenCo, and the rule of law', p. 423.

Page 81 'there was some advantage in refraining from prosecutions': Taylor-Lehman, *Sealand*, p. 61.

Page 83 conducting a 'diplomatic offensive': Taylor-Lehman, *Sealand*, p. 70.

Page 83 'No one knows why various European businessmen …': Grant Hibberd, 'The last great adventure of the twentieth century: The Sealand affair in British diplomacy', *Britain and the World*, 2011, 4(2): 272.

Page 83 'asked the Australian Embassy for visas in their Sealand passports': Grimmelmann, 'Sealand, HavenCo, and the rule of law', p. 425.

Page 84 'the United Nations is an organisation of governments, not gun platforms': Taylor-Lehman, *Sealand*, p. 70.

Page 84 'engaging in fraudulent business based in an imaginary country': Taylor-Lehman, *Sealand*, p. 70; Grimmelmann, 'Sealand, HavenCo, and the rule of law', p. 426.

Page 84 'Luxembourg's financial name should not be sullied …': Taylor-Lehman, *Sealand*, p. 71.

Page 84 The court rejected his petition: *In re Duchy of Sealand* (1978) 80 ILR 683.

Page 85 'light weapons should be installed to fend off enemies': This quote and the following quote appear in Katrin Langhans, 'Newer Sealand', *Süddeutsche Zeitung*, 25 April 2016, <https://panamapapers.sueddeutsche.de/articles/57207ab2a1bb8d3c3495bd29/>.

Page 86 In a pre-dawn raid …: Material in this paragraph is drawn from Bates, *Holding the fort*.

Page 86 'Is there any chance of a British patrol vessel "passing by" the Fort …': Urbina, 'The pint-size nation off the English coast'.

Page 87 'The German national Gernot Ernst Putz is being held prisoner ...': Taylor-Lehman, *Sealand*, p. 79.

Page 87 'outside British jurisdiction': McGill, 'The princess on sentry go'. See further Grimmelmann, 'Sealand, HavenCo, and the rule of law', p. 429; Taylor-Lehman, *Sealand*, p. 79; 'Secret government Sealand revelations', *Ipswich Star*, 31 December 2008, <www.ipswichstar.co.uk/news/secret-government-sealand-revelations-1-169303>.

Page 88 'I've killed a lot of Germans in my time': Taylor-Lehman, *Sealand*, p. 428 n. 191; Taylor-Lehman, *Sealand*, p. 80.

Page 88 'could not understand why the British authorities appeared unable to unwilling to intervene': Dan van der Vat, 'Appeal by wife of "Sealand" prisoner', *The Times* (London), 6 September 1978, p. 2.

Page 88 Sealand's new foreign minister: 'German is freed from Sealand in North Sea', *The Times* (London), 29 September 1978, p. 4. See also 'Attempt to free captive from private "island" fails', *The Times* (London), 5 September 1978, p. 3.

Page 89 'is it not the case that what this time may be a harmless and colourful escapade ...': United Kingdom, *Parliamentary Debates*, House of Lords, 5 December 1978, vol. 397, col. 5–6.

Page 90 'their own "Malvinas" right on Britain's doorstep': This quote and the following two quotes appear in Taylor-Lehman, *Sealand*, pp. 88, 67.

Page 91 'In a raid on the ring's offices ...': Adela Gooch, 'Police swoop on Sealand crime ring', *The Guardian*, 12 April 2000, <www.theguardian.com/world/2000/apr/12/3>.

Page 91 Several countries appeared to have been taken in by Sealand 'ambassadors': 'Storm warning', *The Guardian*, 28 March 2000, <www.theguardian.com/theguardian/2000/mar/28/features11.g2>.

Page 91 'a $50 million deal ...': Urbina, 'The pint-size nation off the English coast'. See also Langhans, 'Newer Sealand', and Jo Bowman, 'Officials in dark on claims 4,000 hit by passport scam', *South China Morning Post*, 16 April 2000, <www.scmp.com/article/314252/officials-dark-claims-4000-hit-passport-scam>.

Page 92 'We're very vulnerable – we are the smallest state in the world': 'Storm warning'.

Page 92 'no-questions-asked data storage web hosting and encrypted communication': Taylor-Lehman, *Sealand*, p. 109; Grimmelmann, 'Sealand, HavenCo, and the rule of law', pp. 445–457. See further Nate Anderson, *Internet police: How crime went online, and the cops followed*, W.W. Norton & Co, New York, 2014.

Page 92 'a combination of first-world infrastructure and third-world regulation': Grimmelmann, 'Sealand, HavenCo, and the rule of law', p. 451.

Page 92 'HavenCo will allow for gambling, pyramid schemes ...': Simson Garfinkel, 'Welcome to Sealand. Now bugger off.', *Wired*, 1 July 2000, <www.wired.com/2000/07/haven-2/>.

Page 93 'right now, we aren't even concerned with something like Sealand': Taylor-Lehman, *Sealand*, p. 116.

Page 93 'was bad for Sealand's image and quest for sovereignty': Grimmelmann, 'Sealand, HavenCo, and the rule of law', pp. 455–456.

Page 93 'Then they can keep running WikiLeaks and nobody can touch them': Jana Winter and Jeremy Kaplan, 'Exclusive: WikiLeaks to move servers offshore, sources say', *Fox News*, 31 January 2012, <www.foxnews.com/tech/exclusive-wikileaks-to-move-servers-offshore-sources-say>.

Page 94 the 'path of purity [they] would endeavour to walk': Taylor-Lehman, *Sealand*, p. 73.

Page 95 'replete with a teller window and a banner reading "Post Office"': Taylor-Lehman, *Sealand*, p. 97.

Page 96 'you can't be a real country unless you have a beer and an airline': Frank Zappa, *The real Frank Zappa book*, Simon & Schuster, New York, 1989, p. 231.

Page 96 CONIFA has rejected Sealand's application ...: Matthew Engel, 'World Football Cup an alternative to Fifa and a lesson in geopolitics', *The Guardian*, 2 June 2018, <www.theguardian.com/football/2018/jun/01/world-football-cup-alternative-fifa-lesson-geopolitics>.

Page 97 'Our story still fires people up ...': Mike MacEacheran, 'Sealand: A peculiar "nation" off England's coast', *BBC Travel*, 6 July 2020, <www.bbc.com/travel/article/20200706-sealand-a-peculiar-nation-off-englands-coast>.

Page 98 'with a faint gurgling sound': Urbina, 'The pint-size nation off the English coast'.

4 Libertarian paradise: The Republic of Minerva

Page 100 The Republic of Minerva – Land of the Rising Atoll, was born: Lawrence Horn, 'To be or not to be: The Republic of Minerva: Nation founding by individuals', *Columbia Journal of Transnational Law*, 2013, 12: 520–528; Samuel Menefee, '"Republics of the reefs": Nation-building on the continental shelf and in the world's oceans', *California Western International Law Journal*, 1994, 25(1): 95–102.

Page 100 On the top of the marker, they raised a flag ...: President Morris Davis explains that 'the blue represents the sea, while a golden torch of freedom "I guess is for our economic system", in Roy Bongartz, 'How to launch a country', *The Saturday Review*, 17 February 1973, pp. 10, 11.

Page 102 a 'fascist-socialist' state: Peter du Bois, 'Utopia on the rocks: Or, the short, unhappy life of the Republic of Minerva', *Barron's National Business and Financial Weekly*, 26 March 1973, p. 5.

Page 102 'enough collectivist clauses to ensure a steady drift toward totalitarianism': Michael Oliver, *A new Constitution for a new country*, Fine Arts Press, Reno, NV, 1968, p. 5.

Page 102 a 'genuine underground bestseller, selling over 20,000 copies': Anthony van Fossen, *Tax havens and sovereignty in the Pacific Islands*, University of Queensland ePress, Brisbane, 2012, p. 110.

Page 102 'Government, under this constitution, can be construed as a private corporation ...': Michael Oliver, *A new Constitution for a new country*, p. 105 (emphasis in original).

Page 103 'Only 200 years have elapsed since the idea of the necessity to separate church and state ...': Bongartz, 'How to launch a country', pp. 10–11.

Page 103 'The first thing is to limit government only to protection against force and fraud': 'Designing a free country: An interview with Mike Oliver', *Reason*, December 1972, p. 5 (emphasis in original).

Page 104 'A surprising number of nearly uninhabited, yet quite suitable places ...': Oliver, *A new Constitution for a new country*, pp. 21, 22.

Page 104 'morally on par with forced labor': Robert Nozick, *Anarchy, state, and utopia*, Basic Books, New York, 1974, p. 169.

Page 105 'it could be drowned in a bathtub': Ed Kilgore, 'Starving the beast', *Blueprint Magazine*, 30 June 2003.

Page 105 'from high taxes, riots, drugs and crime': AP, 'South Sea reef proclaimed a republic by 3 Americans', *New York Times*, 30 January 1972, p. 11.

Page 105 'none of these efforts has succeeded': Lynn Kinsky and Robert Poole, 'Abaco: Birth of a new country?', *Reason*, October 1974, <https://reason.com/1974/10/01/abaco/>.

Page 106 'a new libertarian polity needed its own sovereign powers': van Fossen, *Tax havens and sovereignty*, pp. 111–112.

Page 106 The Minerva Reefs take their name from a whaling ship: Material in this paragraph is drawn from Lili Song, 'The curious history of the Minerva Reefs: Tracing the origin of Tongan and Fijian claims over the Minerva Reefs', *Journal of Pacific History*, 2019, 54(3): 417.

Page 107 would 'sparkle like a jewel in the blue South Pacific': Roy Bongartz, 'Nations off the beaten track', *New York Times*, 28 March 1976, p. 292.

Page 107 'the new nation could compete with Liberia and Panama ...': du Bois, 'Utopia on the rocks', p. 24.

Page 107 a 'new Venice' of perhaps 30,000 settlers: 'Designing a free country'.

Page 107 it is not clear whether they would be offered (or allowed to take up) citizenship: van Fossen, *Tax havens and sovereignty*, pp. 111–112.

Page 108 'investors showed little interest': Erwin Strauss, *How to start your own country*, 3rd edn, Paladin Press, Boulder, CO, 1999, p. 116.

Page 108 a 'peaceful and free republican system of government in adherence to democratic principles': Horn, 'To be or not to be', p. 524.

Page 108 'only one head of state, His Majesty The Sultan of Occussi-Ambeno ...': du Bois, 'Utopia on the rocks', p. 24; Horn, 'To be or not to be', p. 526; van Fossen, *Tax havens and sovereignty*, p. 113.

Page 109 sending an emissary to neighbouring Tonga: Quotes in this paragraph appear in Doug Jenkins, 'A true record of the Minerva Reef saga of 1972 and the part played by the Tongan Shipping Company vessel Olovaha', *Queen of the Isles*, n.d., <www.queenoftheisles.com/HTML/Republic of Minerva.html>.

Page 109 'people will be free to do as they damn well please': Mark Parsons, 'Ashes to ashes', *The New Internationalist*, July 1981, p. 101, <https://newint.org/features/1981/07/01/phoenix>.

Page 110 'I have long dreamed of buying an island owned by no nation ...': Harry Blustein, 'The libertarian dream was tried here', *History News Network*, 15 October 2017, <http://historynewsnetwork.org/article/166946>.

Page 110 'the world's most unusual new country ...': 'The Republic of Minerva coin', *Libertarian Review*, December 1975, IV(12): 11.

Page 110 The Kingdom of Tonga in particular had a connection to the reefs: Material in this and the following paragraph draws from Song, 'The curious history of the Minerva Reefs', p. 420. See also 'Minerva Reef: 1962 mishap', *Fiji Times*, 15 November 2020, pp. 16–17.

Page 112 'If these people can claim Minerva ...': 'Minerva Reefs "republic" fails to impress PM', *Fiji Times*, 28 January 1972, p. 1; Robert Trumbull, 'Pacific Islanders fight reef plan', *New York Times*, 27 February 1972, p. 5.

Page 112 'all other reefs in the ocean would start announcing themselves as independent nations': Bongartz, 'How to launch a country', p. 16.

Page 113 'Tonga would always look upon the reefs with special concern and had strong feelings about any claim': 'Tonga opposes reef "republic"', *Tongan Chronicle*, 3 February 1972, p. 1.

Page 113 New Zealand 'seemed generally too busy to care': Horn, 'To be or not to be', p. 526.

Page 113 'Heaven forbid for this kind of thing to happen': 'South Seas: The Minerva ploy', *Newsweek*, 23 October 1972, p. 52.

Page 113 Tonga's 'longstanding connection with the reefs': Tongan Ministry of Information and Communications, *1972: Mission to Minerva*, 22 March 2010.

Page 113 the issue was considered further at the South Pacific Forum: Material in this paragraph is drawn from South Pacific Forum, *Leaders' Communique*, Canberra, 23–25 February 1972; Trumbull, 'Pacific Islanders fight reef plan'.

Page 114 'it was in the best interest of Tonga ...': 'King goes to Minerva Reefs to investigate', *Tonga Chronicle*, 1 June 1972, p. 1.

Page 114 'to build a permanent structure above high water': Song, 'The curious history of the Minerva Reefs', p. 423; Menefee, '"Republics of the reefs", p. 100.

Page 114 Ninety convict labourers were sent to the reefs: 'King to lead flag raising on Teleki on Monday', *Tonga Chronicle*, 22 June 1972; 'Republic of Minerva', *Pacific Islands Monthly*, July 1972, 43(7): 121.

Page 114 'WHEREAS the Reefs known as North Minerva Reef and South Minerva Reef ...': Tonga Royal Proclamation, 15 June 1972.

Page 115 'had just completed an engineering survey': 'Designing a free country'.

Page 116 Upon my arrival in Nuku'alofa: Bongartz, 'How to launch a country', p. 16.

Page 116 'We can't for the life of us understand why ...': Song, 'The curious history of the Minerva Reefs', p. 423; Bongartz, 'How to launch a country'.

Page 116 The Ocean Life Research Foundation issued a press release: 'Minerva update', *Reason*, October 1972, <https://reason.com/1972/10/01/trends-160/>.

Page 116 'an airline, low-voltage television station ...': van Fossen, *Tax havens and sovereignty*, p. 113.

Page 117 'Members of the Forum recognised Tonga's historical association ...': South Pacific Forum, *Leaders' Communiqué*, Suva, 12–14 September 1972.

Page 117 the Fijian navy has reportedly destroyed ...: See for example Michael Field, 'Fiji, Tonga war over Minerva Reef', *Stuff*, 16 May 2011, <www.stuff.co.nz/world/south-pacific/5008060/Fiji-Tonga-war-over-Minerva-Reef>.

Page 117 After Oliver gave up, a memo was issued by a man styling himself as Major Travers: Strauss, *How to start your own country*, pp. 117–118.

Page 118 they were expelled by the Tongan military: Philip Hayward, 'Oecusse and the Sultanate of Occussi-Ambeno: Pranksterism, misrepresentation and micronationality', *Small States & Territories*, 2019, 2(2): 188.

Page 118 'more or less reclaimed by the sea': Katherine Mangu-Ward, 'Hope floats', *Reason*, August/September 2008, p. 72.

Page 118 a hastily formed 'Greater Abaco Council': Material in this paragraph is drawn from Rick Lowe, *Forgotten dreams: A people's desire to chart their own course on Abaco, Bahamas*, Nassau Institute, Bahamas, July 2010, p. 8.

Page 119 'the outspoken black nationalism of a few members of the Pindling Government': Richard Severo, 'Some in Bahamas prefer the Queen to independence', *New York Times*, 8 July 1973, p. 18.

Page 119 Local militias flew to facilities in Florida and Georgia: Andrew St. George, 'The amazing new-country caper: Capitalist revolution, the ultimate solution', *Esquire*, 1 February 1975, <https://classic.esquire.com/article/1975/2/1/the-amazing-new-country-caper>.

Page 119 under the auspices of Mitchell WerBell III: Raymond Craib, *Adventure Capitalism: A history of libertarian exit, from the era of decolonization to the digital age* (PM Press, 2022).

Page 119 the British would not intervene to prevent the 'harassed' Abaconians: United Kingdom, *Parliamentary Debates*, House of Lords, 10 June 1974, vol. 352, col. 227–230.

Page 119 The first issue of the *Abaco Independent*: Material in this paragraph and the following block quote appears in Kinsky and Poole, 'Abaco: Birth of a new country?'.

Page 120 Oliver and WerBell outlined their plans in a briefing to a potential investor: Quotes from this briefing appear in St. George, 'The amazing new-country caper'.

Page 122 WerBell may also have been connected to the Watergate break-in: van Fossen, *Tax havens and sovereignty*, pp. 115–116; John Beasant, *The Santo Rebellion: An imperial reckoning*, University of Hawaii Press, Honolulu, 1984, p. 54; Kinsky and Poole, 'Abaco: Birth of a new country?'.

Page 122 were left to rot in a southern Florida warehouse: Strauss, *How to start your own country*, p. 119.

Page 122 the 'pandemonium': David Robie, *Blood on their banner: Nationalist struggles in the South Pacific*, Pluto Press, Sydney, 1989, p. 68.

Page 123 'Vemarana Development Corporation' that was to run the island: R.T. Naylor, *Hot money and the politics of debt*, McGill-Queen's University Press, Montreal, 2004, p. 44.

Page 123 In May 1980, Stevens seized Espiritu Santo ...: Patrick Cox, 'Wun niu fela kuntri', *Reason*, September 1980, <https://reason.com/1980/09/01/wun-niu-fela-kuntri/>.

Page 123 Stevens' troops were armed with 'spears, bows and arrows and a few submachine guns': R.W. Apple Jr., 'New Hebrides calling for help to put down rebellion', *New York Times*, 31 May 1980, p. 11.

Page 123 'Some reports say Mr Stevens' rebellion ...': AP, 'New Hebrides rebel urges peace', *New York Times*, 9 June 1980, p. 10.

Page 123 In response to inquiries about his role: The two quotes in this paragraph appear in Joseph Treaster, 'U.S. land developer aids New Hebrides dissidents', *New York Times*, 7 June 1980, p. 20.

Page 124 was permanently banned from entering Vanuatu: van Fossen, *Tax havens and sovereignty*, p. 126; 'Vemarana in a nut shell', the *New York Times*, 8 June 1980, p. 18.

Page 125 'independence-minded' people on the Isle of Man: Strauss, *How to start your own country*, p. 122.

Page 125 'entangled in bureaucracy, corruption, and the free lunch philosophy': This quote and the following appear in 'Oceania', *Reason*, June 1993, pp. 50, 51.

5 Liberty on the high seas: Reef republics and seasteads

Material on the Grand and Triumph Reefs is drawn from Adam Clanton, 'The men who would be kings: Forgotten challenges to US sovereignty', *Pacific Basin Law Journal*, 2008, 26(1): 12–15; Imogen Saunders, 'Artificial islands and territory in international law', *Vanderbilt Journal of Transnational Law*, 2019, 52: 670–671.

Page 127 the reefs were 'outside the Constitutional Boundaries of the State of Florida ...': This quote and the next two appear in *Atlantis Development Corporation v United States*, 379 F.2d 818, 820, 821 (5th Circuit 1967).

Page 127 'to hold and own and develop ...': William T. Anderson, 'Classified notice', *Orlando Evening Star*, 23 November 1962, p. 7.

Page 127 Anderson envisioned a 'new sovereign nation' ...: Material in this paragraph is drawn from *United States v Ray*, 294 F.Supp. 532, 535–536 (S.D. Fla. 1969) and 'New Atlantis, Isle of Gold', *Orlando Evening Star*, 19 January 1963, p. 4.

Page 128 'I went out there and I sat on that island': *United States v Ray* (1969), 535; see also 'Ocean law: Homesteading at sea', *Time*, 24 January 1969, <https://content.time.com/time/subscriber/article/0,33009,900580,00.html>

Page 129 The US District Court for the Southern District of Florida disagreed: Quotes from the court decision appear in *United States v Ray* (1969), 538, 542.

Page 130 'The dreams of the separate group for a new nation must perish ...': 'Ruling kills hope for new Atlantis', *Shreveport Journal*, 23 January 1970, p. 17.

Page 130 'I know it sounds fantastic ...': Hal Stewart, 'Pair planning island nation off San Diego', *Pasadena Independent*, 31 October 1966, p. 11.

Page 132 The US Department of the Interior agreed not to sue the promoters: Sherry Eckhardt, 'Recent cases: international law – continental shelf – proprietary interest of United States in continental shelf precludes claims of acquisition by private entrepreneurs. *United States v. Ray* (S.D. Fla. 1969)', *San Diego Law Review*, 1969, 6: 498–499; Samuel Menefee, '"Republics of the reefs": Nation-building on the continental shelf and in the world's oceans', *California Western International Law Journal*, 1994, 25(1): 102–103.

Page 132 Two other groups were also interested in building a new country on the Cortes Bank: Material in this paragraph appears in Bill Duncan, 'The grand plan for building an island paradise off our coastline', *Press-Telegram*, 18 December 1966, p. 111; Menefee, '"Republics of the reefs"', pp. 103–104.

Page 132 In 1968, Werner Stiefel gave it a try: Material on Operation Atlantis is drawn from Isabelle Simpson, 'Operation Atlantis: A case study of libertarian island micronationality', *Shima*, 2016, 10(2): 18; and Erwin

Strauss, *How to start your own country*, 3rd edn, Paladin Press, Boulder, CO, 1999, pp. 68–75.

Page 133 True freedom required the prohibition of all forms of regular payments: Werner Stevens, *The story of Operation Atlantis*, Atlantis Publishing Company, Saugerties, NY, 1968, p. 17.

Page 133 'Why have a government at all?': Simpson, 'Operation Atlantis', p. 24.

Page 133 'test the hypothesis that a free, capitalist society ...': This quote and the next two appear in Stevens, *The story of Operation Atlantis*, pp. 8, 26.

Page 134 based 'on market-rule, the protection of private property and individual rights': Simpson, 'Operation Atlantis', p. 18.

Page 134 The book attracted 'a sizeable number' of enthusiastic libertarians ...: Strauss, *How to start your own country*, pp. 68–69.

Page 134 'like John Galt's speech in *Atlas Shrugged* ...': Roy Halliday, 'Operation Atlantis and the radical libertarian alliance: Observations of a fly on the wall', *Formulations*, 2001, 30, <https://web.archive.org/web/20020910220252/http:/libertariannation.org/a/n030h2.html>.

Page 134 'closely simulat[ing] a land-locked ship': This and the following quote appear in Stevens, *The story of Operation Atlantis*, pp. 23–24.

Page 135 'Operation Atlantis is a real mind-blower ...': Hugh Gardner, 'Your global alternative: Communes, experiments, jails and hidey-holes', *Esquire*, September 1970.

Page 135 'for people to flee to when the United States, like Germany ...': Simpson, 'Operation Atlantis', p. 24.

Page 135 The tide went out, and the ship was left lying on its side in the mud: Strauss, *How to start your own country*, p. 71.

Page 138 'out Cayman the Caymans': Tim Hulse, 'Prince Lazarus rules the waves', *The Independent*, 31 May 1998, <www.independent.co.uk/arts-entertainment/prince-lazarus-rules-the-waves-1157051.html>.

Page 138 'Venice-style waterways': Alex Heard, 'Libertarian paradiso', *New York Times Magazine*, 9 August 1998, p. 28.

Page 139 there would be no need for personal income taxes: Wheeler Dixon, *Visions of paradise: Images of Eden in the cinema*, Rutgers University Press, New Brunswick, 2006, pp. 40–41.

Page 139 'a free-market oasis ...': Hulse, 'Prince Lazarus rules the waves'.

Page 139 'classic securities swindle': 'It's good to be king', *Wired*, 1 March 2000, <www.wired.com/2000/03/kingdoms/>.

Page 139 In 2000, the US District Court for the Northern District of Oklahoma ...: *Securities and Exchange Commission v Lazarus R. Long (a/k/a Howard Turney individually and doing business as New Utopia)*, USDC/NDOK/TULSA Ca No 99CV 0257BU(M), 20 January 2000.

Page 141 that 'it was even a Soviet submarine base': 'The true story of Rose Island', *Travel Emilia Romagna*, 31 August 2021, <www.travelemiliaromagna.it/en/rose-island/>. See generally Menefee, '"Republics of the reefs"', p. 105.

Page 141 the Convention 'granted a right to the free use of the high seas ...': This quote and the following appear in *Chierici v Ministry of the Merchant Navy* (14 November 1969) (1986) 71 ILR 258, 259.

Page 143 'arranged into atolls and archipelagos': Surabhi Ranganathan, 'Seasteads, land-grabs and international law', *Leiden Journal of International Law*, 2019, 32(2): 205.

Page 143 'peacefully test new ideas for government ...': Carly Jackson, *Support The Seasteading Institute for #GivingTuesday*, The Seasteading Institute website, 2018, <www.seasteading.org/givingtuesday/>. See also Patri Friedman and Brad Taylor, 'Seasteading: Competitive governments on the ocean', *Kyklos*, 2012, 65(2): 218.

Page 143 'Decades from now ...': Alexis Madrigal, 'Peter Thiel makes down payment on libertarian ocean colonies', *Wired*, 18 May 2008, <www.wired.com/2008/05/peter-thiel-makes-down-payment-on-libertarian-ocean-colonies/>.

Page 143 'Let's think of government as an industry ...': Sophie Elmhirst, 'The disastrous voyage of Satoshi, the world's first cryptocurrency cruise ship', *The Guardian*, 7 September 2021, <www.theguardian.com/news/2021/sep/07/disastrous-voyage-satoshi-cryptocurrency-cruise-ship-seassteading>.

Page 143 'as incubators for new forms of government': Grace Wyler, 'Silicon Valley's next disruption: Floating, autonomous city-states', *Vice*, 6 May 2013, <www.vice.com/en/article/8qqpbb/silicon-valleys-next-disruption-floating-autonomous-city-states>.

Page 144 'What about pirates?': The Seasteading Institute, *FAQ*, The Seasteading Institute website, 2021, <www.seasteading.org/faq/#qaef-32848>.

Page 144 'facilitating the tax evasion of the world's greatest fortunes': Alexandre Taliercio, quoted in Julia Carrie Wong, 'Seasteading: Tech leaders' plans for floating city trouble French Polynesians', *The Guardian*, 2 January 2017, <www.theguardian.com/technology/2017/jan/02/seasteading-peter-thiel-french-polynesia>; see also 'Hundreds march in Tahiti against building of floating islands', *Radio New Zealand*, 9 April 2018, <www.rnz.co.nz/international/pacific-news/354491/hundreds-march-in-tahiti-against-building-of-floating-islands>.

Page 145 to 'deteriorate the independence of the state': Alan Weedon, 'Bitcoin couple could face death penalty in Thailand for "seastead" floating home in international waters', *ABC News*, 19 April 2019, <www.abc.net.au/news/2019-04-18/bitcoin-couple-face-death-penalty-in-thailand-for-seastead/11031336>.

Page 145 'a vibrant workplace for innovative industries to bloom': Anthony Fisher, 'Blueseed: The Googleplex of the sea', *Reason*, 9 January 2012, <https://reason.com/2012/01/09/blueseed-the-googleplex-of-the-sea/>.

Page 145 'coworking spaces, high-speed wifi, 24-hour concierge services, and a gym': Wyler, 'Silicon Valley's next disruption'.

Page 145 'homage to Satoshi Nakamoto': This quote and the next appears in Elmhirst, 'The disastrous voyage of Satoshi'.

6 Fighting for change: Political protest and law reform

Page 148 Ruddock claimed the bill was needed to protect the 'institution of marriage': Commonwealth of Australia, *Parliamentary Debates*, House of Representatives, 27 May 2004, p. 29356 (Philip Ruddock).

Page 148 the 'Marriage Discrimination Bill': Commonwealth of Australia, *Parliamentary Debates*, Senate, 12 August 2004, p. 26544 (Bob Brown).

Page 150 'On the 14th day of June 2004 ...': Judy Lattas, 'Queer sovereignty: The Gay and Lesbian Kingdom of the Coral Sea Islands', *Shima*, 2014, 8(1): 67.

Page 150 'Homosexual people have honestly endeavoured ...': Gay and Lesbian Kingdom, *Declaration of Independence*, Gay and Lesbian Kingdom website, 2004, <https://web.archive.org/web/20150121095825/http://gaykingdom.info/sovereign.htm>.

Page 150 'Your letter raises a number of issues...': John Faulkner, letter to Dale Anderson, n.d..

Page 151 'Thank you for your letter ...': Rob Whiddon, letter to Dale Anderson, 30 July 2004.

Page 151 'under Australian law (Australia is a Kingdom) ...': Gay and Lesbian Kingdom, *History*, Gay and Lesbian Kingdom website, 2007, <https://web.archive.org/web/20150121095310/http://gaykingdom.info/history.htm>

Page 153 'oppressed people of overseas territories': Gay and Lesbian Kingdom, *History*.

Page 153 'As a nation, Australia maintains appalling laws ...': This quote and the next appear in Gay and Lesbian Kingdom, *About Us*, Gay and Lesbian Kingdom website, 2007, <https://web.archive.org/web/20150121095448/http:/gaykingdom.info/aboutus.htm>.

Page 154 'only sovereign states and territories can access an international court ...': Lattas, 'Queer sovereignty', p. 65.

Page 155 'The government's obviously not going to recognise it': 'Gay kingdom for Coral Sea', *Star Observer*, 20 April 2008, <www.starobserver.com.au/news/national-news/new-south-wales-news/gay-kingdom-for-coral-sea/8000>.

Page 156 'I reached back explaining the problem': Tobin Low and Kathy Tu (hosts), 'Make Australia gay again' [podcast], *Nancy*, WNYC Studios, 21 April 2020, <www.wnycstudios.org/podcasts/nancy/episodes/nancy-podcast-make-australia-gay-again>.

Page 157 'you realise this particular flag ...': This quote and the following quote appear in Estimates, Senate Finance and Public Administration Legislation Committee, Parliament of Australia, 28 February 2017, p. 39.

Page 158 'the largest narcotics network in America': On the value of the drug trade in Miami, see Gerald Posner, *Miami Babylon: Crime, wealth, and power – a dispatch from the beach*, Simon & Schuster, New York, 2009; Susan King, 'A look back at Miami's vices: Drugs, cash, killings', *Los Angeles Times*, 30 October 2006, <www.latimes.com/archives/la-xpm-2006-oct-30-et-weekmovies30-story.html>.

Page 159 no one 'doubted that drugs were trafficked widely in the Keys by road and by boat': Robert Kerstein, *Key West on the edge: Inventing the Conch Republic*, University Press of Florida, Gainesville, FL, 2012.

Page 159 the roadblock was none of the mayor's business: Darien Cavanaugh, 'Key West declared a faux war on the United States in 1982', *War is Boring*, 3 April 2015, <https://medium.com/war-is-boring/key-west-declared-a-faux-war-on-the-united-states-in-1982-f2c40b429e75>.

Page 160 'We're the Conchs and we've had enough ...': This quote and the following quotes appear in Neil Brown, 'Balmy Key West secedes from United States – sort of', *Charlotte Observer*, 24 April 1982, p. 2.

Page 161 'everybody's going bananas': Kathy McCarthy and Karen Payne, 'Secession near: Key Westerners still asleep', *Miami News*, 23 April 1982, p. 3.

Page 161 some 'very high speed boats familiar with clandestine night operations': Brown, 'Balmy Key West secedes from United States', p. 2.

Page 162 Balbontin rushed over to two US naval officers ...: Katherine Alex Beaven, 'That time the Florida Keys tried to secede from the US by dropping conch fritter bombs', *Vice*, 22 April 2017 <www.vice.com/en/article/4x9n8d/that-time-the-florida-keys-tried-to-secede-from-the-us-by-dropping-conch-fritter-bombs>.

Page 162 'We're kind of like the mouse that roared': McCarthy and Payne, 'Secession near', p. 3; UPI, 'Key West, in protest on aliens, "secedes"', *New York Times*, 25 April 1982, p. 12; Neil Brown, 'Key Westers "secede," declare own republic in row over blockade', *Miami Herald*, 24 April 1982, p. 172.

Page 162 'this victory is very sweet for our country': '"Conch Republic" claims first "victory" over U.S.', *Tampa Tribune*, 25 April 1982, p. 36.

Page 162 Florida Governor Bob Graham became the first foreign dignitary ...: Material in this paragraph appears in Neil Brown, 'A coup review: Conch Republic has fans, foes', *Miami Herald*, 25 April 1982, p. 676.

Page 163 'We've had a lot of fun and a lot of publicity': 'Conch Republic in Florida wins first "skirmish" with America', *Tyler Courier-Times*, 25 April 1982, p. 9; see further William Barnett, 'Inventing the Conch Republic: The creation of Key West as an escape from modern America', *Florida Historical Quarterly*, 2009, 88(2): 139, 171.

Page 164 'You just can't buy the kind of advertising that we got with the mock secession': Brown, 'A coup review', p. 676.

Page 164 'one of the best publicity stunts ...': Judi Bradford, 'Founders create *much* more than a state of mind', *Miami Herald*, 17 April 2004, p. 131.

Page 164 'patrolmen were making only spot checks of passing vehicles': '"Conch Republic" claims first "victory" over U.S.', p. 36.

Page 164 Anderson 'decided to take the job seriously': 'Peter Anderson: Driving force behind the Conch Republic', *Florida Keys News*, n.d., <https://fla-keys.com/news/article/8890/>.

Page 164 The Conch Republic now has its own pledge of allegiance: Material in this and the following paragraph appears in '10 days of fun mark birth of a nation', *Miami Herald*, 17 April 2004, p. 131.

Page 165 'We're keeping alive a tradition ...': Nancy Klingener, 'Annual fest celebrates "liberation"', *Miami Herald*, 15 April 1992, p. 103.

Page 166 'I got a letter from the Conch Republic ...': John Lantigua, 'Snubbed Conch Republic wants in on historic summit', *Miami Herald*, 6 December 1994, p. 25.

Page 166 A few months later tensions flared again: Material in this paragraph is drawn from Cavanaugh, 'Key West declared a faux war on the United States in 1982'

Page 167 'There was nobody home in Washington to ask': Peter Anderson, *Report to the nation: The taking of Fort Jefferson*, The Conch Republic website, n.d., <https://web.archive.org/web/20150304095044/https:/conchrepublic.com/fortjef.htm>.

Page 168 'what we're hoping to accomplish is to thoroughly embarrass the federal government': Susana Bellido, 'Conch rebels on the warpath again', *Miami Herald*, 30 December 1995, p. 113; Susana Bellido, 'Conchs: End shutdown, open fort!', *Miami Herald*, 3 January 1996, p. 51.

Page 168 'You get a lot of scrutiny ...': Material in this and the following paragraph is drawn from Jennifer Babson, 'FBI examining Conch "passport" link', *Miami Herald*, 3 October 2001, pp. B1–B2.

Page 169 'Since the federal government decided in its infinite wisdom ...': 'Conch Republic "takes" old Seven Mile Bridge', *South Florida Sun Sentinel*, 14 January 2006, p. 36.

Page 170 'With all due respect ...': 'Conch Republic "takes" old Seven Mile Bridge', p. 36.

Page 171 The Greater London Council had adopted a scorched earth policy to deter squatters: The Leverhulme Trust, 'The Independent Republic of Frestonia', *Squatting London*, 5 August 2017, <https://squattinglondon.wordpress.com/2017/08/05/frestonia/>.

Page 173 'We appeal to the United Nations ...': This quote and the following quote are drawn from David Rappaport-Bramley, letter to the United Nations, 30 October 1977, <http://www.frestonia.org/application-to-the-united-nations/>. See further A.O. Sulzberger Jr, 'A new nation in London?', *Evening Standard* (Union Town, Pennsylvania), 5 November 1977, p. 20.

Page 175 'the ideal size for a nation is about 100 to 200 citizens': Nicholas Exelby-Bramley, 'Nicholas Exelby-Bramley', *Built Environment*, 1979, 5(3): 232.

Page 176 'All Hail, Frestonia': *Daily Mirror*, 4 November 1977, p. 11.

Page 176 'As one who had a childhood enthusiasm for the Napoleon of Notting Hill Gate ...': Sir Geoffrey Howe, letter to Nicholas Exelby-Bramley, 20 July 1978, <www.frestonia.org/letter-from-the-rt-hon-sir-geoffrey-howe-qc-mp/>.

Page 177 'All I can say is were you not to exist it would be necessary to invent you': Sir Horace Cutler, letter to Nicholas Exelby-Bramley, 25 July 1978, <www.frestonia.org/response-from-horace-cutler-leader-of-the-glc/>.

Page 177 'it was a snowball that started rolling ...': John Harris, 'Freedom for Frestonia: The London commune that cut loose from the UK', *The Guardian*, 30 October 2017, <www.theguardian.com/cities/2017/oct/30/frestonia-london-commune-squatters>.

7 Environmental micronations: Creating a country to save the planet

Page 180 'knuckles grazed and still in an extreme state of fear ...': John Vidal, '"Hello Mum, I'm on Rockall": The £100bn piece of rock', *The Guardian*, 1 January 2011, <www.theguardian.com/theguardian/2011/jan/01/john-vidal-rockall>.

Page 180 'Hello Mum, I'm on Rockall ...': Vidal, '"Hello Mum, I'm on Rockall"'.

Page 181 'the most isolated small rock in the oceans of the world': James Fisher, *Rockall*, Geoffrey Bles, London, 1956, pp. 12–13.

Page 181 'just moss, seaweeds and one black lichen': The Rockall Club, *Facts*, The Rockall Club website, 2019, <www.therockallclub.org/The_Rockall_Club_Facts.html>.

Page 181 'more people have landed on the moon than have landed on Rockall by sea': United Kingdom, *Parliamentary Debates*, House of Commons, 13 December 1971, vol. 828, col. 199 (William Ross).

Page 181 'a dreadful place': United Kingdom, *Parliamentary Debates*, House of Lords, 18 November 1971, vol. 325, col. 754–755 (Lord Kennet).

Page 181 the final 'territorial expansion of the British empire': Fleet Air Arm Officers Association, *On this day 18 September 1955*, Fleet Air Arm Officers Association website, 18 September 2014, <www.fleetairarmoa.org/news/on-this-day-18-september-1955>.

Page 182 On her dominions the sun never sets: 'The British Empire', *Caledonian Mercury*, 15 October 1821, p. 4.

Page 182 'The fleet set sail for Rockall ...': 'Rockall' from *Fresh Airs* by Flanders & Swann, 1955, composed by Michael Flanders and Donald Swann. All efforts have been made to contact the copyright holder for permission to reproduce the lyrics.

Page 184 Donald Swann noted that … : Stephen Royle, '"This mere speck in the surface of the waters": Rockall aka Waveland', *Shima*, 2014, 8(1): 75–76.

Page 184 'hostile agents' might install 'themselves on the island …': Gurpreet Narwan, 'UK feared Rockall could be used to spy on missiles', *The Times* (London), 16 May 2017, <www.thetimes.co.uk/article/uk-feared-rockall-could-be-used-to-spy-on-missiles-bsdd3bb0z>.

Page 184 'My old father, God rest his soul …': Ondřej Daněk, *Rockall* [survey report], 2009, p. 20, <https://dokufunk.org/upload/rockall_en.pdf>.

Page 184 'the MacLeods of the Western Isles': United Kingdom, *Parliamentary Debates*, House of Lords, 18 November 1971, vol. 325, col. 753 (Lord Tanlaw).

Page 185 'Oh the Empire, it is finished …': Composed by Brian Warfield of The Wolfe Tones, 1974. Lyrics reproduced with permission of Dwyer McClorey, DMC Event Promotions (managers of The Wolfe Tones).

Page 186 'mere speck in the surface of the waters': Basil Hall, *Fragments of voyages and travels: Volume III*, Robert Caddell Press, Edinburgh, 1831, p. 179.

Page 186 'You get a lot of wind …': Nichola Rutherford, 'Rockall: The adventurers who lived on a craggy outcrop', *BBC News*, 11 June 2019, <www.bbc.com/news/uk-scotland-48582267>.

Page 186 'staying in an accommodation pod strapped to a rock': Royle, '"This mere speck in the surface of the waters"', p. 78.

Page 187 Greenpeace was increasingly focusing on oil exploration projects in the North Atlantic: Material from this paragraph and the next is drawn from Chris Rose, *How to win campaigns: 100 steps to success*, Earthscan, London, 2005, pp. 91–93, 107–10; Grant Jordan, *Shell, Greenpeace and the Brent Spar*, Palgrave Macmillan, Basingstoke, UK, 2001.

Page 188 'Let the sun and wind do their work. Leave the oil beneath the waves': Vidal, '"Hello Mum, I'm on Rockall"'.

Page 188 'We reject the governance of a country which permits new oil exploration …': Greenpeace, *World has a new country: Sun rises on new flag as Greenpeace declares a new global state from Rockall* [media release], Greenpeace, 15 June 1997, <http://roundrockallrace.com/2010/06/waveland.html>.

Page 188 'The seas around Rockall …': Rutherford, 'Rockall'.

Page 188 'Without violence and by bearing witness …': Greenpeace, *World has a new country*; Royle, '"This mere speck in the surface of the waters"', p. 80.

Page 189 The activists stayed on Rockall for 42 days … 'territorial claim': Peter Morris, 'Rockall 1997 – no new oil' [blog post], *Stuff: Peter Morris ramblings*, 8 October 2017, <https://petermo.wordpress.com/2007/10/08/rockall-1997-no-new-oil/>.

Page 190 The council also threatened to charge a tax …: 'Rock and a hard place', *The Herald* (Scotland), 29 July 1997, <www.heraldscotland.com/news/12312785.rock-and-a-hard-place/>.

Page 190 'freed from the threat of development': Greenpeace, *World has a new country*.

Page 190 'Rockall is British territory': The Rockall Club, *History*, The Rockall Club website, 2019, <www.therockallclub.org/The_Rockall_Club_History.html>.

Page 190 'No New Oil …': Peter Morris, 'Rockall 1997 – No new oil'.

Page 190 'although it may not be down to the Greenpeace campaign …': Royle, '"This mere speck in the surface of the waters"', p. 80.

Page 190 'the fools are still wasting time and money': Morris, 'Rockall 1997 – No new oil'.

Page 191 'draw attention to glacier retreat and global warming': Jorge Daniel Taillant, *Glaciers: The politics of ice*, Oxford University Press, Oxford/New York, 2015, p. 224.

Page 191 The republic has pledged to maintain its assertion of sovereignty …: Taillant, *Glaciers*, p. 224; Kristen French, 'Copper versus ice: Chilean mine would excavate five glaciers', *GlacierHub*, 1 October 2014, <https://glacierhub.org/tag/glacier-republic/>.

Page 191 This has not stopped activists …: The quotes in this paragraph appear in Marianela Jarroud, 'A new "republic" to save Chile's glaciers', *Inter Press Service*, 4 February 2015, <www.ipsnews.net/2015/02/a-new-republic-to-save-chiles-glaciers/>.

Page 194 'Welcome to the Independent State of Aramoana': This quote and the following quote appear in Angela Findlay, '"Vive Aramoana": The Save Aramoana campaign, 1974–1983' [master's thesis], University of Otago, 2004, pp. 20, 72.

Page 195 'for the entire universe … so long as its owner could still laugh': Andreas Baum, 'Kernkraftgegner rufen im niedersächsischen Gorleben die "Freie Republik Wendland" aus', *Deutschlandfunk Kultur*, 3 May 2005, <www.deutschlandfunkkultur.de/kernkraftgegner-rufen-im-niedersaechsischen-gorleben-die-100.html>.

Page 196 Polynesian sailors may have first sighted the region …: Laura Geggel, 'Antarctica was likely discovered 1,100 years before Westerners "found" it', *Live Science*, 16 June 2021 <www.livescience.com/indigenous-people-discovered-antarctica.html>.

Page 198 'complicated political situation …': Encyclopaedia Westarctica, *Achaean Territory of Antarctica*, Encyclopaedia Westarctica website, 2020, <www.westarctica.wiki/index.php?title=Achaean_Territory_of_Antarctica>.

Page 198 'If no one had bothered to claim …': Westarctica, *The story of Westarctica*, Westarctica website, 2022, <www.westarctica.info/our-story>.

Page 198 'I have been heavily studying the continent of Antarctica …': Katherine LaGrave, 'A very big little country', *AFAR*, 14 October 2021, <www.afar.com/magazine/westarctica-antarctica-a-micronation-with-a-

mission>. See further: John Ryan, George Dunford and Simon Sellars, *Micronations: The Lonely Planet guide to home-made nations*, Lonely Planet, London, 2006, p. 111.

Page 199 'Western Antarctica is one of the most fragile ecosystems on the planet ...': Westarctica, *What we do*, Westarctica website, 2022, <www.westarctica.info/what-we-do>.

Page 201 'an official partner with the People's Climate Movement': This quote and the following quote appear in LaGrave, 'A very big little country'.

Page 201 'I wanted it to be useful...': Julien Oeuillet, 'Springtime of micronations spearheaded by Belgian "grand-duke" Niels', *Brussels Times*, 29 July 2020, <www.brusselstimes.com/all-news/magazine/35805/springtime-of-micronations-spearheaded-by-belgian-grand-duke-niels/>.

Page 201 'that seeks its own destruction': Olivier Touzeau, 'Everything you wanted to know about Angyalistan' [unpublished conference presentation], *3rd International Conference on Micronations*, Free Republic of Alcatraz, 4–5 July 2015.

8 Humour and boredom: Playing a king

Page 202 Up to eight hours a week serving as king: Alex Blumberg, 'It's good to be king', *Wired*, March 2000, p. 132.

Page 203 'mewing gulls, a few hardy sheep ...': Wendy Arundel, 'The strange tale of Outer Baldonia', *Maine Boats, Homes and Harbors*, March/April 2020, <https://maineboats.com/print/issue-163/strange-tale-outer-baldonia>.

Page 203 the world's largest international sport tuna fishing tournament: On Outer Baldonia generally, see Lachlan MacKinnon, '"Give me fish, not federalism": Outer Baldonia and performances of micronationality', *Shima*, 2014, 8(2): 105.

Page 204 denied any wrongdoing ...: 'Pepsi head denies loan to McCarthy', *Hartford Courant*, 7 May 1953, p. 39; 'Russell Arundel, 75, dies, Pepsi official, sportsman', *Washington Post*, 3 February 1978.

Page 204 'Back in Washington, the deed in my pocket ...': This quote and the following quote appear in Vernon Pizer, 'Mirth of a nation: A three-acre principality gives the USSR a raspberry', *Esquire*, January 1954, p. 82.

Page 206 Barkley 'wanted to handle a treasury with no money, no assets ...': Nancy Coe, 'Outer Baldonia struggles for its fishy place as a somewhat emergent nation', *Sports Illustrated*, 18 September 1967; Ted Kerr, 'Outer Baldonia: Defender of fishermen's rights', *Ottawa Citizen*, 22 September 1977, p. 79.

Page 207 'The principality is only three acres in all ...': This quote and the following quote appear in Pizer, 'Mirth of a nation', p. 82.

Page 208 'what to do in the event of an atomic attack': Ian Sclanders, 'How propagandists (of both sides) distort innocence', *Macleans*, 7 October 1961, p. 109.

Page 208 'The world's newest state may never be eligible for the United Nations': Robert J. McCleave, 'All women barred in newest state: Outer Baldonia Principality is strictly for men only', *Edmonton Bulletin*, 22 October 1949, p. 81.

Page 209 'Did the late Liberal government let the U.S. set up a satellite regime ...': Ronald Grantham, 'Weekly summary of events: Canada', *Ottawa Citizen*, 27 July 1957, p. 17.

Page 210 In 1952, the Soviet literary magazine *Literaturnaya Gazeta* published ...: Quotes in this section are from L. Chernaya, 'The state of Baldonia', cited in Department of External Affairs (Canada), 'Outer Baldonia – a Soviet view', *External Affairs*, 1952, 4(1): 408–410. The story was reproduced in 'Outer Baldonia – a Soviet view', *Ottawa Citizen*, 24 January 1953, p. 32.

Page 211 'a capitalistic cannibal preparing to gobble up the humble fishermen of the island': 'Outer Baldonia "state" invites Russian writer', *Calgary Herald*, 15 December 1953, p. 3.

Page 211 'Russians Rise to Defend Poor Islanders from Fauquier Ruler': John Toler, 'The "whimsy state" of Outer Baldonia', *Piedmont Lifestyle*, 2 August 2021, <https://piedmontlifestyle.com/uncategorized/the-whimsy-state-of-outer-baldonia/>.

Page 212 'so-called principality exists only in the playful minds ...': This and the following quote appear in The Canadian Press, 'Russia finds "savagery" on N.S. fishing club island', *Ottawa Citizen*, 21 January 1953, p. 34.

Page 212 'break off diplomatic relations with the Soviets' ... 'Who do these Russians think they're pushing around?': 'Brave Baldonia', *Ottawa Citizen*, 19 July 1956, p. 6.

Page 212 'made a speech excoriating Russia ...': This quote and the following quote appear in Coe, 'Outer Baldonia struggles for its fishy place as a somewhat emergent nation'. Alas, a search of the 1953 Nova Scotia House of Assembly Hansard reveals no evidence of such a speech. Thanks to David McDonald of the Nova Scotia Legislative Library for assistance on this matter.

Page 212 'We have been able to determine that L. Chernaya ...': Pizer, 'Mirth of a nation', p. 82.

Page 213 'a rod-and-reel guy, he massively disapproved of their fishing practices': Arundel, 'The strange tale of Outer Baldonia'.

Page 213 'filled with the spirit of Christmas' ... 'Getting out of Russia ...': 'Outer Baldonia "state" invites Russian writer', p. 3.

Page 213 'One thing is sure – when the Soviets attack Outer Baldonia our only reaction is to feel sorry for them': Pizer, 'Mirth of a nation', p. 82.

Page 213 'We just couldn't handle the number of phone calls': This quote and the following two quotes appear in Kerr, 'Outer Baldonia: Defender of fishermen's rights', p. 79.

Page 214 'In the midst of international snarling, consider today the good news from the principality of Outer Baldonia': Arthur Edson, 'In peaceful Outer Baldonia there is nothing – absolutely', *Arizona Republic*, 17 April 1956, p. 1.

Page 214 he 'spent only one uncomfortable night there ...': Arundel, 'The strange tale of Outer Baldonia'

Page 215 'an unparalleled role in micronational development': John Ryan, George Dunford and Simon Sellars, *The Lonely Planet guide to home-made nations*, Lonely Planet, London, 2006, p. 63.

Page 215 'idea of tiny nations like Monaco...': This quote and the following quote appear in Kristy Totten, 'There's a tiny nation in northern Nevada – kind of', *KNPR's State of Nevada*, Nevada Public Radio, 30 July 2018, <https://knpr.org/knpr/2018-07/theres-tiny-nation-northern-nevada-kind>.

Page 216 'why you should probably Google things before you use them': Maggie Fuller, 'Go inside the quirky "micronation" of Molossia through these brilliant photos', AFAR, 27 October 2017, <www.afar.com/magazine/go-inside-the-quirky-micronation-of-molossia-through-these-brilliant-photos>.

Page 216 'There's a place beneath the western sun ...': Republic of Molossia, 'Our new national anthem', *Khamsin Molossia News*, 28 January 2014, <www.molossia.org/article307.html>. Lyrics reproduced with permission of Kevin Baugh.

Page 217 'ever-present foreign menace from over the border': Quotes in this paragraph appear in Republic of Molossia, *General government information*, Republic of Molossia website, n.d., <www.molossia.org/generalinfo.html>.

Page 218 'Most have kings or dukes and queens and emperors ...': This quote and the following quote appear in Fuller, 'Go inside the quirky "micronation" of Molossia'.

Page 218 'It's an expression of personal sovereignty ...': Carmen Machado, 'The imaginary republic of Molossia', *Vice*, 27 April 2013, <www.vice.com/en_us/article/vdywxm/the-imaginary-republic-of-molossia>.

Page 218 'Can I lower the drinking age? ...': 'Molossia and Vikelsand? Leaders of (fake) nations gather in L.A.', *CBS News*, 10 April 2015, <www.cbsnews.com/news/molossia-and-vikesland-leaders-of-fake-nations-gather-in-l-a/>.

Page 219 'it's good to have an eternal enemy that you can blame all your ills and woes on': Fuller, 'Go inside the quirky "micronation" of Molossia'.

Page 219 'to allow micronations not recognised by the macronational Olympic Committee ...': Republic of Molossia, *Intermicronational Olympic Games: Overview and rules*, Republic of Molossia website, n.d., <www.molossia.org/olympics/olympicabout.html>.

Page 219 'I believe that all micronations should exist as much as possible in the real world ...': This quote and the following quote appear in Mark Hay, 'The absurd history of the Intermicronational Olympic Games', *Good*, 14 October 2016, <www.good.is/sports/micronations-play-sports-too>.

Page 219 Popular fiction launched a micronation boom in Japan in the 1980s: See Jennifer Robertson, 'Empire of nostalgia: Rethinking "internationalization" in Japan', *Theory, Culture & Society*, 1997, 14(4): pp. 108–110; Adam Pasion, 'The will to secede: Japan's micro-nation boom', *Japan Daily*, 9 February 2016, <https://japandaily.jp/will-secede-japans-micro-nation-boom-2573/>.

Page 221 'It's fun to get together and exchange ideas ...': This quote and the following quote appear in Fuller, 'Go inside the quirky "micronation" of Molossia'.

Page 221–228 The Great Bitter Lake Association: Material in this section is drawn from Cath Senker, *Stranded in the Six-Day War*, Cath Senker, Brighton, UK, 2018. We also thank Peter Valdner for his valuable comments on this material. Any errors remain our own.

Page 222 'produced bows and arrows ...': This quote and the following quotes appear in Senker, *Stranded in the Six-Day War*. On the English World Cup victory, see also 'uber alles!' *Daily Express*, 30 September 1968, p. 2.

Page 224 'We don't know if the Israelis are going to push further ...': This quote and the following two quotes appear in Alan Howe, 'The Yellow Fleet was stuck in the Suez Canal for eight years', *The Australian*, 29 May 2021, <www.theaustralian.com.au/inquirer/the-yellow-fleet-was-stuck-in-the-suez-canal-for-eight-years/news-story/ddea6174667333e43c1914686408d037>.

Page 224 'a moat between enemies': This quote and the following quote appear in 'World: The Suez Canal's bleak centennial', *Time*, 21 November 1969, <http://content.time.com/time/subscriber/article/0,33009,841641,00.html>.

Page 224 'There was little the stranded sailors could do except wait and play cards': Senker, *Stranded in the Six-Day War*; 'Great Bitter Lake Association', *99% Invisible*, Invisible Inc., 29 October 2019, <https://99percentinvisible.org/episode/great-bitter-lake-association/>.

Page 225 'The first month was like a holiday ...': 'Ship crews keep lonely Suez vigil', *New York Times*, 11 August 1974, p. 9.

Page 226 'At a recent meeting ...': See image of announcement, supplied by George Wharton, in 'Great Bitter Lake Association', *99% Invisible*.

Page 227 'One wonders what future archaeologists in a few thousand years' time will think of this': Simon Edge, 'Meet the seafarers who were stranded in the Six-Day War', *Express*, 3 June 2017, <www.express.co.uk/life-style/life/812599/six-day-war-seafarers-stranded-suez-canal>.

Page 227 'a sense of stability in an incredibly unstable place': This quote and the quotes in the following paragraph are from Senker, *Stranded in the Six-Day War*.

Page 229 'a thousand percent more profitable': Senker, *Stranded in the Six-Day War*.

Page 229 'to keep in touch after their service': 'Almost eight years in the Great Bitter Lake', *Florida Journal of Commerce/American Shipper*, August 1975, p. 16.

9 Frauds and scams: The great micronation rip-offs

Page 230 'delightful and most valuable': This quote and the following quote appear in Thomas Strangeways, *Sketch of the Mosquito Shore, including the Territory of Poyais*, William Blackwood, Edinburgh, 1822, p. 355.

Page 232 'to attach their country to the Empire': This quote and the following quote appear in David Sinclair, *The land that never was: Sir Gregor MacGregor and the most audacious fraud in history*, Review, London, 2003, p. 6. Material in this chapter draws on Sinclair's excellent biography. See also 'The king of con-men', *The Economist*, 22 December 2012.

Page 235 'one of the most healthy and beautiful spots in the world ...': Strangeways, *Sketch of the Mosquito Shore*, pp. 19–20.

Page 235 'a sinister coast of disillusion': Victor Allan, 'Gregor MacGregor, the Prince of Poyais', *History Today*, 11 July 2018, <www.historytoday.com/miscellanies/gregor-macgregor-prince-poyais>.

Page 237 'I am sick and tired of this bluffer, or Quixote': Sinclair, *The land that never was*, pp. 152–155.

Page 238 the presence of a 'body of [armed] Blacks from St Domingo': Rafe Blaufarb, 'The western question: The geopolitics of Latin American independence', *American Historical Review*, 2007, 112(3): 752–753; Charles Bowman Jr, 'Vicente Pazos, agent for the Amelia Island filibusters, 1818', *Florida Historical Quarterly*, 1975, 53(4): 428.

Page 239 'understood the value of the printed word and the official-looking document': Sinclair, *The land that never was*, p. 316.

Page 239 the founding father of securities fraud: Louis Straney, *Securities fraud: Detection, prevention, and control*, Wiley, Hoboken, NJ, 2011, p. 35.

Page 240 'Dear Ed ...': David Passage, letter to Ed Ride, 18 April 1978.

Page 240 The counsellor to the Yugoslav Embassy: P.J. Lloyd, memorandum to R.J. Smith, 21 June 1978.

Page 241 'enjoy the purity of true fruit juices ...': Alison McClymont, 'Trouble in baron's "peace state"', *Sun-Herald*, 26 August 1990, p. 23.

Page 241 'sick of hearing about nuclear missiles, the daily poisoning of the environment and ruthless corporations': Alison McClymont, '$50,000 paid to live in "ideal" state, claim', *Sun-Herald*, 2 September 1990, p. 23.

Page 241 after a jury failed to reach a verdict the case was abandoned: Malcolm Brown, 'Clouds cleared on baron's reign', *Sydney Morning Herald*, 24 June 1992, p. 10.

Page 243 'drawing on Bougainville's sense of having been exploited by international capital': Nick Bainton and John Cox, 'Parallel states, parallel economies: Legitimacy and prosperity in Papua New Guinea', Discussion Paper 2009/5, Research School of Pacific and Asian Studies, ANU, Canberra, p. 2.

Page 243 'Bougainville's first international financier': John Cox, 'The magic of money and the magic of the state: Fast money schemes in Papua New Guinea', *Oceania*, 2013, 83(3): 176. See further John Cox, *Fast money schemes: Hope and deception in Papua New Guinea*, Indiana University Press, Bloomington, IN, 2018, ch 2.

Page 243 'before the Australian Securities and Investments ...': Grant Wyeth, 'Musingku: Bougainville's "royal" pyramid scheme problem', *The Diplomat*, 27 January 2021, <https://thediplomat.com/2021/01/musingku-bougainvilles-royal-pyramid-scheme-problem/>; Australian Securities and Investments Commission, 'Enforceable undertaking: Noah Musingku and U-Vistract Finance Corporation Limited', 28 October 1999, <https://download.asic.gov.au/media/1297837/008547394.pdf>.

Page 244 'the financial foundation of a new state': Cox, 'The magic of money', p. 177.

Page 244 'We had to set up our own home-grown international government': *Papaala Chronicles*, 2005, 3(9), cited in Anna-Karina Hermkens, 'Like Moses who led his people to the promised land: Nation- and state-building in Bougainville', *Oceania*, 2013, 83(3): 202.

Page 245 a Fijian militia of between 30 and 100 men: Stan Starygin, 'The gangs of Bougainville: Seven men, guns and a copper mine', *Journal of Conflict Transformation and Security*, 2013, 3(1): 67.

Page 245 'people are still visiting him to invest more money ...': Liam Fox, 'Bougainville's conman "king" still on the run as island edges closer to independence', *ABC News*, 15 November 2020, <www.abc.net.au/news/2020-11-15/bougainville-conman-king-still-on-the-run-independence-png/12879932>.

Page 246 In 2021, the President of the Bougainville government ...: Wyeth, 'Musingku: Bougainville's "royal" pyramid scheme problem'.

Page 247 filling the text with 'idiosyncratic metaphysics': Peter Jamison, 'Fantasy Island: The strange tale of alleged fraudster Pearlasia Gamboa', *SF Weekly*, 6 July 2011.

Page 247 The Pedley family denied an FBI request to fingerprint David Pedley's body: Bertil Lintner, 'Cyberfraud: The fictitious "Dominion of Melchizedek"', *The Nation* (Bangkok), 30 May 1999.

Page 248 'The Dominion of Melchizedek is an Ecclesiastical, Sovereign, Independent society': Dominion of Melchizedek, *About the government of Melchizedek*, Dominion of Melchizedek website, 2021, <www.melchizedek.com/the-government/>.

Page 248 'the great three monotheistic religions': Dominion of Melchizedek, *General statistics of the Dominion of Melchizedek*, Dominion of Melchizedek website, 2021, <www.melchizedek.com/general-statistics/>.

Page 248 An alleged 'serial scammer' herself: Jamison, 'Fantasy Island'.

Page 249 a group of 'like-minded fraudsters': Lintner, 'Cyberfraud'.

Page 249 'with the wave of his financial wand'...: Robert Tillman, *Global pirates: Fraud in the offshore insurance industry*, Northeastern University Press, Boston, 2002, p. 111.

Page 249 In 1991, a man calling himself Branch Vinedresser: Terrence O'Hara, 'D.C. home to shadowy banking web', *Washington Business Journal*, 18 February 1991; Terrence O'Hara, 'District probes off-shore companies for fraud: U.S. agencies also look into shell banking firms in district', *Washington Business Journal*, 25 February 1991; Terrence O'Hara, 'D.C. Office of Banking probes shell "banks": Banking agency says firms chartered without prior OK', *Washington Business Journal*, 4 March 1991.

Page 249 In 1995, an Austrian man named Gerhard Bacher ...: Manuel Gren, 'Young pretender jailed for princely fraud', *South China Morning Post*, 14 July 1995, p. 1.

Page 249 Bacher had used his Melchizedek 'diplomatic passport' to visit several countries in Asia: Lintner, 'Cyberfraud'.

Page 250 were worthless instruments issued by the German Weimar Republic: Michael Gillard, 'SFO enters the inner sanctum', *The Guardian*, 24 September 1995, p. 3.

Page 250 bogus policies through a company purportedly based in Melchizedek: David Pasztor, 'No man is an island', *Dallas Observer*, 27 June 1996, <www.dallasobserver.com/news/no-man-is-an-island-6403643>; Tillman, *Global pirates*, pp. 106–108.

Page 250 'Credit Bank is not a bank, Melchizedek is not a country and Rosemount is not an ambassador': Tillman, *Global pirates*, p. 114.

Page 250 By the time they were caught they had allegedly made US$1 million from the scam: Lintner, 'Cyberfraud'; Manuel Gren, 'A "paradise" struggling for identity', *South China Morning Post*, 21 November 1998, p. 3.

Page 250 'more on tax laws than territory' ...: Richard Leiby and James Lileks, 'The ruse that roared', *Washington Post*, 5 November 1995.

Page 252 'especially with regard to its location, economic and political data': Ministry of Foreign Affairs of Grenada, letter to the Office of the President of the Dominion of Melchizedek, 6 August 1998, <www.melchizedek.com/wp-content/uploads/2015/04/DoM-Grenada011.pdf>.

Page 252 'This letter has been drawn to set forth the Central African Republic's official and formal recognition of the government of the Dominion of Melchizedek': Général d'Armée André Kolingba (President, Central African Republic), letter to Branch Vinedresser (Minister Plenipotentiary, Embassy of the Dominion of Melchizedek), 3 June 1993, <www.melchizedek.com/wp-content/uploads/2015/04/TPR-With-Central-African-Republic.pdf>.

Page 253 'will soon exchange ambassadors with this country': Tillman, *Global pirates*, p. 112.

Page 253 'the Honorable Mike Sonpon as Emissary Extraordinaire to the Republic of Liberia': Dominion of Melchizedek, *New appointment as emissary extraordinaire – Mike Sonpon* [media release], Dominion of Melchizedek, 5 September 2021, <www.melchizedek.com/new-appointment-as-emissary-extraordinaire-mike-sonpon/>.

Page 253 'As you know I no longer take an active role in the DoM': This quote and the following quote appear in Dominion of Melchizedek, *Denouncing the Melchizedek Bible* [media release], Dominion of Melchizedek, 26 March 2012, <www.melchizedek.com/denouncing-the-melchizedek-bible/>.

Page 254 'More Information Will be added as we move forward in clearing up allegations and assumptions about the State's assorted history': Dominion of Melchizedek, *Dominion of Melchizedek* [website], 2021, <www.melchizedek.com>.

Afterword

Page 255 'Historically, women have gotten the short end of the stick': Jessica Muddìtt, 'The country that became a "micronation capital"', *BBC Future*, 19 April 2022, <www.bbc.com/future/article/20220407-the-country-that-became-a-micronation-capital>.

Page 256 'the world's only feminist micronation': This quote and the following quotes in the paragraph appear in Ambulatory Free States of Obsidia, *The Ambulatory Free States of Obsidia* [website], n.d., <www.obsidiagov.org>.

Page 257 'I've always been attracted to the idea of statehood ...': Jennifer Parker, 'The royal me', *Saturday Evening Post*, 2 February 2016, <www.saturdayeveningpost.com/2016/02/royal-me/>.

Page 257 'Borders are the enemy of mutual aid ...': Heather Buckner, 'You probably didn't know, but leaders from 26 micronations just gathered in Atlanta', *Atlanta*, 30 June 2017, <www.atlantamagazine.com/news-culture-articles/probably-didnt-know-leaders-26-micronations-just-gathered-atlanta/>.

ACKNOWLEDGMENTS

We hope that you find this book as enjoyable to read as it was to research and write. Micronations are an object of fascination and sometimes bemusement to many. Why on earth would someone decide to create their own country? Does it work? And do you still have to pay tax if you manage it? Micronations can give rise to strange legal questions. More interesting, however, are the stories behind those would-be Queens, Kings, and Emperors. No micronation may have yet succeeded in becoming a recognised country, but they have had a lot of fun pretending to do so.

We have had a lot of support in writing this book. Harry thanks Annabel Johnson for her love and support – even though she refuses to accept her royal title as the Princess of Petersham. George thanks Emma, Edward and Eleanor for their patience as he regaled them with stories about the antics of micronations.

We would like to thank the team at NewSouth Publishing, including Joumana Awad, Emma Hutchinson, Caitlin Lawless, and Harriet McInerney for their care and enthusiasm for this project. We also thank our copyeditor Emma Driver, for her excellent proofing and for pushing us to strengthen the narrative in key places as well as Anne Savage for her granular proofread. Special thanks must also go to the many people who gave us permission to reproduce their images – of stamps, coins, passports, windswept rocky atolls, and photos of micronational heads of state – that have enriched this book and hopefully instilled the same interest we have in this topic in you.

Finally, this book could not have been written without those micronationalists themselves. We thank the very many people who – for thousands of different reasons – decided 'enough is enough' and tried to rule their own country.

INDEX

Index

Index